I HOPE THEY SERVE BEER IN HELL

I HOPE THEY SERVE BEER IN HELL

TUCKER MAX

CITADEL PRESS
Kensington Publishing Corp.
www.kensingtonbooks.com

CITADEL PRESS BOOKS are published by

Kensington Publishing Corp.
850 Third Avenue
New York, NY 10022

All Kensington titles, imprints, and distributed lines are available at special quantity discounts for bulk purchases for sales promotions, premiums, fund-raising, educational, or institutional use. Special book excerpts or customized printings can also be created to fit specific needs. For details, write or phone the office of the Kensington special sales manager: Kensington Publishing Corp., 850 Third Avenue, New York, NY 10022, attn: Special Sales Department; phone 1-800-221-2647.

CITADEL PRESS and the Citadel logo are Reg. U.S. Pat. & TM Off.

First printing: January 2006

20 19 18

Printed in the United States of America

Library of Congress Control Number: 2005934008

ISBN 0-8065-2728-5

CONTENTS

APPENDIX

ACKNOWLEDGMENTS

TheBunny—For whatever issues we've had, and there have been many, no one has been more solidly in my corner. Not my parents, not my friends, not even my dogs. She is a very special person. [BTW, she is an excellent writer in her own right and I suggest you check out her site: thebunnyblog.com. But finish my book first.]

PWJ—I am a proud and complex man, and as a result I have to face most of my problems alone. But sometimes even I need someone to go to, and PWJ was there to help pull me out of the two lowest points of my life. Friends like this are beyond rare; they are priceless in the truest sense of the word.

Nils Parker (aka Drunkasaurusrex)—I would call him the Robin to my Batman, but that underestimates the importance that his contributions make. Robin is replaceable; Nils might not be.

Donika Miller—It's hard to describe why Donika has been so important to my development as a writer. She is someone who really gets it, but isn't seduced by my bullshit. She sees through the crap to the real issues, she isolates the problems I don't see, she does more than just add value—her critiques turn good writing into great writing.

My law school friends get a separate mention, not only because they've had to put up with more shit from me than almost anyone, but because more than half these stories wouldn't exist without them playing the foils: PWJ (he gets two mentions), SlingBlade, Hate, Credit, JoJo, GoldenBoy, El Bingeroso, JonBenet, and Carolyn (my first year roommate). In a very real way, these guys helped mold the person I am today.

Those who have always been there to help whenever I asked, who've saved my ass in several situations, and who otherwise have contributed something tangible to this book: Luke Heidelberger (without whom my site probably wouldn't work at all), Max Wong (my mentor in the entertainment business; plus she gives great critique), D-Rock (who has gotten me out of lots of fights and always calls my shit out when I need it), TheCousin (the JV me), Dickless Vonboffinsheep Bedwettter, the Turd (always willing to give me a vacation spot), Junior, Skippon, Sharts, Ford, Zach Albarron (the craziest guy I know), Laura, Christine (whose commentary was golden) and all my other 'real life' friends.

I have to thank my agent and my editor. My agent Byrd Leavell has not only believed in me from day one, he has fought for me where almost no one else would. I am probably too fucked up to ever get married or even have another serious long term relationship with a woman, but I can't imagine dumping Byrd. As for my editor, Jeremie Ruby-Strauss: I'll get all the press and the credit, whatever there is, for this book, but he deserves some of it. He not only got my vision for this book, but actually fought all the bullshit bureaucratic battles to maintain that vision. Without these two guys, I would still be just an Internet writer.

To anyone I've forgotten who should have been in here: I am a bad person and I'm sorry, but if you know me well enough to deserve to be in the acknowledgments, you already know that.

[I'm also going to throw in a thank you to the moderators on the Tucker Max Message Board. It's a weird place, but they do a great job making it fun (and making me enough money in the process so I could finish this book in peace without having to worry about paying bills): Joseph "JoeyHustle" Hansen, Jon Tando, Ben Hanson, Erin O'Leary, Jess Allen, Brian Stieglitz, Mike Gill, AncientMariner, Boozy, SoylentGreen, CJ*, Dark Helmet, DietCokehead, Foxfyre, Wahoo, KimChi, madd scientist, Slappybird, SqueekyCleen, and WillyDuer.]

AUTHOR'S NOTE

My real name is Tucker Max. Unless a full name is used, all other names are pseudonyms.

All the events depicted in the stories are completely true. Only certain dates, characteristics, and places are changed to protect me from criminal prosecution or civil liability.

I hope you enjoy reading this as much as I enjoyed living it.

The Famous Sushi Pants Story

Occurred—July 2001
Written—July 2001

I used to think that Red Bull was the most destructive invention of the past 50 years. I was wrong. Red Bull's title has been usurped by the portable alcohol breathalyzer. The same device that cops have been using for 10 years to conduct field sobriety tests is now available to the public. It is the size and shape of a small cell phone with a clear round tube sticking up from the top, almost like an antenna. One blows into the tube, and a few seconds later a Blood Alcohol Content (BAC) reading is given. Though not as accurate as a blood test, they are accurate to within .01, which is good enough for my purposes.

I was living in Boca Raton, Florida, when I bought one to take out with me on a Saturday night. This is the story:

9:00pm: Arrive at the restaurant. I am the first one of the group there, even though our reservations are for 9pm. The restaurant is crowded full of the abysmal type of people that infest South Florida. Already depressed, I order a vodka and club soda.

9:08: No one else has arrived. I order another vodka and club. I consider checking my BAC, but doubt that it would show anything thus far.

9:10: Two 30+ year-old Jewish women on my left keep eyeing me. Both have fake breasts. One has exceptionally large fake breasts. They are beckoning me from her shirt. She is not highly attractive. I begin drinking faster.

9:15: No one else has arrived. I order my third vodka and club. While I wait for it, I try out my portable breathalyzer. I blow a .02. This is the greatest invention ever made. I am giddy. I show the breathalyzer to the fake-breasted Jewish women next to me. We begin a conversation.

9:16: They both have thick Long Island accents. I summon the bartender over and change my order to a tall double vodka on the rocks, splash of club.

9:23: Four people at the bar have tried my breathalyzer, both of the fake-breasted women included. Everyone wants to know their BAC. I am the center of attention. I am happy.

9:25: The first member of my group arrives. I show him the breathalyzer. He is enthralled. He buys a round. The fake-breasted women loudly inform us they would like drinks. My friend buys them drinks. I order a double vodka on the rocks. No splash.

9:29: I blow again, a .04. I've been drinking for half an hour, and am on my fourth drink. My wheels of intellect begin grinding through the vodka haze that is already forming . . . four drinks . . . a .04 . . . that must mean that each drink only adds .01 to my BAC. I begin to think that I can drink a lot. I tell one of the fake-breasted women that she is very interesting.

9:38: Six of the eight are here. I lie to the hostesses, and they seat our incomplete party. Everyone is talking about my breathalyzer. I am the focus of adulation. I forgive everyone for sucking so bad. I think this night may go OK after all.

9:40: I blow again, a .05. This confuses me. I haven't ordered another drink since I blew a .04. I have a vague memory from a long distant D.A.R.E. class about the rate of alcohol absorption being constant, regardless of speed of drinking. This memory quickly fades when two hot girls at the table next to me inquire about my portable breathalyzer.

9:42: Hot girl #2 is into me. She begins telling me a story about how she got pulled over once for DUI, and had to blow into something like this, and the cop let her off. She tells me that she always wanted to be a cop, but couldn't pass the entrance exam to the police academy, even though she took it twice. I tell her that she must be really smart. She stops paying attention to me. Hot girl #2 is apparently smart enough to detect thinly veiled sarcasm.

10:04: The novelty of the portable breathalyzer has passed. The table has moved on. I am no longer the center of attention. I am not happy with my table. If the spotlight is not shining directly on me, I feel small inside.

10:06: The people at my table begin talking about energy healing. Everyone is mesmerized by a girl who took a class in it. I tell them that energy healing is a worthless and solipsistic pseudo-science. They think energy healing is a real science because the instructor of the girl's class went to Harvard. One guy calls it a "legitimate, certifiable science," while making air quotes with his fingers. I tell them that they are all (while imitating his air quotes) "legitimate, certifiable idiots" because they believe in horse-shit like energy healing. Two girls call me close-minded. I tell them that they are so open-minded that their brains leaked out. They all glare at me with disapproval. I hate everyone at my table.

10:08: I have completely tuned out their inane conversation. I am slamming down straight vodka as fast as the low-rent wanna-be Ethan Hawke waiter can bring it. I blow every three minutes, watching my BAC slowly creep up.

10:10: .07

10:17: .08. I am no longer legally eligible to drive in the state of Florida. I announce this fact to no one in particular.

10:26: .09

10:27: I decide that I am going to see how drunk I can get and still be functional. I know that .35 BAC kills most people. I think that .20 is a good goal.

10:28: I get up, saying nothing to the seven sophists at my table, and go back to the bar. I don't leave money for my drinks.

10:29: The fake-breasted women are still at the bar. They want drinks. Upset that I'm only at .09 after a good hour and a half of aggressive drinking, I decide to do a round of shots. I let the women pick the shots, with the explicit instruction that it cannot be whiskey, cannot smell like whiskey, cannot even resemble whiskey (I once went to the ER drinking whiskey, but I don't tell them this).

10:30: The shots arrive. Tequila. Judging by the bill, very good tequila. It is smooth. We order another round.

11:14: I blow a .15. I have passed a milestone. Only .05 away from my goal. My pride swells. I show everyone my .15. The bar crowd is impressed. I am their idol. Someone buys me a shot.

11:28: I feel queasy. I realize that I didn't even stick around the table for dinner. Not wanting to either go back to my table or eat at the bar, I walk across the street to a sushi restaurant.

11:29: There is a lingerie party at the sushi restaurant. Half of the people are in some form of pajamas or other bedtime clothing. Everyone here sucks as bad as the last place, except they are in their underwear.

11:30: I am confused. I only want sushi. I stand at the door, mesmerized by the shifting masses of near nakedness. A mildly attractive girl who apparently works at the restaurant wants me to put on lingerie. I tell her I don't have any. I just want some sushi. She says I should at least take off my pants. I ask her if this will get me sushi. She says it will. I take off my pants.

11:30: I pause while unzipping my pants, wondering what type of underwear, if any, I have on. I consider not taking my pants off. I realize that getting food quickly is more crucial than my dignity.

11:31: I take off my pants. I have on pink and white striped Gap boxers. They are too tight. I make sure my package is tucked in. People watch me do this.

11:32: I order sushi by pointing at the pictures and grunting.

11:33: I show a guy at the sushi bar my breathalyzer. He is impressed. He shows it to everyone. People begin congregating around me. I am a star again.

11:41: I blow a .17. I tell everyone my goal. Someone orders me a shot.

11:42: I do the shot. Something that has a familiar taste, makes me feel warm inside. I ask what it is. "Cognac and Alize." There is a God, and he hates me.

11:47: My sushi arrives. I slosh soy sauce over it and shovel it into my mouth as quickly as my hands will get it there.

11:49: My sushi is finished. No one is paying attention to my table manners, as everyone is crowded around the breathalyzer, waiting their turn to find out their BAC.

12:18: I blow a .20. I AM A GOD. The sushi bar erupts. Men are applauding me. Girls are pining for me. Everyone wants to talk to me. I forgive them their flaws, as they are all paying attention to me.

12:31: My deity status is lost. Someone blows a .22. This is a challenge to my manhood. I order a depth charge with a Bacardi 151 shot. And a beer back. The crowd is in awe.

12:33: I finish the depth charge, and the beer. I talk shit to my challenger, "Who runs this bar now, BITCH??" The crowd erupts. Momentum has swung back in my direction. I am Maximus. I am winning the crowd. I will rule the sushi bar.

12:36: I take a better look at my challenger. He is a tall, broad-shouldered, heavily muscular man. His natural facial expression is not one of happiness. He quietly watches me, then orders a shot, throws it back without noticeable effect, and smiles at me. I consider that talking shit to him was a bad idea. At this point I also realize that my stomach is very upset with me. I ignore it. I still have a public that needs to adore me.

12:54: I blow a .22. Only mild cheers this time. Everyone is waiting for the challenger to blow.

12:56: He blows a .24. He smiles condescendingly at me. I order two more shots.

12:59: I do the first shot. It doesn't go down well. I decide to take a short break from drinking. The crowd is not impressed.

1:10: Reality sets in. I am going to vomit. A LOT. I try to discreetly make it outside.

1:11: I knock a girl over as I sprint through the door.

1:11: I trip over a bush, stumble into it, and begin throwing up. Out of my mouth. And nose. It is not pleasant.

1:14: I can't figure out why my legs hurt so much. I look down at them in between heaves. I have no pants on. Thorns and branches are embedded in my shins.

1:18: The vomiting is over. I am now trying to stop the bleeding. A bright light hits my eyes. I am not happy. I tell the owner to "get that fucking light out of my face." The owner of the light identifies himself as an officer of the law. I apologize to the officer, and ask him what the problem is. A long pause ensues. The light is still in my eyes. "Son, where are your pants?" Remembering past encounters with the law, and realizing there is no one around to bail me out of the county lockup, I summon every bit of adrenaline in my body to sober myself up. I apologize again, and explain to the officer that my pants are in the restaurant that is less than 50 feet away, and that I came outside to share my sushi with the bush. He doesn't laugh. Another long pause.

"You're not driving tonight are you?", "Oh, NO, NO, NO . . . no sir, I don't even have a valid driver's license."

1:20: He tells me to go back inside, put on my pants, and call a cab.

1:21: I go back into the sushi restaurant. A few people stare at me in a peculiar manner. I look down, and then tuck my partially exposed sack back into my boxers. I don't know what to do about my bleeding legs. I look around for my pants.

1:24: I can't find my pants. My breathalyzer is in clear sight. I blow. A .23. Someone informs me that my challenger just blew a .26. They add that he hasn't thrown up yet. I tell them to "kiss my fucking ass." My last clear memory.

8:15am: I wake up. I don't know where I am. It is very hot. I am sweating horribly. It smells like rotting flesh.

8:16: I am in my car. With the windows up. The sun is beating down directly on me. It is at least 125 degrees in my car. I open the door and try to get out, but instead I fall onto the pavement. The scabs that cover my legs tear and reopen as I move. My penis falls out of my pink Gap boxers and lands, along with the rest of me, in a dirty puddle on the asphalt.

8:19: The fetid standing water finally jars me into full consciousness. I can't find my pants. Or cell phone. Or wallet. But I do have my breathalyzer. I blow. A .09. I am still not eligible to drive in the state of Florida.

8:22: I drive home anyway.

Let me be clear about this night: it was in my top 5 drunkest nights ever. I was completely shit-housed. I threw up multiple times, some of them through my nose. JESUS CHRIST, I WOKE UP blowing a .09. That's fucking ridiculous. That device is awful. It is the devil dressed in a transistor.

My advice to you: avoid it at all costs.

The Night We Almost Died

Occurred—April 1999
Written—July 2001

There are fun nights, there are crazy nights, and then there are those nights that make men legends.

It was a Saturday night in law school. Me and about 4 friends (Hate, GoldenBoy, Brownhole, and Credit) had collected at El Bingeroso's apartment. El Bingeroso had a college fraternity brother in town, Thomas, and wanted to show him a good time. We got there at around 7pm, and immediately began cooking large quantities of meat and drinking lots of alcohol.

El Bingeroso, who lived with his fiancée, was excited about seeing his college friend and began attacking the Natural Light. His fiancée, Kristy, knowing El Bingeroso's proclivity towards unruly drunken behavior, caught me in a corner and made me promise to stay sober so I could drive. Owing her a favor, I agreed. Though pissed at the time, it became the best decision I have ever made in my life.

All the meat and liquor in the apartment consumed, we headed out. It was decided that we needed to try a new bar. Someone mentioned that a place called "Shooters II" had a mechanical bull. This was an easy call.

By the time we arrived, El Bingeroso and Thomas were so drunk they were singing Johnny Cash songs and kicking cars in the parking lot. The rest of the party was not doing much better. Hate, normally an edgy person anyway, was so drunk he was eyeing Stop signs suspiciously. Having wrestled with Jim Beam for the past two hours and lost, he was ready for a fight. Brownhole and GoldenBoy were already staggering. I mentally prepare for the worst.

We paid $2 to get the obligatory bracelets. The girl behind the counter was dressed in a tight red Lycra cowgirl outfit, replete with white lace and frills. Her boots were black and white snake skin. But it was the white leopard print ten-gallon hat really brought the outfit together.

The bar was decorated in classic neo-Western Roadhouse: long-horns, oil cans, and saddles decorate the walls. I half expected Patrick Swayze to be smacking around unruly townies. I was so busy looking at the redneck paraphernalia, I failed to notice it before I heard Hate gasp, "No way! This is awesome!"

In the center of the bar was something I had never seen before in my life: Live professional wrestling.

Let's be clear about this: there was a ring, a full wrestling ring set up in the middle of the bar, and there were people, ostensibly professionals, in the ring, wrestling each other. I must have stood there for a good three minutes, trying to let my brain catch up with my eyes.

A real life ring, right in the middle of the bar. Two sweaty, out of shape wrestlers grappling, and a white banner behind the ring, proclaiming for all to see, "THIS IS THE SOUTHERN WRESTLING ASSOCIATION."

Hate is the first into action. Being an ex-high-school wrestler, completely shit-housed, and constantly filled with rage, he immediately pushed his way though the layers of crowd to arrive ringside, and began yelling curses at the wrestlers.

"THESE FUCKING CLOWNS ARE AWFUL! MY GRANDMOTHER COULD WRESTLE BETTER THAN THIS! YOU'RE LUCKY I'M NOT IN THERE, YOU COCK-SUCKING PUSSIES!! LET ME WRESTLE, I'LL KICK THEIR FUCKING ASSES!!"

This continued for a good five minutes. All of us were mesmerized, drunkenly fixated on this surreal comedy playing out before our eyes. To Hate's credit, the guys in the ring were not in good shape. If by "not in good shape," I mean "fat and disgusting."

A mere one beer later, Hate made his move. He stepped over the ropes that separated the crowd from the ring, and began banging on the canvas, yelling at the wrestlers. A bouncer told him to stop. Hate takes this as a cue to get into the ring, and beer firmly in hand, tried to climb into the ring. Two bouncers pulled him out of the ring before he could climb all the way in. We collected Hate from the bouncers, promised that he will behave, and gave him another beer. Hate continued repeating "My grandmother could kick their asses, this is a complete joke," over and over to himself.

Then I noticed how much we stood out. We were dressed in the standard grad-school uniform; khaki's and button down's. No one around us shared our fashion sense. They were dressed in "redneck casual;" dirty blue jeans and assorted trailer-park shirts (e.g. WWF shirts with logos like, "Come Smell What the Rock is Cooking"). The better dressed had on cowboy hats, cowboy boots, flannel shirts and clean blue jeans. Having grown up in Kentucky, I knew that these sorts of people generally don't take kindly to those they perceive as rich and snobbish, especially when they've been drinking. I filed that thought under "obvious foreshadowing."

By this time, Hate had separated from us and found his way into a discussion with a group of younger rednecks about the relative merits of the North versus the South. Hate is from Pennsylvania. They did not share his views. He claimed that he could whip any wrestler in the bar that night. Two of the rednecks, one very fat, claimed to be cousins of one of the wrestlers, the one called "Motorbike Mike," or some such bullshit. Hate questioned the sexuality of their cousin. A girl in the group claimed to be the girlfriend of "Motorbike Mike." Hate questioned her taste in men, her moral turpitude, and her intelligence.

The fat one, the alleged cousin of Motorbike Mike, who was apparently also somehow a relative of the girl, took exception to this. He was about 6'1", making him a good 8 inches taller than Hate. He had thick glasses, so horribly smudged I wanted to rip them off his face and clean them on my shirt (remember, I'm sober). His white tank-top shirt had grease and ketchup stains on it, partially covering the "George Strait" concert logo.

The redneck desperately needed a course in logic. He was losing an argument to someone so drunk he tried to climb into a wrestling ring:

Hate "The south is full of in-breds and rednecks. How are you related to both of them?"

The redneck tries to explain. I'm not able to follow. Hate ignores him.

Hate "None of this changes the fact that they're dating, and they're related. That is incest. You are southern in-bred trash."
Redneck "Yeah, well the north is just a bunch of rich bitches."
Hate "Possibly, but that doesn't change the fact that you have not responded to me. You are obviously an idiot also."
Redneck "Wa, well . . . You ain't worth a shit, and neither is the north."
Hate "Oh, that's a great comeback. You're making my point for me, moron."
Redneck "Bitch, I'll fight'cha ass. Well see who's better then, ya rich bitch."

A few more minutes of this, and the wrestling round mercifully ended, creating a short break in the action. I pulled Hate away from this stimulating conversation, and we joined everyone else at the bar. Hate ordered shots for the group.

After a post-shot round of beers, the mechanical bull started up. Hate not only signed himself up, but continuously yelled across the bar at the fat redneck with the smudged glasses until he came over and signed up also. El Bingeroso slammed a ten dollar bill on the bar, and called the redneck out.

El Bing "Hey FATASS, ten bucks says my friend rides longer than you."
Redneck "Screw you, northern bitch. I'll fucking outride your mom."
El Bing "What? My mother's not here, idiot. You just have to outride him," pointing at Hate.

The redneck walked off without answering. After a few girls rode the bull, the redneck got on and was thrown after about 4 seconds. A poor showing. We mock him mercilessly. He flips us off. We cheer loudly.

Hate rode for the full 8 seconds, an eventful 8 seconds at that. The first four or so he was doing fine, until the bull reared back, and flung him forward. Hate, had he been like the redneck, would have flown off into the cushions. But Hate is sort of like a British pitbull: once his jaws are locked, nothing short of death can get him to release. As a result, his entire body landed on his crotch, which hit his hand, which he had tied to the saddle horn. You could almost see him turn green as his entire body weight crushed his testicles against his wrist. To his credit, he stayed on for the full 8 seconds.

Hate, along with El Bingeroso and Thomas who have joined in the North vs. South discussion, begin taunting the fat redneck.

Hate "Hey, Jethro, how'd I stay on longer than you? Your fat ass alone should have kept you on for more than 4 seconds."
Thomas "Can anyone from the South do anything right?"
El Bing"Maybe if you weren't fucking your cousin, you'd be able to hold on tighter."
Hate "I thought the North wasn't worth a shit? I've never even seen a mechanical bull before tonight, and I outrode your sorry ass."

The redneck flips us off again, yells a stream of non-sequiturs that he presumably intended as disparaging remarks, and storms off with his friends. This enrages Hate,

Hate "HE OWES YOU TEN DOLLARS!!"

El Bingeroso and I convince Hate that it's OK, in this case, a moral victory is sufficient.

The mechanical bull interlude over, wrestling began again. Everything stayed calm for a while. The two wrestlers were incredibly fat, but they were using props (trash cans and such) and fake blood, so it was entertaining.

I went to the bathroom and when I get back Hate had disappeared again. I found him up against the ring, trying to grab one of the wrestlers by the ankle. I run over to the ring, where the bouncers had pulled him off the ring, and were trying to calm him down. He did not respond to them agreeably.

At this point, dealing with Hate was like taking a leashed pit bull to the Westminster Dog Show. I assist the bouncers on moving Hate away from the ring, and he and I end up in the area where the fat redneck and his entourage are. By this time, Motorbike Mike has come down to hang out with his myriad cousins and girlfriend. Hate, seeing the fat redneck, demands El Bingeroso's ten dollars. Motorbike Mike and I try to break them up, when Hate realizes who he is, yells at him,

"YOU FUCK YOUR COUSIN! YOU INBRED BITCH, GIVE ME MY TEN DOLLARS. I'LL KICK BOTH YOUR SOUTHERN WHITE TRASH ASSES."

And then hell starts breaking loose.

The bouncers lose their patience with Hate, and three of them, plus Motorbike Mike, picked him up and literally threw him out the back door. It was a scene straight out of "Roadhouse." I go to find everyone else, still at the bar, to tell them that Hate has been thrown out. El Bingeroso and Thomas are drunk, hanging all over each other, telling college stories to each other that both were there for. Brownhole is talking to the only female bartender with a full set of teeth, and GoldenBoy is cheering the wrestlers, urging them to spill more fake blood.

When El Bingeroso gets drunk, violence tends to follow. Provoked by the knowledge of Hate's ejection from the bar, El Bingeroso begins smashing ashtrays and flinging them off the bar. This upsets the bar manager, who pulls me aside.

Manager "Son, I think it's time you and your friends left."
Tucker "Yes sir, I agree wholeheartedly. Let me just get them together, and we'll promptly leave."

I huddle everyone together, and explain the situation. We are getting kicked out. As I herd them toward the door, Hate walks up.

Hate "Hey guys."
Tucker "What are you doing here? You just got kicked out."
Hate "It'll take more than that to keep me out of here. I paid my two dollars, I've got a bracelet, and I'm getting my goddamn money's worth."

Fine, I tell him we've been kicked out anyway, it's time to leave. I get everyone moving towards the door. El Bingeroso is one of the first outside, and as he waits for the rest of the group, he sees a truck parked right next to the door. He rears back and kicks the front grill of the truck. Twice. I am still trying to round everyone up, when a large redneck comes out the front door, and walks up to El Bingeroso.

Redneck "Hay boy . . . hay, did-jew juss kick dat truck?"

El Bingeroso is unsure how to answer. The redneck is large, and El Bingeroso knows he's guilty of the offense charged, but he doesn't seem to want to admit this to the redneck. So he just glares at him.

Redneck "I asked you a question, boy, did you kick that truck?"
El Bingeroso " Who the fuck are you?"

That was apparently the magic phrase, because the redneck immediately open fist slapped El Bingeroso right in the face. Thomas, who was standing there watching, throws his beer bottle on the ground, takes a little crow hop, and swings at the redneck. His aim is not good, and the fight degrades into a poorly choreographed dance, where El Bingeroso, Thomas and the large redneck are each swinging at each other and alternately moving away so as to not be struck by any counter punches.

Before I can even intervene (I was a good ten yards away as the first punch was thrown), ten more rednecks pour out the door. Brownhole and I successfully pull El Bingeroso and Thomas away from the increasingly large group of rednecks, and manage to settle things down for a second.

Tucker "OK, we are leaving. Sorry about any problems, but we're going."

The group of now twenty to thirty rednecks crowded around the door are staring and yelling at Brownhole, Credit, GoldenBoy and I as we try to pull Thomas and El Bingeroso away from the door.

A few seconds later Hate pushed his way through the crowd of rednecks, emerging on the other side just as one of the rednecks yelled something derogatory at El Bingeroso. Hate, being both loyal and drunk, immediately tackled this redneck, pinning him up against the very truck that El Bingeroso was kicking three minutes prior.

The events of the next minute are somewhat unclear, but I do remember these images:

- Hate with his head buried in someone's stomach, waling at his ribs, as other rednecks descended upon him.
- GoldenBoy and a redneck trying desperately to strangle the life out of each other.
- El Bingeroso and Thomas, back to back, swinging at anything that came close.
- Credit standing in the street debating.
- Me and Brownhole trying to pull Hate off of his redneck punching bag.

Then, the defining words of the night rang from out of Brownhole's mouth: "DUDE, HE'S GOT A FUCKING GUN! GUN! GUN! GUN! A FUCKING GUN!"

The word "gun" can do strange things to a fight. In this case, it ended it immediately. At those few words, El Bingeroso and Thomas were immediately out in the street with Credit, and GoldenBoy and Hate began retreating, hesitantly, with me and Brownhole, into the street.

Brownhole and I succeed in pulling everyone down the street, towards the first safe place we can find, a bar called the Oak Room. We walk up a flight of stairs, and there are 3 girls standing at the top of the landing. Hate is the first one to make it to them.

Girl "Hey guys, welcome to the Pi Phi Fall Philanthropy Event. It's two dollars to get in. Which fraternity are you guys from?"
Hate "Two dollars? I just paid two dollars and got into a fight, what the hell is this? Tucker? Take care of this, I'm not paying shit. Where's the damn beer?"

He pushes his way past the girls towards the bar area.

Girl "Hey! You can't do that! It's two dollars to get in. Um, excuse me!"

I really don't need this right now. I try to walk past the Pi Phi police, but she grabs me, "Excuse me, you have to pay two dollars, and two more for your rude friend."

That was my limit.

Tucker "What are you, fucking kidding me? Do you even work here?"
Girl "Uh, no. But it's a sorority philanthropy event; it's for charity."
Tucker "If you don't work here, then get the fuck out of my way. I'll drink to charity."

Brownhole ends up paying for the group to get in, and throws in an extra twenty to make the girls feel better. He'll do anything to get girls to like him.

We all get a beer, myself included. El Bingeroso buys the round, and then huddles everyone together. His speech is not entirely lucid.

El Bing "Alright guys, seriously . . . guns. OK? We cannot go anywhere without each other. We could die. For real. From the guns. We cannot leave this bar, except as a group. We have to stay together. We could get shot. Understood? Everyone together."

We agree. At the time, the group, mired in a fog of drunkenness, misses the irony of this statement. I smirk and head to the bathroom. Alone.

On my way back, I smile at a beautiful girl, and she gives me a cute little acknowledgment smile back. I wrote the book on pickup lines, so I head over to her and drop one of my favorite: "Did you invite all these people? I thought it was just going to be the two of us?"

She laughed, and I spent the next twenty minutes staring into her deep green eyes, pretending I was interested in the stupid things she was saying. A beautiful house, it's a shame no one was home.

Eventually remembering my shepherding duties, I looked around the bar to make sure everyone was OK. Much to my dismay, NONE OF MY FRIENDS WERE THERE.

I sprint off from the girl, she still in mid-sentence, and find Brownhole standing near the door, talking to the girl who wanted us to pay to get in.

Tucker "Dude, where is everyone?"
Brownhole "Oh, the rednecks came up and got them, but I think it's best for us to stay up here."
Tucker "WHAT!!! ARE YOU A FUCKING RETARD!! WE'RE THE ONLY SOBER ONES HERE!!!"

I fly down the stairs, and stumble out to what can only be described as something straight out of a bad '90s remake of *West Side Story.*

On the near side of the courtyard are my friends, El Bingeroso, Thomas, GoldenBoy, Hate and Credit, standing up on benches, pointing, gesticulating and yelling, in a fashion similar to agitated African savanna baboons.

On the far side of the courtyard are about twenty rednecks, engaged in the same type of ritual male-dominance displays. In between this are 5 large bouncers, trying to maintain calm and keep the warring factions apart.

Hate chooses this point to try and charge across the courtyard towards the rednecks. Thankfully for him, one of the bouncers intercepts him and places him in a headlock. Hate does not like this at all, and begins swinging at the bouncer's ribs. Presumably, he would have swung at his face, but Hate is 5'6", and the bouncer's face was about a foot above Hate's reach. I help the bouncer move Hate back over to our side and out of the demilitarized zone in the middle of the courtyard. The bouncer takes this as a sign that I'm the sober one in the group, and says something to me I heard many times in my law school career:

Bouncer "You need to take your friends and get out of here."
Tucker "Look man, our cars are out in that parking lot. You are going to have to walk us out there. Those fucking guys have guns, and they are very angry with us."

The bouncer sees the logic in this, and explains the situation to the other bouncers. They encircle us, and begin walking us towards our car. The rednecks are none too happy about this, but the lead bouncer has somehow managed to convince them to not launch a full-scale assault on us. I can only assume he threatened violence and inevitable police involvement.

We finally make it to Credit's car, when I notice that Brownhole is nowhere to be found. Fucking great. I should leave that disloyal coward cocksucker back in the Oak Room. Scanning the parking lot, I see him. He is walking next to the very truck that El Bingeroso had been kicking earlier, talking to the older redneck driving it.

Thomas sees this, and yells out, "Oh shit, guys, Brownhole is gonna get fucked up."

El Bing "What? Where? Brownhole! WE HAVE TO BACK HIM UP!," and he tears off running towards Brownhole and the truck.

The subsequent conversation I did not hear, but was reported pretty much the same from both Brownhole and El Bingeroso. Brownhole had apparently made headway into calming the old redneck driving the truck. This guy not only owned the truck in question, but also the very bar that everything had started in. He was on the way to convincing the old redneck to call off his henchmen, when all of the sudden El Bingeroso runs up.

Old redneck "Son, your friends are lucky you're here to get them out of this. I kill people like them."
Brownhole "Yes sir, I'm glad we can resolve this peacefully."
El Bing [As he runs up] "Brownhole, what the fuck? Let's get the fuck out of here. He's got a gun!"
Old Redneck "A gun? Boy, I got two guns." At which point the old redneck pulled a 9mm pistol out from a hidden compartment in the truck, and held it up along with his sawed-off shotgun from before.
El Bing "OH SHIT!"
El Bingeroso tried to back up so fast he fell over.
Brownhole "El Bingeroso, go away, go back to the car, I'm taking care of this."
Old Redneck "Hey, hey boy, you're the one who kicked my truck. You got to pay for a new grill."
Brownhole "El Bingeroso, come on, let's go. Sorry sir, my friend needs to get home, he's very drunk. Your grill looks fine."
Old redneck "Who's gonna pay for a new grill for my truck? Goddammit!"

The bouncers thankfully re-intervened at this point, and everyone piled into Credit's car. Being the sober one I drove over to GoldenBoy's car, and GoldenBoy and Brownhole got out. We sat there and watched them get in, and then pull off.

This is important, because the conversation in the car for the next twenty minutes as we drove to Chapel Hill revolved around this event. El Bingeroso was convinced that we had left GoldenBoy and Brownhole to die by the hands of the rednecks. Hate refused to believe that there were any guns involved. Thomas was convinced we were being followed. Credit fell asleep. It went something like this:

Hate "Dude, we fucking left GoldenBoy and Brownhole. They're fucking dead, man. We left them to die, man. What the fuck?"
Thomas "Tucker man, speed up, those lights have been behind us since we left Durham."
Tucker "Guys, everyone relax. GoldenBoy and Brownhole are fine, the redneck with the gun parked his truck, we are fine, so everyone just shut up."
Hate "What gun are you guys talking about? There was no gun."
Bingeroso "Fuck you Hate, I saw the fucking gun. I saw the gun that

the rednecks are using right now to kill Brownhole and GoldenBoy. How the fuck could we leave them? They've been shot. We left them for DEAD. THEY'RE DEAD! FUCK!!"
Hate "There was no gun."
Bingeroso "FUCK OFF HATE, I SAW THE FUCKING GUN. THERE WERE TWO GUNS, ASSHOLE!!"
Thomas "Seriously, just pull into a police station. The rednecks are following us."
Hate "Who cares? They don't have any guns."
Bingeroso "FUCK YOU MAN, I SAW THE GUN. I SAW THE FUCKING GUN! GOLDENBOY AND BROWNHOLE ARE DEAD! WHAT THE FUCK?!? WE ABANDONED THEM!"
Thomas "Those are totally the same truck lights. They've been behind us since Durham. Tucker, seriously, start evasive maneuvers or something."
Bingeroso "We left our friends . . . WE'RE COWARDS."
Hate "Speak for yourself."
Bingeroso "FUCK YOU HATE! I'LL FUCKING KILL YOU!"

We eventually made it to Chapel Hill. GoldenBoy and Brownhole were fine, no one was following us, Credit woke up, and everyone told Hate that there were indeed guns. We drank some beers, calmed down, and headed home.

I was exhausted. Being the only sober one in a group of nine retarded drunks is not fun. Fuck this; from now on, I'm drinking and driving. El Bingeroso and Thomas were the last two I dropped off, and I headed into El Bingeroso's place with them to get a beer; I figured I had earned it.

El Bingeroso decided he was hungry, so he took out a roll of unopened, pre-made cookie dough from the refrigerator, tore off the package, plopped the whole thing down on a cookie sheet, and threw it in the oven, setting the temperature at somewhere around "Lowest Level of Hell." He tossed us a few beers, and we relived the night for a while, filling each other in on the parts that the other two had missed. After two beers, Kristy came out of her room, groggy and sleepy-eyed, and said to El Bingeroso,

Kristy "What is that smell?"
El Bing "Oh, sorry baby, that's cookies burning."

Kristy "Umm, OK. Can you guys keep it down, I've got to be at work early tomorrow."

At this, Thomas stood up and said, "Keep it down? WOMAN, WE'RE LUCKY TO BE ALIVE!!!"

The Blowjob Follies

Occurred—various 1994–2004
Written—July 2004

Blowjobs . . . the sweet sounds of silence. The problem with oral sex is that it's like writing. When done right, it's amazing, but there are just so many ways it can go wrong, and when it goes wrong, it's just not worth it. These are some of my funnier blow job stories:

Say it, Don't Spray it

High school was the first time I realized that blow jobs would be a painful pleasure. I was dating a girl from another school in my area. Besides being one of the hottest girls I've ever known, she was also one of the very first girls to give me head. We were both new at it, and she liked me to courtesy tap. This was because I had convinced her that—I'm not making this up—it wasn't "real" oral sex as long as I didn't cum in her mouth. Aren't 17-year-old girls funny?

The first few dozen times she went down on me I courtesy tapped just like she asked. One time we were in my car, parked right out front of her house because I was dropping her off after a date. Instead of a kiss goodnight, I suggested she blow me goodnight. She thought this was a brilliant idea.

I quickly got carried away with the risk and thrill of having her suck my dick twenty yards away from her house where her father, who I hated, was waiting for her to come home. I was lost in the sexual ecstasy of the dangerous youthful blowjob when I heard her let out a little yelp. She immediately sat up, her mouth half open, full of splooge, the excess dripping off her chin, and uttered a muffled,

"You asshole!"

Then she spit the cum all over my face. Sprayed it all over me.

I was still recovering from getting *my own* jism spat into *my own* face as she jumped out of my car and sprinted into her house. I quickly drove off. I had no desire to face her rifle-wielding father with my face covered in my sperm.

Once I was out of imminent danger, I couldn't help but laugh. I had no idea that this would only be the first in a long line of strange blowjob incidents.

Miss Chokesondick

One girl I was dating the summer after I graduated high school, "Jayne," had never given head before she started seeing me. Now, my experience has taught me that whenever a girl tells me she "doesn't normally give head," she inevitably ends up giving me an incredible blowjob. It's the ones who say they never do it that do it the best. Jayne was the exception.

She was the absolute worst I've ever experienced. I've never even heard of girls worse at fellatio than Jayne. Her teeth were all over my dick, she had no rhythm, no enthusiasm, and had a mouth that mysteriously never got moist. It was awful.

It was a month of painstaking instruction before she finally got good enough that I didn't just stop her after 5 minutes and tell her to jerk me off—she was that bad. After another month or so, she got good enough that she could at least come close to finishing me off by herself. Here's the weirdest part: no matter how much she improved, ***she never moved her head***. She kept her head still and I would have to move my hips. This was annoying, but I was patient with her because she was stunningly beautiful and I was still young enough to think I was actually capable of love.

One night she was doing a pretty good job and I got very enthused with my hip thrusts when I felt a warm, wet sensation on my crotch. I was laying on my back and I looked down and saw what looked like A LOT of splooge.

This confused me because even though I was close to coming, I didn't think I had actually achieved orgasm. The cum was chunky to the touch, very dark, and much more viscous than any semen that I've ever seen shoot out of my dick. My first thought was that she had given me some crazy hybrid VD that made my discharge all thick and chunky. I dismissed that, but my mind was still racing; I couldn't figure out what could be wrong, so I said, "What did you do to my dick?"

She looked up at me. The expression on her face immediately gave it away:

"Oh my god—did you just throw up on my dick? Did you just VOMIT ON MY FUCKING DICK?"

Yes, Tucker. Yes she did.

I ended up dating her for another two years (beauty does strange things to the male mind), but she stopped going down on me and we just focused on vaginal sex from that point forward.

Bull's-eye

The next incident was a few years later, in college, right after I had discovered the art of coming on a girl's face. Even before I made the term "dotting her eyes" famous, I was a fan of giving the facial.

As my climax approached, I moved her onto her back and pulled out just in time, covering her face with a solid 5-roper. Being the neophyte, I had no idea how to aim, and accidentally shot the first—and strongest—rope right in her eye. As I finished and collapsed, very happy with myself and proud of my prodigious paint job, I noticed the look of agony and pain on her face.

Tucker "Baby, are you OK? What's wrong?"
Girl "I . . . I can't see . . . Jesus, it hurts . . . it's burning."

I helped her scoop most of it out of her eye and, both of us still naked and sweaty, I led her into the bathroom where she washed her eye out for a good five minutes.

Apparently, semen does not agree with the eye. I called her "Red Eye" for the next few hours, until she got mad and refused to ever give me head again. Then I apologized profusely. She forgave me until she realized that she had ejaculate in her hair and had to wash it twice to get it all out. Needless to say, there were no more facials for her. After that, she swallowed every bit of my seed like a nun taking communion.

The Phantom Menace

One time when I was visiting some friends and family in DC, I went out drinking and ended up going home with a girl. I'll be honest: this girl was not attractive. But she was into me, and she was there, and perhaps most importantly—she just gave off a blowjob vibe. You know the type; they aren't good looking or exceptional in any way, but they just give off a look that says 'I suck dick like I invented it.'

I was pretty drunk when we got back to her place, but that didn't seem to faze her. We didn't even make it to the bedroom. She grabbed me right as we came in the door, undid my pants as she pushed me onto her white sofa and knelt on the ground in front of me, working me right there in her living room.

My God was I right: She blew me away, literally and figuratively. She must have spent at least 20 minutes fellating me, never once taking her mouth off my penis, slurping at the exact right moments in the exact right places. She was so good even my ankles started sweating. God bless whoever taught her.

As soon as she finished, she went to the bathroom to wash out her mouth (she's one of those), and I stood up to rifle through my pants pocket and get a condom when I saw the sofa: there was a HUGE skid mark prominently displayed on her WHITE sofa.

I laughed at first. Then I remembered that she drove me to her place . . . and she lived a good 30 minutes away from where I was staying. As the thought of having to hitchhike 45 miles walked through my mind, she appeared out of the bathroom. Fuck.

Thinking fast, I put my pants on the sofa and "romantically" whisked her into her bedroom, where I had to fuck her at least 3 or 4 times to get her to go to sleep. Once she was safely out, I snuck out of her room and flipped the cushion.

I still don't know if she ever found that stain.

Blowjob Betty

Those incidents were from back when I was young and cared about things like feelings and emotions. As I grew older and my soul became jaded, I realized that I could be an asshole and get away with it, so I became more risky with my blowjob activities.

One time I was with a girl, we'll call her "Betty." She lived in a house with three other girls, but they were all out, so we hooked up in her living room. Betty was a master of her craft, and especially loved going down on me. She was hitting the crescendo of her well-conducted symphony of knob-slobbing, but right before I felt myself let loose into her mouth, the door to her house opened.

Her roommate was barely inside when she saw Betty on her knees sucking me off like she was auditioning for a porn movie. Betty, lips still wrapped firmly around my penis, hand wrapped around my shaft, heard the noise and looked up. Momentarily the eyes of the two roommates locked, one walking in the door, the other with my dick in her mouth. At that exact moment in time, two things happened simultaneously:

- I shot my load into Betty's mouth.
- The roommate screamed and ran back out the door.

I had not cum for about three days before this encounter, and thus I had a Peter North sized 8-roper waiting for her. This did not sit well with Betty, especially because she was not expecting it.

Betty tried to take the porn star load, but it was just too much. She was not ready and still trying to process the fact that her roommate saw her sucking dick, so she started choking. Not coughing or a slight choke—the bitch was turning red and dying right in front of me, with my seed as the instrument of death.

I was unsure what to do; I'd never seen a girl choke on dick before. I thought that only happened in rap songs.

After about five seconds of watching her retch, the words from the Too Short song "Blowjob Betty" rang through my head, "A young girl died just last night, she choked on sperm in her windpipe . . ." so I did the only thing I could think of: I gave her the Heimlich Maneuver.

I grabbed her around her chest just below her breasts and pulled my fists into her ribcage with all my force. After about three times she heaved, coughed my splooge all over her couch and started yelling at me, "STOP IT! [cough] YOU'RE HURTING ME! [cough] STOP ASS-HOLE!"

I ended up having to take her to the hospital. Not for asphyxiation—she wasn't choking after all, the cum just surprised her and got in her nose. Nope . . . in my enthusiasm to save her life, I had succeeded in breaking one of her ribs.

The highlight of the night was at the ER when the doctor told me that I did a very good job with the Heimlich. Apparently, you're actually *supposed* to break a rib if you do it right.

We never could get the old magic back after that night. It might have been because she couldn't take a deep breath for two months.

A Satisfying Meal

My personal favorite blowjob story happened with a girl I hooked up with only once. I met her in some city, out at some bar, on some night—I barely even remember what she looked like (thank you, Dollar Beer Night). I am pretty sure she was engaged, but it wasn't to any of my friends, so I didn't care.

The girl did a pretty decent job sucking me off, especially considering how much I drank, and I finished in her mouth. Like a pro, she kept her lips wrapped around my dick till it was dry, but when she came up, there was a strange look on her face. She contorted her expression a little, opened her mouth like she was going to vomit, which of course made me pull back quickly, then all of the sudden:

"BUUUUUURRRRRRRRRRRPPPPPPPPP!"

The girl belched like a drunken sailor—OFF OF MY CUM!

Easily one of the proudest moments of my life.

EVERYONE HAS "THAT" FRIEND

Occurred—various, 1999–2001
Written—June 2005

While at Duke Law School, I made some of my best friends on earth. Guys like PWJ, GoldenBoy, El Bingeroso, Hate, JoJo and Credit made my three years there some of the best of my life. Even though all of them were awesome in their own way, one friend stands out: "SlingBlade."

SlingBlade is white, about 6'1", a generally good looking guy except for his huge nose. Picture a younger Owen Wilson, fucked up nose and all, but with a buzz cut. The first time I met SlingBlade was in the law school library. JoJo was sitting with him at a table shooting the shit and I joined them. Even though I didn't know him at the time, when SlingBlade started talking about a movie he'd just seen, saying things like, "It was so bad I had to hit myself in the hand with a tack hammer to take my mind off the pain it caused me," and "I'd compare watching that thing to masturbating with sandpaper," I knew that this kid was hilarious and I wanted to hang out with him some more.

Over the ensuing months and years I've gotten to know him much better, and it seems like every layer I uncover is weirder and more hilarious than the next:

OCD, GI Joe, and his nickname

When I first went over to SlingBlade's apartment, it was to pick him up on the way to a bar. This was about a month or so after I met him in the library and I was a little weirded out: his place was a shrine to obsessive-compulsive disorder. He kept it meticulously clean and Spartan to the extreme. The only thing in the living room was a TV on a stand, a single chair in front of it, and a PlayStation2 at the base of the TV. The controllers had the cords wrapped around them, placed on each side, equidistant from the PS2 base, which itself was perfectly perpendicular with the TV stand. On his shelf were about 300 DVDs, perfectly in line and arranged alphabetically by genre. He had a lot of the standard guy movies like *Scarface* and *Godfather*, but most of his collection was sci-fi. He had every *Star Wars* and *Star Trek* DVD I've ever heard of, and lots I hadn't.

His bedroom had only a bed and a desk. The bed had Batman sheets and a Green Lantern comforter. Just about every free piece of space in the room was occupied with dolls, or as he calls them, "action figures." He must have had like 70-100 various toys all over the place, most of them were set up like they were fighting each other; the GI Joes were battling the Spawn characters, Superman and the Justice League were squared off against Star Wars figures, and dozens of other genres that I didn't recognize were locked in frozen combat with each other. I was momentarily encouraged by the hot Jeri Ryan poster on the wall . . . until I realized that she was dressed as Seven of Nine (the character she plays on *Star Trek*). The kicker was a talking Yoda doll that he had on his desk. I walked by and the thing blurted out, "Size matters not." I punched it and it chirped at me, "Beware the Dark Side":

Tucker "Dude, have you ever brought a girl back here?"
SlingBlade "Yeah . . . once."
Tucker "What did she say when she saw all this?"
SlingBlade "I don't know. Nothing. It was dark."

I am not a toy expert, but one thing I did notice was that he had both the older and the newer GI Joes. Because I loved my GI Joes—when I was TEN—I jokingly asked him about them:

Tucker "Are the new GI Joes better than their 80's counterparts? I don't see how you can beat the old school Snake-Eyes."
SlingBlade [the exactness of this response is due to the fact that he rewrote it for me. From memory. You think he might be OCD?]:

"The answer is a resounding yes. The old figures suffered from a potent and debilitating malaise known as Wasting Rubber-Band Syndrome.

WRBS occurred when you held the legs of Duke or Roadblock, the only two GI Joes you had since your parents were poor and hated you, and spun around the top portion to create a 'super-spinning punch' wherein the figure would triumph over his enemy, much to my adolescent delight. This punch was an amazing tool, used only under dire circumstances, such as when Cobra (populated by conscripts from my sister's Barbie collection who were sold into white slavery) was about to overrun your Lego fortress. Why Lego, you ask? Because your parents wouldn't spring for the GI Joe base. God forbid you should spend twenty dollars so your lonely son who spent his formative years confined to quarters for things like "backtalk" and "auto theft" could have a cool fortress for his only friends. Coincidentally enough, I won't be springing for the silver package when I stuff those two idiots into the old folks home in a few years. Payback's a bitch, isn't it?

Anyway, after enough of this the rubber band would snap and your GI Joe would be cleaved in two. You would then cry, as your supply of friends had been effectively cut in half.

There was also a secondary problem named Fatigued Thumb Syndrome. FTS was when the GI Joe received a constructive form of leprosy due to overuse and their thumbs would fall off, rendering them incapable of holding a weapon. Once the thumb was gone these figures became almost useless. At this point the only thing they were good for was renaming them for one of your enemies at school and then melting them on an open flame or destroying them with a firecracker. Neither problem exists in the current version, from what I can tell.

In unrelated news: I'm still single."

Looking through his DVD's, I saw a movie that didn't really fit with the sci-fi/gangster themes of the rest of his titles: *Slingblade.* I love that movie, and asked him why he had it. He told me it was his favorite movie, and started reciting lines from memory, in the same low, baritone gravely voice that Billy Bob Thornton used in the movie.

[In case you have never seen it, *Slingblade* is a fantastic movie about a semi-retarded man named Karl Childers. My buddy SlingBlade relates on a very personal level with the main character (played by Billy Bob Thornton) because they are both very sensitive people who feel disconnected and hurt by a world that doesn't understand or appreciate them, and as a result must wear a social mask that is different from their inner self. The only major difference is that SlingBlade is a fucking genius, while Karl Childers is mildly retarded.]

This was only like the fourth or fifth time I'd ever hung out with him, so I didn't really understand how unpredictable and random he could be. After we got to the bar and had some drinks, I was talking to a hot UNC soccer player and SlingBlade was playing wingman with her friend. I guess the girl he was talking to was an idiot, because eventually he got bored, and when he gets bored you never know what he'll do to entertain himself:

Girl "So, do you like Duke?"
SlingBlade [imagine his voice in a low, baritone rumble, like Billy Bob Thornton in the movie] "Some folks call it a Kaiser blade, but I call it a sling blade, hrmmmm."
Girl "Excuse me?"
SlingBlade "I reckon I want me some of them French fried taters, hrmmm."
Girl "What did you say?"
SlingBlade "I reckon you bout dumb as post, hrrmmm."
Girl [to me] "Your friend is scaring me."
Tucker "Me too."

After a few nights of this, I stopped trying to fight it and just went along, because after all—it is pretty damn funny. We'd be talking to some girls, and if they bored us or pissed us off, we'd just bust out with these improvised mini-montages from the movie. Usually, I'd play the role of Doyle Hargraves, the abusive boyfriend (played in the movie by Dwight Yoakum):

SlingBlade "I reckon this'n girl bout to fuck you, hrmmmm."
Tucker [in a redneck voice] "Boy, you shut yer mouth or I will beat the dog shit outta yew."
SlingBlade "I want me some of that there vaginer, hrrmmmm."
Tucker "Dat's it! Linda—I'm bout fed up with this retard hangin' round the house!"
Random Girl "What is wrong with you two?"

The McGriddle Argument

Even though he can be weird in a lot of ways, SlingBlade is a legit comedic genius. The purest example of this is "The McGriddle

Argument." On the message board attached to my site, SlingBlade and I we were talking about a McDonalds breakfast sandwich called the McGriddle. This is the basic transcript of the discussion:

Tucker: "Dude—that thing looks disgusting. It has to be nasty, with the syrup shit in it. What is that?"

SlingBlade: "I can only assume from your cavalier attitude that you have yet to partake of the wonderment that is the McGriddle. Let me enlighten you. What happens is the One True God grows them on trees in the Elysian Fields using a heretofore unused incantation. He then proceeds to magic them down to your local eatery where whatever Ghetto Bastard cook your McDonalds has rescued from welfare that week proceeds to wrap it in cellophane and pass it along to you, the fortunate consumer. You proceed to ingest this finery in the vain hope that your obviously overmatched taste buds can somehow grasp the delectable intricacies it is suddenly faced with. Is that egg? Why yes it is, and bacon too. But wait—they didn't add . . . yes they did, yes they did indeed. They added cheese. And then, then my friends, they wrapped it in a sumptuous pancake bun! As your taste buds try to process that amazing piece of information, IT hits them...the syrup nugget. THE MOTHERFUCKING SYRUP NUGGET! It announces itself with a burst of confectionery grandiosity the likes of which your palate has never seen."

Tucker: "So you like them?"

SlingBlade: "If you EVER speak ill of the McGriddle again I will personally force-feed you one while I fuck you in the butt using the wrapper as a condom and then donkey punch you when the infused syrup nuggets explode in your mouth."

Ironically, I think more people on my message board have commented on that than anything I've ever written there.

"Welcome to my life"

But of all his little quirks, one characteristic truly defines SlingBlade: his issues with women. The first few times we went out, the same basic thing happened: I'd hit on a hot girl, he'd play wingman and hit on her friend, but invariably he'd get depressed and/or upset with her, insult her, and she would run off crying or get mad at him. At first this was bothersome, because the hot girl I was talking to would usually leave with her pissed off/upset friend. But after I got used to it, I was more intrigued than upset. This was a decent looking guy who was not only blowing pussy, he was doing it on purpose. Who does this?

I had to drag it out of him, but I discovered what is perhaps the most defining story of his life: He and his high school girlfriend, the love of his life, went to different undergrads. He never cheated on her because he is an honest and moral man, but she did not possess the same integrity. She fucked half her school, and never told him. At least not until he went down to visit her and didn't understand why all these guys kept coming by her room asking her what she was doing later . . . until she dumped him and asked him to leave. He has never recovered, and still cannot deal with women on a meaningful romantic level.

After that sort of trauma I can understand having issues with intimacy, but he should still be able to hook up. You don't have to be in love to fuck, right? Even though SlingBlade agreed with that notion in principle, it didn't work for him in practice.

You know that saying, "Any club that would let me be a member, I wouldn't want to join?" SlingBlade assumed that any girl that he liked enough to want to fuck, wouldn't want to fuck him. But any girl who did want to fuck him without first knowing him and respecting him, he automatically thought was a whore . . . and he refused to sleep with a girl he regarded as a whore. This absurd Catch-22 pretty much guaranteed that SlingBlade got no ass.

Add in his low tolerance for stupidity and his utter disdain for whorish female behavior, combine it with the fact that many of the girls I hit on fit right into either the dumb or slutty categories that he hated, and you have a recipe for hilarity. This is only one example:

A few months after law school graduation I went up to DC to visit SlingBlade for a weekend. He was in bad shape, even for him. Working 70 hours a week doing document review as a temp (the lowest level of legal work), living in a crappy over-priced apartment in Alexandria, no women or prospects, SlingBlade was as thoroughly depressed as I've ever seen him. From what I could tell, the only thing that brought him joy was beating his roommate at Tetris. I decided to take him out, get him drunk and see if I couldn't get him out of his despair.

We pre-partied at his place and get hammered, then went to some bar in Clarendon that was packed with hot girls. Across the bar I see what I think is a super hot girl.

Tucker "Look at her; that girl is hot."
SlingBlade "She probably looks alright when it's dark.
Tucker "What are you talking about? She's hot."
SlingBlade "Here's a shock. Let's see: she's a tall slutty blonde, and you are drunk. Cupid has spoken."

We walk over there, but before I can hit on her I realize much to my dismay that SlingBlade was right: Her hot face and great tits are paired with ghetto booty and elephant legs. This girl had a cover-of-Maxim upper body and a World's Strongest Man lower body.

SlingBlade "HAAHHAHAHHAAH—Welcome to Zerosville, population: Her."
Tucker "I need some more shots."
SlingBlade "Well, you know who to go to if your car gets stuck and you need a push."
Tucker "Dude . . . just leave me alone right now. If I hook up with her, you can make fun of me all you want tomorrow, but let me have my illusion tonight."

She comes over and starts flirting with me before I can even get my shots down. I played it coy as I talked to her, but not because I was trying to run advanced game; I was trying to hurry up and get drunk so her legs would look skinnier.

Tucker "So, what do you do?"
ElephantLegs "Well I'm about to finish school, but I've been doing some modeling and I'll probably do that full time when I graduate."
SlingBlade "You're a model? Right, and the red 'S' on my chest means that I'm Superman." [Did I mention that he was wearing a Superman shirt . . . to a bar?]
ElephantLegs "I model!"
SlingBlade "I might believe you were a model if you didn't have such fat legs. Oh wait—have you been in a Lane Bryant catalog? That kind of modeling?"
ElephantLegs "NO!!"
Tucker "In her defense, do you realize how much money plus-sized models can make? It's shocking."

ElephantLegs "I DON'T PLUS SIZE MODEL!! I'll have you know that Ford signed me to a contract just last week!"
SlingBlade "Whatever. You did that on your back."

One great thing about SlingBlade's attitude was that he was truly great at unintentionally playing "The Bad Guy." When you are picking up girls, sometimes having an asshole friend can actually work towards your advantage. Though this girl was all pissed off and huffy at SlingBlade, it made her more into me. Not only is it easy to be The Good Guy when a Bad Guy is there, but that little exchange made her really want to fuck me, just to prove that the Bad Guy was wrong and that she was desirable.

But there is a limit to what a girl will endure before she gets pissed and leaves. I talked to her for a while longer, solidified my position, and then took SlingBlade around to try and get him in with another girl. And of course if I can trade up too, that's always a plus.

The next group of girls we talked to were really cute, and one seemed into SlingBlade.

Girl "I totally recognize you from somewhere."
SlingBlade "Perhaps we go to the same comic book store."
He said that sarcastically, but she didn't get the joke.
Girl "No, no, that isn't it. I think I saw you riding a bicycle the other day, over in Ballston."
SlingBlade "Are you fucking stupid?"
Girl "What?"
SlingBlade "Yeah, I was riding my bike to the porn store. I take my bike there so no one will recognize me."
Girl "I have to go find my friends."

I get us in with another pair of really cute girls. Things were going great for me . . . sadly SlingBlade's girl was not quite up to the task:

Girl "I am hoping to get my masters in psych after I get my BA."
SlingBlade "It takes someone very smart to get a psych degree."
Girl "I'm smart."
SlingBlade "The smartest thing to ever come out of your mouth is a penis."
Girl "I'm NOT STUPID!"

SlingBlade "IT STOPS TALKING TO ITS INTELLECTUAL SUPERIOR OR IT GETS THE HOSE."

She turns and walks away.

SlingBlade grabs his nipples like Buffalo Bill in *Silence of the Lambs*, "I'D FUCK ME!!"
Tucker "Dude, do you realize that when you insult one girl, you aren't just fucking it up with her, you are polluting her entire group of friends. See those girls that she's sitting with? Now as far as that group is concerned, we might as well be lepers."
SlingBlade "Did you hear the nonsensical prattle spewing from her pie-hole?"
Tucker "Dude, I am your best friend. Help me out here."
SlingBlade "Best friend? I can't begin to elucidate my hatred for you."
Tucker "That's the funny thing: I really am your best friend, but if I died tomorrow, I don't know if you'd come to my funeral."
SlingBlade "I don't know. Maybe . . . if nothing good was on TV."

I try one more time to get him set up with another girl, but that ends before I can even get them both drinks. As I am ordering, he yells out:

"FELLATIO WON'T FILL THE HOLE IN YOUR SOUL!!"

That pretty much sealed his fate with all the other girls at the bar, so we head back to ElephantLegs. In a stroke of luck, this time she's with some other girl. OtherGirl is very pretty, has a great body, and seems sweet, so she and SlingBlade get along well enough that when the bar closes, the four of us decide to go to IHOP together. As we are walking out, I pull SlingBlade aside:

Tucker "Dude, be cool, this one likes you and wants to hook up. Just be yourself and everything will be fine. She seems like a good girl."
SlingBlade "Yeah, I think so. And if she doesn't find my unique blend of caustic wit and political satire amusing, I'll just pull out the 'B' game: potty humor and slightly veiled masturbation references."

I should have just pushed him into traffic right then to save us all time, but what can I say, I'm a loyal friend.

We get to IHOP and there are about thirty people, mostly black and Hispanic, waiting in line. SlingBlade storms in front of them, yelling:

"There are white people who need to eat, make some room, white people need a table, outta the way."

It was obviously a joke, and most people got it and laughed. The Alexandria City cop working the door did not.

Cop "If your attitude doesn't improve, you are going to sort it out in the tank."
SlingBlade "OK, Mr. Plastic Badge. So, which section of the police academy entrance did you fail, hmm? Perhaps it was the hospitality portion."
Tucker "Dude—he's a real cop."
SlingBlade "Oh . . . we'll be leaving now."

We take the girls across the street to Denny's. I guess they have lower standards for seating drunk idiots than IHOP because they give us a table immediately. SlingBlade goes to the bathroom and when he gets back he tells the table:

"Dude, taking antibiotics and then drinking beer is a bad idea. I just let loose a symphony of bowel movements, each in different pitches and melodies. It was like a poop xylophone in there."

I think this is hilarious, while the girls do not. Some people just don't get good potty humor. After we order, SlingBlade and OtherGirl start getting to know each other.

OtherGirl "So what do you do in your free time?"
SlingBlade "Cut up Guatemalan hookers and bury them in shallow graves by the interstate."

OtherGirl "What was your family like?"
SlingBlade "My dad was so mean, he'd give my sisters and me ten dollars on Christmas Eve, steal it back from us that night when we were sleeping, and then beat us on Christmas Day because we lost it."

She was a nice girl, but wasn't getting the jokes. Sensing the night slip away, I tried to shift the focus by talking about ElephantLegs' ex-boyfriend. He was a complete tool, and I figured this sort of gossip would be more OtherGirl's intellectual speed.

ElephantLegs "Yeah, he was 26 and I was 20 when we met. We met at a Macaroni Grill my friends and I were eating at, in [a very rural college town]."

SlingBlade "He is an assistant manager at a Macaroni Grill? In that city? HAHAHAHAH. This one sounds like a winner. Was he a townie? Did he have a goatee and drive a rusted out Firebird?"
ElephantLegs "No, he was a really good guy. He was cool."
SlingBlade "He sounds like the type of guy who would profess his love for a girl in spray paint across a highway overpass. I bet his busy schedule includes screaming into his pillow and crying himself to sleep, because his life sucks."

SlingBlade decides that his food is taking too long and that he can do better than the current line cook, so he leaves the table and goes into the kitchen. There is no one in there, so he messes with the griddle, flipping knobs and switches until it turns on. The female cook comes around the corner, she sees him, stops and stares at him in astonishment for a few seconds as he pours some pancake mix on the griddle. He sees her, and she questioningly shrugs her shoulders at him, to which he replies:

"I'm hungry. I'm gonna make me some flapjacks."

She didn't think it was funny, and we had to leave our second restaurant of the night.

The girls drove their own car, and in the parking lot we tried to figure out what to do. OtherGirl came up with a good idea:

OtherGirl "You know . . . I have a hot tub at my place. What would you two say if I asked you back there?"
SlingBlade "Heeellllloooo staph infection."
Tucker "He has health insurance. We'll follow you."

In the car, SlingBlade looked about as a happy as a Mormon getting a lap dance.

Tucker "Hello staph infection? What the fuck is wrong with you?"
SlingBlade "Why do so many women disgust me?"
Tucker "Because you are fucked up and can't get over your ex. Are you gonna hook up or what? That girl seemed into you."
SlingBlade "Yeah, I guess. She seems nice. I don't know."

We go back to their place and there are already a bunch of people at the house; apparently one of the other roommates was having a party that night. OtherGirl mixes us a few drinks, and we sit around and talk awhile before ElephantLegs and I get into the hot tub and start making out. A few minutes later, I hear him screaming from inside:

SlingBlade "Oh you don't want to hook up with me? What, my fetid, hoppy beer breath bothering you? Oh yeah, daddy drinks too much!"
SlingBlade comes out to the deck:

SlingBlade "I am leaving."
Tucker "Why? What happened?"
SlingBlade "I'm going home to get my gun so I can kill everyone here."

He storms off before I can put my shorts on (ElephantLegs had them off in the hot tub) and catch him. I find OtherGirl:

Tucker "What the fuck happened? Why did he leave?"
OtherGirl "I don't know—your friend is weird."
Tucker "There has to be a reason. He wouldn't just storm out."
OtherGirl "Well, I think he got mad when he tried to kiss me."
Tucker "What happened?"
OtherGirl "I backed away."
Tucker "WHAT? Why would you invite him back here if you didn't like him?"
OtherGirl "I don't know. I thought I did, I just didn't feel like it."

I could not believe that this bitch flirted with him all night—and she was FLIRTING—and then dissed him AT HER PLACE, AFTER SHE INVITED HIM BACK THERE. It's not like she had to fuck him, but to deny even a kiss after all that is really bad. Especially for him; it's not like this guy has lots of self-esteem with women to begin with.

He wouldn't pick up his cell, so I just go back to the hot tub and ElephantLegs, who after 20 beers looked surprisingly good in a bathing suit. We get pretty hot and move inside to finish off, when she drops a bomb on me:

ElephantLegs "I'm not sure if we can hook up. Let me ask my friend."
Tucker "What do you mean?"
ElephantLegs "Well—I don't live here. I am visiting from Ohio. All those bedrooms belong to her roommates. I'll see if she'll let us use her room."

No fucking way. NO FUCKING WAY.

Of course OtherGirl says no. OK, fine, I can understand not wanting other people to fuck in your bed. So I go through the other options. ElephantLegs wouldn't hook up on the patio, "Someone might see us" or on the sofa bed we had to sleep on, "There are other people passed out in the living room. What if they wake up?"

In a last ditch attempt to save the night, I make what I think is a very reasonable suggestion: ElephantLegs takes OtherGirl's car, and the two of us go to SlingBlade's place and hook up. He has an extra bed.

Do you want to guess what Princess CockBlock told her friend? No.

I was furious. OtherGirl had taken what could have been a great night, and totally ruined it, for no fucking reason other than her whim. That's OK bitch: I got summin' for you.

The next morning I woke up early, went into the bathroom and locked the door. I took off the lid of the toilet tank and dropped a gargantuan shit, right in the tank. I have hit many homeruns in my life, but this was my first upper-decker.

Then I took a Sharpie marker I found in her house and wrote on the underside of the lid:

"This is for [SlingBlade]. Whore."

I put the top back on the tank and used about half a roll of toilet paper to wipe my ass, putting all of it in the bowl. As I expected, the toilet clogged when I flushed it, spilling shit water all over her bathroom floor.

I immediately get a taxi back to SlingBlade's, stopping to say goodbye to ElephantLegs on my way out. I am laughing hysterically.

ElephantLegs "What's so funny?"
Tucker "Tell your friend I'm NOT sorry. She'll understand."

I take the taxi back to SlingBlade's, laughing the whole way, and walk into his place at like 7am, still giddy. I find him sitting in his chair in front of the TV, soaking wet, fists clenched up in rage and a look of exasperated anger on his face the likes of which I've never seen.

Tucker "Dude—what's wrong?"

He points out the window to his car. The front and rear windshields are completely out, and the hood and roof have massive dents in them.

Tucker "OH MY GOD! What happened to your car?"
SlingBlade "I don't want to talk about it."
Tucker "Why are you all wet?"
SlingBlade "I don't want to talk about it."
Tucker "Have you been sitting here all night?"
SlingBlade "I DON'T WANT TO TALK ABOUT IT. God obviously hates me. HATES ME. Nothing ever goes right. ALL I WANT IS PEACE AND QUIET AND A SMALL LIFE WITH MY NINTENDO AND COMIC BOOKS. IS THAT SO MUCH TO ASK???"

After a few hours he calmed down and I found out what happened:

It was raining heavily on the interstate as he drove home. He was cruising along in the right lane, still mired in self-loathing over his rejection, not noticing that he was riding in the blind spot of a truck. He noticed too late that the truck was swerving from the left lane across his lane in order to make it onto an off-ramp. SlingBlade had to swerve violently to avoid the truck careening across his lane, and since he was going fast and it was slick, he ended up driving right into a road sign at about 60 miles an hour.

It impacted on his bumper, smashed into the hood of his car leaving a huge dent, then somersaulted and crashed into the roof—popping both the front and rear windshields out—before flying off behind him. The truck kept driving, never having seen what it did. In his own words:

SlingBlade "After the sign destroyed my car, I slammed on the brakes and stopped. Once my heart rate dropped below 200, I was able to pry my fingers off the steering wheel and thank all major and minor deities that I was still alive. I had to kick the front and rear windshields fully out, because they were both cracked and falling in. Once I regained enough of my motor control to drive, I pulled off, and realized that even though they saved my life, the gods were still mocking me . . . and every drop of rain that hit my face through the gaping hole where my windshield used to be was proof of this."
Tucker [not even holding back my laughter] "That SUCKS."
SlingBlade "Yes it does. Welcome to every day of my life."

Tucker "Hold on now dude—fate may fuck with you, but I fuck with fate right back."

I filled him in on my upper-decker. He told me I was a bad person, but it was one of the few times I've ever seen him crack a genuinely warm smile, even if it was wet and fleeting.

"I prefer vaginally-challenged"

SlingBlade and I interned at the same law firm in the summer after our second year. There is one night that summer in particular that really exemplifies our friendship and explains SlingBlade as a person:

We lived a bit south of San Francisco and were driving into the city for a party. On the way there, a cop in front of us, not in any hurry and with no lights or siren on, ran a stop sign. SlingBlade flipped out. Even though he hangs out with me, SlingBlade is a very moral and righteous person. To him you are either right or you are wrong, and this cop was wrong. He started honking, flashing his brights at him and motioning for the cop to pull over.

Tucker "What are you doing? That's a cop!!"
SlingBlade "I AM GOING TO CITE HIM! HE RAN THAT STOP SIGN!"
Tucker "What the fuck? Are you crazy?"
SlingBlade "Give me your cell; I am calling 911."

Thankfully he would not take his hands off the wheel long enough to wrestle the phone away from me, I calmed him down, and we got to the party. It was a launch party for a company called Eveo.com at a clubish-type place, Ruby Skye. Almost as soon as we got there, two girls dressed in clubbing outfits and smeared with make-up came up to me:

Girl 1 "Holy shit—I totally recognize you."
Tucker "I'm not your baby's daddy."
She giggles a little and gives me a coquettish smile.
Tucker "Just kidding. So how do you think you know me?"
Girl 1 "You're that guy with the website, with the date application on it?" [This was a big deal to me at the time because it was back when my site got no traffic and I only had the Date Application on it.]
SlingBlade "Oh dear God. What kind of whores are these?"

Tucker "Stop it dude—anyways, yes ladies you are correct, I am that guy."
Girl 1 "YAY! I knew it! What do I win?"
SlingBlade "An incurable case of Hepatitis C and years of emotional pain."
Tucker "STOP IT."
SlingBlade "LINE UP THE SHOTS MAX. YOU KNOW THE DRILL—I GET SHOTS OR THEY LEAVE CRYING!"

For the most part, the only way he will play wingman with girls he doesn't like is if he is intensely drunk . . . cue five shots of Jagermeister, it's time to loosen up SlingBlade.

We get a table and drink and talk. The girl SlingBlade was talking to, Girl 2, thought he was funny and laughed at his jokes, and everything is going great until Girl 1 decides to fuck it up by telling SlingBlade that she has a boyfriend but cheats on him all the time, especially with guys like me. Oh man . . .

SlingBlade "Well aren't you just spectacular. I'm glad to see that those 'Worthless Whore' lessons turned out well for you."
Girl 1 "Uh, you can't make fun of me. You are wearing a Batman shirt out to a club."
SlingBlade "I'd rather fellate a hot curling iron than listen to fashion advice from you."
Girl 1 "You NEED fashion advice, you dress like an action figure."
SlingBlade "Better an action figure than a Bowery prostitute."

I tried to calm this down, but they got started again.

SlingBlade "Do you have anything else in your life besides work and fellatio? I'm not counting the empty syringes and used condoms decorating your apartment floor."
Girl "YES! I do lots of things! What do YOU DO besides work? Watch Batman cartoons all day?"
SlingBlade "Woman, do not disparage Batman, or you will find this fork sticking out of your eye. Not only do I watch Batman, I go to the gym. You should try it some time."
Girl "Excuse me jerk, I run."
SlingBlade "Run?!? What, do you run to the refrigerator during commercial breaks? Huh, fatty?" [This girl wasn't fat at all, but SlingBlade likes to push the obvious female insecurity buttons]

Girl "You are a real asshole."
SlingBlade "Settle down slim, don't hate the messenger. Just curious: Have you ever eaten just one of anything?"
Tucker "Stop it."
SlingBlade "She has—the forbidden apple."
Tucker "Hey dick head, here's my beer bottle, go peel the label and shut the fuck up."

I took Girl 1 to the bar to calm things down, because unlike Colonel Masturbation, I wanted to fuck the girl I was talking to. Girl 2 actually thought SlingBlade was funny, so she stayed at the table to talk to him:

Girl "So you're single?"
SlingBlade "I prefer 'vaginally-challenged'."
Girl [laughing] "You're so funny. I can't believe you're single."
SlingBlade "I'm a 25 year old socially anxious, pre-mature ejaculator and I'm wearing a Batman t-shirt. Is it really that implausible?"

After a few drinks I got Girl 1 settled down and back to the table, and Girl 1 and Girl 2 immediately went to the bathroom together.

Tucker "So, your girl seems into you. And she's kinda hot. You going to finally close a deal?"
SlingBlade "I don't know. She has a 2 year-old kid . . . oh well, at least I know she fucks."
Tucker "You want more shots?"
SlingBlade "Yeah, whatever. It's not like I can hate myself anymore than I do now."

I think it was George Burns who said, "It takes only one drink to get me drunk. The trouble is, I can't remember if it's the thirteenth or the fourteenth." The same could be said for SlingBlade about hooking up. For him to hook-up he has to perfectly hit his drinking sweet-spot. It's got to be enough alcohol that he is truly fucked up, but not so much that he loses control. The problem with this is that his tolerance is terrible, which leaves him without much margin for error. If he doesn't drink enough he still thinks the woman is a slut and he won't touch her, but if he drinks too much he throws up and/or passes out. It's a delicate balance to get him into his Hook-up Zone.

We do one shot, and then another. At this point the girls return from the bathroom, and he smiles when he sees Girl 2. I get excited because I think I may have hit the spot exactly. I look over about 30 minutes later and his head is buried in his hands and he is muttering to his drink:

SlingBlade "Alcohol, I know I can trust you. You won't leave me like that dirty whore did, will you?"
Girl 1 "What's wrong with your friend?"
Tucker "He has a problem with women. And alcohol."
SlingBlade "My liver hurts, my liver is dying."
Girl 2 "He is really funny."
SlingBlade "If you aren't completely repulsed by me, you haven't been paying attention."
Girl 2 "You aren't repulsive."
Girl 1 "Yes he is."

At that moment a guy with crutches walked by our table.

SlingBlade "I wish I had crutches like him, because then I could beat myself to death with them, which would be preferable to my night thus far."

Since the bathrooms are the small one-person-at-a-time type, the crippled guy had to put his crutches outside the door while he pees. Seeing this opportunity, I decided to lighten the mood at his expense. I run back there and throw his crutches in the empty girls restroom. At the table, I cannot control my giggling, because I know what is coming next:

"WHERE THE FUCK ARE MY CRUTCHES?"

Girl 2 "Hehehehhe—you two are both so funny!"
SlingBlade [in the SlingBlade voice] "How would a man go'bout contactin' da' po-lice, were he so inclinded, hrrrmmm."
Tucker "Oh Christ . . . not again."

Girl 1 and I decide to take her car and go back to her place (you know, for sex—something normal people do), leaving Girl 2 and SlingBlade to the Fates. Though I did not see what happened next, SlingBlade recounted it to me the next day:

He kept drinking until Girl 2 left. Without him. Apparently she got fed up with him alternately passing out and calling her a whore in the

SlingBlade voice. After her departure he wandered around the bar, finally deciding that he needed to go to the bathroom.

As he walks to the bathroom, he starts veering to the right, and in an attempt to correct this he flings himself to the left. Instead of correcting himself he ends up slamming head first into the wall, which lays him out straight on his back. This is directly in front of a bunch of people, all of whom naturally laugh at him.

He's so hammered that he just lays there for a minute, trying to remember how to stand up. Eventually he rolls himself over, but can't get up on his feet. Instead he starts to crawl, arm over arm, military-style, to a nearby chair. Once there, he pulls himself up on the seat, looks over to the crowd who was watching and laughing, points to himself and yells:

"Still single ladies!"

Where is he now?

SlingBlade is a different person now than he was when all these stories took place (most of them occur between 1999-2002). Even though I begged him and begged him to start a site similar to mine where he could display his prodigious comedic talents, he repeatedly declined, instead pursuing a very different field. It ended up working out well for him, and he is a much happier person now, mainly because of this new job. He has asked me not to write anything about his current occupation, and of course I'll respect his wishes.

And yes, though he has sold all his action figures on eBay (for a profit, as he likes to note) and no longer sleeps on Batman sheets, SlingBlade is still very single.

TUCKER FUCKS A FAT GIRL; HILARITY ENSUES

Occurred—March 2000
Written—August 2004

We've all done it.

We've all accidentally fucked a fat girl.

You start the night with the best intentions, but somehow you end up in one of those blacked-out, where-the-fuck-are-my-pants drunken states, and wake up with some girl who is packing more ass than a Sir Mix-a-Lot video. Getting smashed and goin' hoggin' is almost a rite of passage for the American male. There's no shame in that.

This being said, very few of us have fucked a fat girl *on purpose*. I will be honest; I may be a member of that club, but it's up for debate. Let me explain:

It all started in February of 2000, the first month my website was up. I was 23 years old and in my second year of law school. TuckerMax.com originally started as a Date Application Page that I put up to settle a bet. My friends thought the page was hilarious, but wanted to see some results:

PWJ "Tucker, the site is awesome, but you need to actually meet a girl through it."
Tucker "I don't know."
Hate "Max! How could you put that site up and not hook up with at least one girl through it? That's weak."
Tucker "I don't know; there have been some crazies emailing me."
Hate "When has that stopped you in the past?"

SlingBlade "This is opposed to the crazies that you pick up in bars?"
PWJ "Dude, you can't put this thing up and never go on a date or hook up from it. You have to. At least one girl."
Tucker "Fine. Might as well. What's the worst that could happen??"
Hate "OH YEAH! That line of thought always serves you well!"

But I didn't just promise my friends that I'd go out on a date with a girl I met through the site. I ended up promising that I'd do my very best to hook up with her.

So of course as soon as I make this promise, I get no applications from any girls near the Durham, NC area. I know this sounds ridiculous now, as I get dozens of propositions a day from girls, but you have to remember that back when the site started, it was almost totally unknown outside my circle of friends. Maybe 30 people a day saw it, if that. There were only like three of my stories up, and the notion that this site would become anything beyond a silly joke never even crossed my mind. If you had told me then that within two years my webpage would become my launching pad to fame, I would have laughed at you and told you stop sucking the glass dick.

One week went by, nothing. Two weeks, nothing. I was starting to get a little desperate, thinking about all the shit I was going to have to eat from my friends because I couldn't even get a date off my own Date Application Page, when finally a girl emailed me. She had just moved to Raleigh for a job, knew no one, and thought I was funny. We emailed a little and she seemed cool and normal enough, but I had to make a couple requests before she sent me a picture of her. Once I got the pic, it was clear why it took her three emails to work up the courage to send one.

Ladies and gentlemen: She's a fatty.

Normally, this would have been an easy decision. I'd just say "Get the fuck away from me and go back to your trough," and everything would be fine, but this time it was different. I had PROMISED my friends that I would hook up with a girl from my webpage, and FatGirl was my only option.

I put her off for a few weeks with cutesy email banter, while I prayed for a girl without a giant oversized pig heart to email me.

One week . . . two weeks . . . nothing. Finally, I consulted my friends on what I should do. I showed them the picture:

Hate "WOOOOOOO-WEEEEEEE! YOU GOT YOURSELF A CHUNK-ER! FORGET THE DATE, LASSO HER AND TAKE HER TO THE STOCKYARDS!"
PWJ "Yeah, you did promise. She might be your only chance."
SlingBlade "Just make sure you take her to a bar that doesn't serve food. You can't afford that kind of date."
El Bingeroso "Wow. Yeah man, that sucks. Wow . . . but you did prom-ise."
Hate "WOOOOOO-HOOOO! MAX YOU ARE MAKING US PROUD! GOD BLESS THAT WEBSITE!"

After some deliberation, I decided to meet FatGirl out. It still makes me laugh to this day, but I legitimately thought that this would be my only shot at hooking up with a girl through my website, and I didn't want to blow it . . . even if it meant I had to go pork diving. I justified it as such:

Tucker "Well . . . maybe she's lost weight. She said it wasn't a good picture."
[Everyone in unison] "HAHHAHHAHAHAHHAHAHAHAHAHAHAH-HAHAHAHA."
SlingBlade "Lost weight? What, you think she caught that secret rubella epidemic sweeping the Carolinas? When was the last time a girl was better looking than her INTERNET DATING PICTURE?"
Tucker "Well, she does have a cute face. You can't fake that."
El Bingeroso "This is not going to end well."
Hate "Max, just when I think you've tapped out, you find a whole new way to fuck up!"
Tucker "Fuck you. I hope all of your children have birth defects."

I agreed to meet Fat Girl at a bar in Durham, The James Joyce. I flatly refused to tell any of my friends where we were meeting, and made them promise not to come looking for me, in case she turned out to be morbidly obese, as opposed to just normal fat, like in her picture. Like an IDIOT, I didn't think about extracting promises for what would happen after the date. A rookie mistake that will haunt me my entire life.

FatGirl was there when I got there, and looked pretty much exactly like she did in the picture—fat. We started talking over beers, and she was exactly like her emails: a nice, sweet girl without a whole lot going for her. It quickly became obvious that she was very much into me, and after about three beers she really started loosening up. The turning point in the conversation was this:

FatGirl [with a seductive, portly, dimpled look] "Tucker, are you a player?"
Tucker "Uh, no . . . I mean, not in the way you are thinking. A player is someone who is only out to have sex for the sake of sex, and will do or say anything to hook up. Yeah, I mean, I like sex, but I won't do anything to hook up with a girl. Well . . . normally, at least."
FatGirl [Still with the seductive, portly, dimpled look] "I think you're a player Tucker Max . . . but I'm not going to sleep with you."

Well, this one is locked up. The night is obviously going to end in sex if I want it, but I still had to decide: Do I bail on this date, avoid the ignominy of having sex with Miss Piggy, and pray that another girl emails me for a date, or do I just suck it up, take the opportunity in front of me and fulfill the promise to my friends? I went back and forth on this in my mind.

Good Tucker "She has a really cute face."
Bad Tucker "She is fat."
Good Tucker "Well, she isn't disgustingly obese. She's only like 30 . . . 40 . . . -ish . . . pounds overweight."
Bad Tucker "What does that mean? Because she doesn't need a crane to leave her house, it's somehow OK? She's FAT."
Good Tucker "But I promised my friends, and this might be my only chance to hook up through the site."
Bad Tucker "Right . . . but SHE'S STILL FAT."

I end the debate by moving my army across the Rubicon: "Bartender, get me a shot."

And then I burned the bridges behind me: "Make it cheap tequila. With a beer back."

Yes, I know that fucking fat girls is against the rules for any self-respecting guy, but the rules have a loophole. That loophole is called alcohol. God bless it.

With each tequila shot and beer combo, she lost weight, and her face, which was previously only cute, became sorta hot. The night started improving.

Then it went to shit. I chose the James Joyce because I knew none of my friends would be there that night, as on Wednesdays they always went to a bar in Chapel Hill. But there are more people that drink in Duke Law School besides my friends. Namely, two loud-mouthed gossiping bitches in my class, Carry and Amy, who were at the Joyce that night.

I tired to hide when I saw them walk in, but it was no use, their scandal radar was too sensitive. They immediately spot me:

Carry "Hey Tucker, I was just about to—"
She stops mid-sentence when she sees the land beast I am with. I wish I had a picture of the look on her face. Complete and utter confusion, with a hint of disgust and twinge of contempt. I almost laughed . . . then I remembered that I was the one with the fat girl.
Tucker "Hey, we were just about leave."
FatGirl is standing behind me waiting to be introduced, but that is not happening.
Carry "Wha— who— uhhh . . . Tucker . . ."

I am out of there before she can finish her thought. There is nothing at the end of that sentence that I want to hear.

FatGirl and I end up back at my place (I knew my roommates, Hate and Credit, would still be out drinking). We have sex, and both pass out afterwards, even though it was only about 11. I'm not sure if it was the alcohol, the fumes, or the PTSD that put me out. Probably some happy combination of all three.

The gods of alcohol often entertain themselves at my expense, but sometimes they throw me a bone. Waking me out of an alcoholic stupor normally requires nothing short of ice water and a fog horn, but somehow I awoke in time to hear Credit and Hate slowly open the front door to our apartment and start creeping towards my door, conspiratorially whispering to each other. I spring out of bed, dive at the door and lock it just in time to prevent them from charging in.

Unfortunately, there was nothing I could do about their yelling and banging on the walls:

Hate "MAX!! BRING OUT THE FATTY!! LET'S SEE HER!!!"
Credit "Tell her I have a cheeseburger!"
Hate "MAX!! LET'S HAVE A LOOK AT HER!! BRING HER OUT!! WOOOOOOOOOO-WEEEEEE!!"

Of course, I couldn't help but laugh. That shit is funny. But it wasn't the best part:
FatGirl "What are they talking about? Should we go out there?"
Tucker "Uh, no. So . . . do you just want to spend the night? It's already like midnight."
FatGirl "I would love to, but I can't. I have to go to work tomorrow, and I can't leave from here for work. In fact, I need to get going real soon."
Tucker "Let's just wait a minute before you go."

Great. Now how do I get her out of here without my roommates meeting her? Hate and Credit eventually settled down in the living room to watch TV, and I devised a plan. Since the door to my room faces the front door to the apartment, I didn't need to move FatGirl through the living room to get her out of the apartment. I could just rush her from my room out the front door and to her car.

Tucker "Alright, you put your clothes on and then we need to get you out of the apartment."
FatGirl "Get me out? What about your friends? Don't they want to meet me?"
Tucker "Trust me, you don't want to meet my friends. They are evil. Rapists and murderers, both of them. Very unsavory characters."
FatGirl "No, I want to meet them. They sound fun."
Tucker "This is not an option."
FatGirl "Tucker, you are not hustling me out of here like some prostitute."
Tucker "Fine, but meeting my roommates is not an option."
FatGirl "But Tucker, I want to meet your roommates. Hold on, let me pee and then I'll put my clothes on and go out and meet them."

Are you kidding? The day I bend my will to a fat girl's is the day I retire.

I considered my options for a second, then very calmly opened the window in my room and heaved all her clothes out into the yard. She was confused when she came out of the bathroom.

FatGirl "Where are my clothes?"
Tucker [As I pointed out my open window] "If you want to meet my friends, you are going to do it naked."

Talk about a priceless facial expression.

FatGirl "WHY DID YOU DO THAT?"
Tucker "You can either go out the window after your clothes, or you can run out the front door and go get them. It's dark out. No one will see you. Or you can meet my friends naked."

She stood there in shock for a good ten seconds. Not about to lose my momentum, I quietly opened the door to my room and pointed to the front door. She looked out the window, and even though I am on the first floor, I guess she didn't like the idea of going through a window to get her clothes, so she jogged, lumbered, whatever, to the front door, opened it and ran out. I followed her and locked the door behind her.

Problem solved.

As I nonchalantly sat down in the living room, my roommates kinda stared at me in a surprised what-the-fuck manner, then they got up and went into my room.

Hate "Max, where is she?"
Tucker "She's gone."
Hate "Wha— how— where is she?"
Tucker "I hustled her right the fuck out. I'm not about to let you jackals see her."
Hate "AHAHHAHAHAHAHAHA."
Credit "I wondered what that stampede sound was."

Postcript

I tell this story a lot, and people, girls especially, often ask me if I regret what I did. Well, first they get real mad at me and act like they are offended, but then they ask me if I regret it. In a way I do; it was kinda mean. But I was only like 23 when it happened; what do you expect from me? Compassion? Caring? Should I have just invited her out to meet my friends and stay for a nightcap? Yeah, I guess that's what most guys would have done. And that's why most guys are hard-up schmucks who couldn't get laid in a monkey whorehouse with a bag of bananas.

What really cracks me up is when girls ask me if I'd do something like this again. Of course I wouldn't. I already fucked a fat girl once, why would I do it again? That's a stupid question.

I found out later that Credit and Hate came home early that night because they saw Carry and Amy out, and those two bitches told them I was home with FatGirl. The next day at law school was quite fun.

SlingBlade "Wait—you threw her clothes OUT your window? HAHHAHAHAHA. She must have been huge."
Tucker "No, she wasn't that fat. Just overweight."
Credit "I don't know Max. I thought we had rhinos on our apartment last night."
PWJ "It was that bad?"
Hate "The floor boards were heaving and moaning."
Credit "I think she drove off in a cattle car."
Tucker "Whatever. As far as I am concerned, this never happened. If your friends didn't see you, it doesn't count. I'm invoking that rule to get out of this."
JoJo "Then you haven't hooked up with a girl from the website."
PWJ "Carry and Amy saw you."

I hate having smart friends. I guess that ends the debate: I fucked a fat girl on purpose.

The Now Infamous Tucker Max Charity Auction Debacle

Occurred—Summer 2000
Written—September 2002

Everything I am about to tell you is true. This is the complete and unadulterated story, as I can best remember it, behind my infamous summer with Fenwick and the very famous "Tucker Max Charity Auction Debacle" email.

Let's start from the beginning:

In May of 2000, my buddy SlingBlade and I drove out to Palo Alto to work as summer associates at a law firm called Fenwick & West. It was the summer between our 2nd and 3rd years of law school at Duke. The internet and tech boom was hitting its crescendo, and as we arrived in Silicon Valley, the Nasdaq was set to pass 5,000. Remember those days?

Almost immediately upon arrival, I realized that I HATED being a lawyer. My mental picture of what being a lawyer entailed did not include spending countless hours every day sitting in a lifeless office, surrounded by boring people, doing idiotic and ultimately meaningless paperwork. Unfortunately, that is all that a corporate lawyer does. When you are a lawyer, your job is to clean up the messes of others, to rubber stamp and make legal someone else's real work, to essentially be a paper custodian for the people who actually do important things. The people at Yahoo and Cisco and Network Solutions (all our clients) actually did something; what did I do? Stupid, mindless, and utterly irrelevant bullshit. I was a junior paper-monkey, and I hated every second of it. Honestly, I wish I could say it was the firm, I wish I could blame the people or the place, but that was not the case. I hated the very nature of the job. Being a lawyer SUCKS.

When I am bored or unhappy, my behavior becomes akin to a crack-addled ADD monkey until I find something to occupy me. The law firm and the work bored me; so what did I do? Did I endure the boredom and soldier on? Or better yet, did I find a productive output for my creativity, like I did with my website in law school?

No. I got drunk and acted like an asshole. Virtually every day, and especially at firm events where the liquor was free. If being a lawyer was not interesting, I was going to make it that way, goddamnit.

The first Friday I was there, the firm had an all-day orientation for the incoming summer associates. The night before, I got my roommate and myself into the SOMA magazine opening party in San Francisco, where I got completely shit-faced and went home with one of the models at the party (at least, she told me she was a model, but who really knows). When I woke up at 6am the next morning, in her house in Oakland, I realized that I had not carefully thought out the ramifications of this act. My firm is far from Oakland, and I had to be at work at 9am for the start of summer associate orientation.

First things first: I rooted around in her purse, noting the large supply of condoms, and found her driver's license so when I woke her up, I'd know her name (it was one of those nights). She said she'd give me a ride, but she can't take me to my place because it was in Mountain View (which is even further away from Oakland than Palo Alto), and she had to be somewhere at ten. That meant I had to wear the same clothes I wore out last night to work Friday. Not really a big deal, except there was liquor, vomit, piss (and probably other fluids) all over them.

Liquor is understandable, but vomit and piss? On the way to her house Thursday night, we had stopped at Jack-in-the-Box. Don't ask me how she could eat that crap and still have such a good body . . . she wasn't a plus-size model, so I guess she was bulimic.

Sitting in the drive-thru, the inhuman amounts of liquor I had consumed caught up to me, so I calmly got out of her car, walked behind a bush, and proceeded to vomit and piss at the same time. It is hard enough keeping from vomiting on yourself when you're drunk; try doing it while also pissing. Whatever; I just put in a breath mint and hid the urine stains until they dried, and she still hooked up with me. Isn't alcohol great?

I show up at orientation, stumbling drunk, eyes still bloodshot, smelling like a speak-easy. I somehow made it through without incident until after lunch, when they partnered us up with another summer associate and had us tell each other all kinds of things about ourselves, and then recite to everyone else in the room what we learned. I didn't know what to say to the guy who was my partner, so I told him I was out all night and I couldn't see anything because my contacts had fallen out when I was hooking up with some random girl. He stood up and told this to everyone. I thought it was funny; the hiring partner did not. Whatever, if he can't take a joke, fuck him.

The next week, the hiring partner, John Steele, came down to the office that I shared with three other summers, and started shooting the shit with us. All of a sudden he started in about the Infirmation.com Greedy Associate boards, how he couldn't believe that the Fenwick summer salary info got up there so fast, and how that thing has really changed the way firms do things. Let me digress here for an important and revealing subplot:

During the spring, Fenwick announced that they were going to pay summer associates only $2,100 per week, which was below the $2,400 that most big firms in New York, LA and Chicago were paying their summers. Yet, right before we arrived in Palo Alto, Fenwick, along with every other Silicon Valley firm, announced that they were going to pay summers $2,400 per week, commensurate with the big firms in other major cities.

What does this have to do with anything? Well, I was almost single-handedly responsible for Fenwick, and basically every other Silicon Valley firm, raising their summer associate salary from $2,100 to $2,400. How is that possible, you ask? The beauty of the internet, and the influence of an amazing website called Infirmation.com.

Infirmation.com is a job-related website that has message boards on it, where anyone can anonymously post anything. The message boards are divided by region, one being for New York associates, one for Silicon Valley, one for Chicago, etc. These message boards, called "Greedy Associate" boards, had vaulted to fame in the preceding months as a means for associates at different firms to anonymously share information with each other about salary, benefits, work conditions, anything they chose. One of the sparking events was when Gunderson, a relatively small firm in Silicon Valley, raised their starting associate salaries from somewhere around the industry average of $100,000 to $125,000. One of the first places this information was posted and disseminated was the message boards on Infirmation.com, and from that event, as well as a few others like it, junior associates at all the major firms started sharing info with each other about the relative benefits and detriments of their particular firms on these Greedy Associate boards.

As a result of these developments, partners at all the majors firms monitored these message boards, looking for the latest gossip about their firms and their competing firms. They had to stay up to date, because a change in benefits in Firm A could mean a flood of associates or law students to that firm, and away from Firm B, before Firm B even knew what was going on.

How does this relate to the story? The summer salaries had already been announced in New York at $2,400, and everyone was waiting for the Silicon Valley firms to announce their summer salaries [Fenwick had three major competitors in Silicon Valley at the time: Cooley, Wilson, and Brobeck (these are abbreviated names of law firms)]. Fenwick was the first to announce; they did so sometime around late April, and they announced at $2,100, which was below NY salaries.

I was unhappy with this, so I immediately posted this info on the Infirmation.com Silicon Valley/SF Greedy Associate board, and then, using four or five different anonymous screen names, proceeded to have a thread discussion on how horrible this was, how Fenwick was insulting its summers, how no one was going to accept their offers because the firm was so cheap it wouldn't fork over the extra $300 a week, etc, etc. I even used one of my aliases to play the other side. It was beautiful. Of the 20 messages on this topic on the first day, I probably posted 10 of them. I kept this up, at a slightly lower output, for about three days.

About a week after Fenwick's announcement, and the resulting Infirmation.com message board "explosion," Wilson announced they were paying summers $2,400. Each of the other Silicon Valley firms quickly fell in line after that, including Fenwick.

Back to the story: So here I was, sitting with the hiring partner at a major Silicon Valley law firm, talking about the very message boards that I used to influence the summer salary structure, when he let the clincher go.

"Yeah, what kills me is that we had decided to pay $2,100. But as soon as we announced, that message board blew up, and other firms decided to pay $2,400. That thing is something else."

Holy shit! The whole time I am thinking, "Ha, ha asshole, the joke's on you, I basically wrote that whole thing myself!" It took everything I had to not laugh in his face.

We all bullshit a little more, when he asks to talk to me in private. He took me into a conference room, closed the door, and began talking to me about my reputation, how I'm starting to get the reputation as the "party guy" in the summer associate class. Yeah, so? At this point, I'm really unconcerned about my reputation; yes, I liked getting paid $2,400 a week for what amounted to summer camp, but I hated this job and I hated being a lawyer. Plus, the way he phrased the conversation, I just thought he was talking about unimportant stuff—I am not very adept at picking up subtle social cues, and even though this was not a subtle one, I wasn't picking it up.

I did a couple of other stupid things in the next few days; I can't really remember, because they were things that don't even register on my radar as "events", yet others found them to be "seismic." For instance, one day, one of the recruiters came into my office, when I was on the phone. She asked who I was talking to, and I said, "Oh, I was just calling a porn line." Obviously, I was kidding; I later found out she was mortified.

The next day I get invited to sit in on a meeting with a prospective client, the managing partner, and a senior associate. The client is a girl who is an aspiring artist, a good one, and is about to graduate from Stanford. A Stanford alumni-VC (venture capitalist) in the area has told her she should incorporate herself, and set up what amounts to a start-up for her artwork. She came to us for legal advice about this venture. Well, I may have been the junior person in the room, but I'm sorry, she was given some serious horseshit advice, and I proceed to tell her this, point blank. Who's ever heard of this? Incorporating a new artist? Is this a joke? I'm not even talking about securitizing her future work and selling bonds, like what David Bowie did; he wanted her to literally set up some sort of corporation with herself, and pass out stock options to get people to work for her. I tell her to ignore this VC, he knows nothing about the art world, and for her to get an agent or a manager, or both, and start producing some art to sell and show, that incorporating herself would be against her interests in both the long and short term, and is completely unheard of in the art world, and for good reason—because it's idiotic. I thought the meeting went well; apparently, the managing partner did not. He was upset that I called the VC's idea, someone who is apparently very important in Silicon Valley, "idiotic."

The next day I get a call from John Steele to come see him in his office. I go up there, and he gives me ANOTHER talk about my attitude. Really, don't let anyone tell you they weren't patient with me at Fenwick, because they were. But he told me that the good news was that the lawyers I was working with, a senior associate and a partner, thought the work I was doing was great, and that they really liked me. Of course, I took this as carte blanche to keep doing what I was doing (As long as my work was good, that's all that matters, right? Not when you act like Tucker Max). Then he says, "Oh yeah, I saw your little bachelor of the week thing on sfGirl.com. That was really funny."

WHAT? How did he find out about that? He continued, "The part about the dog pound, I was in tears reading that. My wife thought it was hilarious. Of course, I wish you hadn't mentioned Fenwick, or a fat Puerto Rican stripper, but you know, I guess that's just you." I didn't think I had told anyone at Fenwick about that. I felt like Tom Cruise in *The Firm*, but unlike Tom Cruise, I just willfully ignored the warning signs and kept on being myself.

Friday rolls around, and we have a firm cocktail party at a partner's house. The liquor was free, and I was drinking, and after an hour or so, I find myself talking to two female partners, "Betty" and "Kathy." Betty is in her forties, married, a kid or two, and is one of the leading lawyers in the firm. I am my normal gregarious, boisterous self, and these two female partners are eating it up. Loving me. As the cocktail party wound down, I convinced them to join me, ten other summer associates, and a few junior associates in a trip to a local Palo Alto bar.

At this point, I'm just inviting them because I want someone to pay. On the trip over to the bar, I'm in the car with Betty and the other partner, and the conversation turns to sex. At first I was a little reticent, being that Betty is married with children and an important partner, but before I know it I'm explaining the BJ rule to them, i.e., what it means to "dot someone's eyes," and why guys do such things. This was eminently interesting to Betty and the other partner. The conversation carried into the bar, and further explored such topics as whether a young man (around 24), would know what to do with an older woman (around 40 or so), whether my lips were pouty, sultry or alluring, etc, etc.

We're all sitting at a long table, and by the time the food comes, I have Betty hand-feeding me calamari. All the while, Jim, another Duke Law student, sat across the table from this scene, unable to believe what he was witnessing, and (I swear this is true), eating ribs with a fork. Needless to say, this scene was just too much for most of the other summer associates. And the look on the face of one of the junior associates was priceless when I leaned over and asked her if the woman feeding me calamari was actually a partner. Yeah, I was a little out of control.

Everyone scatters except me, Betty, Kathy, and one other summer. I'm assuming they saw the train wreck coming, and didn't want to be anywhere near when it hit. Smart decision. My car was still at the firm, so Betty offers to give me a ride to the office to get it. I accept, and then another summer, Brian, invites himself along, "Oh, I need a ride to the office too." I didn't really understand why at the time, but Betty gave him a mean look, but agreed to take him along.

[Side note: The only reason I can tell you this next part is because truth is an absolute defense to libel, and this particular event had a sober witness named Brian, who went to law school at Columbia. Though it may seem libelous, this is the complete truth. I'd been drinking, but I remember this vividly. If you don't believe this, find him and ask him about it. He has no reason to lie for me.]

We get to the firm, and Brian and I get out of Betty's car, and then she turns off the car and gets out herself. She looks up at the building (Fenwick has all of a ten story building in Palo Alto), then looks right at me and says, "It looks like I left the lights on in my office. I should probably go turn them off. What do you think?" I am oblivious to the implied meaning here, and look up and say, "Whatever, who cares—they're halogen, it'll cost like 3 cents for the night. Forget it."

Betty gets a mildly frustrated look on her face, and still staring right at me, says, "I need to go up to my office and turn off my lights. Maybe you should come up there . . . help me out." Did I ever mention how retarded I am when I get drunk? Well, I missed that signal too, "No, whatever, they're fine, don't worry about it." She kind of pauses for a second, looks right into my eyes, and says, "DO YOU . . . want to come . . . HELP ME . . . turn off the lights . . . IN MY OFFICE?"

Bingo. That one registered.

What did I do? Did I go with her up to her office and fuck the shit out of her? Did I dot her eyes right on her desk? Did I show her that this 24 year old knew exactly what to do with that 40 year old?

No. In perhaps the single stupidest move of my life, I quickly said no, jumped into my car, and tore out of the parking lot. The irony here is so fucking thick it's ridiculous. There is no category that Betty falls into that I have not slept with before; I have hooked up with women as old as Betty, uglier, more married, more children, everything. Shit, I have a hard time counting the times I've turned down sex at all, unless the girl was ugly *and* my friends were around.

So why did I chicken out? Why did I pass up such a sure thing? I DON'T KNOW!! That's the worst part. I can't figure out what happened. It's like for about 5 minutes of my life, I was a moral puritan.

The next weekend was the firm retreat at Silverado Ranch in Napa Valley. My roommate and I drove up Friday afternoon, in my car, checked into the hotel, and then met everyone in the reception area. Starting at around 7pm, there were cocktails and hors d'oeurves, and then at 9pm the Charity Auction was starting. I get to the reception promptly at 6:58 to find numerous well-stocked open bars . . . and no food. OK, there was some shrimp, perhaps some baklava, and maybe even a petit four or two, but nothing substantive to eat. Well, HELLO, what do you think is going to happen? Did no one involved in the planning of this thing ever hear of the behavioral effects of alcohol on an empty stomach?

By the time the auction started, I was so drunk I was walking around carrying, seriously, two bottles of wine in my hands; red in my left, white in my right, taking alternating swigs from each. I sat, clutching my wine bottles, at a table right next to the stage, with my roommate, about maybe 5 or 6 other summers, and a few junior associates.

The charity auction was only for the 400+ firm people associated with the firm (and their spouses), and was all firm-specific items. Things like the managing partner would cook you dinner, you could throw things at some other partner, a chair from a partner's office, etc. I forget where the money was going, probably to Our Sisters of the Festering Rectum Orphanage, who knows? Most of the things were stupid, so I just sat there and solemnly poured wine into my face. Then an item came up, which, in my drunken stupor, I simply had to have: The hiring partner, John Steele, would chauffeur you around for a night in his Cadillac. Beautiful, I thought in my inebriated stupor, if I buy this, they have to give me an offer. That's how drunk I was.

The bidding started at $50. It slowly went to 60, then 80, then 100, so I got bored, and just stood up on my seat and held my paddle up. The auctioneer took this as a sign to just start yelling out ever increasing numbers, never even looking at the other bidders. The bid got to around $600, with no one bidding but me, and I yelled at him to quit. One or two other people might have thrown a bid in there, when John Steele got on the mike and said that if a summer won, he'd pay half. This, predictably, doubled the bid immediately.

When the bidding hit about $2000, I thought I had it won. No one else was bidding, when all of the sudden, Aparna, another summer who was good friends with me, knew the condition I was in (shit-housed drunk), and knew that, given my egomaniacal personality, I would not stop bidding, ever, no matter what, regardless of the price. So, with the help of a few partners bankrolling her, she started slowly bidding me up. 2200, 2300, 2400 . . .

The next thing I know, I'm on stage, and I grab the microphone from the auctioneer, and start yelling at her. I'm doing it in a teasing way, but I'm like, "Aparna, what are you doing? You know you can't afford this. You're just trying to mess with me. I have to win this; it's the only way I'm getting an offer." This sends the crowd into fits of laughter. I wasn't even trying to be funny, but hey, put some liquor in me and you never know what's going to come out.

He kicks me off the stage, the betting gets up to about 3300 or so, I climb back on stage, wrestle the mike away from the auctioneer, and start yelling, "This is not fair. You have partners bankrolling you, I only have a few scrubby summers in my corner. Seriously, Aparna, I need this. QUIT!" Again, eruptions of laughter.

The bidding eventually hits $3800, and this time the auctioneer says, "Alright Tucker, come on up here. I know you'll come up anyway." I get on stage, and eventually have to make the call, do I go to $3900 or not?

Microphone in hand, in front of everyone, I say, "Fuck it—go ahead."

The funny thing is, people not associated with the firm think this is why I got fired. Not at all; the managing partner came up to me afterwards and told me it was the funniest thing he had ever seen at a firm event. The name partner, Bill Fenwick, told me, literally, I did Kentucky proud. Another partner I didn't know told me I was awesome. For the rest of the night, I was a star. Believe it or not, that's the absolute truth.

We end up back at the hotel, and the summer associates and some other junior associates go to someone's suite, and we're playing cards, drinking, and socializing. It was about this point that I blacked out. My last clear memory is trying to convince some summer to beat up an associate, because he was cheating at poker. The next day, Eric told me that I tried to hook up with Aparna, but all I could manage to do was pass out on top of her. It was that kind of night.

I wake up the next morning, it's like 11am, and I feel like a bag of ass. All the summer associates were supposed to be at the morning lecture given by the managing partner, and some other guy. They were there, I was not. I throw something on and make it there right as it's finishing.

Someone tells me that Gordie, the managing partner, asked, on the microphone, if I was there when it began at 9am. So I go up to him afterwards, and say, "Hey! I made it . . . eventually." He smiled, shook his head, and said, "There's always one."

Fast forward to Monday. I'm sitting in my office, bored out of my mind, when I decide to write my friends and tell them what happened over the weekend. So I compose the now infamous email. Here it is, exactly as I wrote it that day [just so you know, it's pretty much the same as what I wrote above]:

——-Original Message——

From: Tucker Max
Sent: Monday, June 05, 2000 2:51 PM
To: [name removed]
Subject: The Now Infamous Tucker Max Charity Auction Debacle . . .

Here is the story of what happened to me this weekend at my firm's retreat. That's the last time I ever drink before an auction:

My roommate and I decide to leave for the Silverado Ranch by car instead of taking the bus at 2 pm. You have not lived until you've ridden through three hours of Bay Area traffic with Slingblade at the wheel. By the time we got to Silverado, he was madder than fire.

The first reception starts at like 6pm. There are finger foods, etc., and lots and lots of wine and beer. Not really liking any of the food, I start drinking. Heavily. By the time I know what's going on, I'm talking to the name partner, Bill Fenwick, in a redneck accent. Of course, he is from Kentucky, so we talked about basketball for an hour. It was great.

About 9pm the charity auction began. There were lots of "Fenwick" type items, like a dinner cooked by the managing partner, etc. One of the items was an entire night chauffeured by the hiring partner, John Steele. In my inebriated stupor, I thought that if I won this, then they would have no choice but to give me an offer. The bidding starts at $50. People are bidding here and there, but I get tired of all the slow bidding, so I stand on my chair, and hold up my bidding card. Without getting down. So the auctioneer takes this as a cue to just start yelling price increases, without even identifying other bidders.

When the price hits about $800, John Steele says that he will pay half if a summer associate wins. The bidding automatically doubles (John is a litigator). As the price gets to $2000, I think I have the thing won. I get the "going once" call, and then this other summer, Aparna, goaded on by some partners, decides that she has to beat me. So the bidding hits $2600, and before I know it, I'm on stage, taking the mike from the auctioneer, and yelling at Aparna to stop bidding. My exact quote, "Aparna, seriously, stop. I have to win, this is the only way I'm getting an offer."

So that just inspires more partners/attorneys/recruiting staff to contribute to Aparna's pool. When the bidding hits $3400, I start yelling, on the mike, about how this isn't fair, because she has partners bankrolling her, but I only have a "few scrubby summers in my corner." I keep trying to bid only like 5$ more than her, but the auctioneer gets all mad at me, and is making me bid in hundred dollar increments. When her bid hits $3800, I get back on stage. After some banter, the auctioneer asks me if I want to bid $3900.

I ponder this for a second, and in front of the whole firm and spouses/significant others, with the mike in my face, say, "Fuck it—go ahead."

I won the auction.

Now, as you can see, the email is exactly what happened. I left almost nothing out. I may be an obnoxious asshole, but I don't need to exaggerate or lie in my stories; they are funny enough as it is. I sent this to about ten friends, and thought nothing else about it. They didn't even think it was that great; I had had some much better ones that summer (like the one about the SOMA party, and the one about this Korean girl who raced me home doing 120mph on the 101 . . . you get the picture).

That was Monday. Wednesday comes, and around 4:30 John Steele asks me to come to his office. I stroll up there and notice my key card, which you have to have to operate the elevators or doors, isn't working. This means only one thing . . .

I get into his office, and he's in there with some other lady I've never seen before. John introduces her, some HR lady, and then proceeds to tell me that I have an option to either voluntarily withdraw from the firm or get fired. He cited certain things I had done that led them to this course of action, like my "porn line" comment and some other stuff like that, but said nothing about the really bad stuff I did. If I withdraw, he tells me they will pay me a large separation sum, pay my rent for the summer, and pay the for the item I "won" at the charity auction. In total, this is close to $20,000, plus I get to keep what I've already made in the not quite four weeks I was there. If I get fired, I get nothing.

I'm a little bit in shock, but not really; one of the associates at the firm, who is no longer there, heard about this, and gave me a heads up the day before. I took the money, thanked them, and headed out. It all went rather pleasantly, considering.

Granted, I had acted a little reckless, but I was nonetheless confused. I figured I wasn't getting an offer, but I didn't think I was going to get fired, and the reasons he gave me for them letting me go were bullshit. They had plenty of reasons, don't misunderstand, but the ones John named did not seem like reasons to fire a summer associate.

The next day, I got two calls, both from associates at the firm. One talked to me on the phone, the other met me for lunch a few days later. They both thought I had been dealt with the wrong way, and independently told me basically the same opinion: I got canned mainly because of the Betty incident, and not because of the charity auction. The one who met me for lunch claimed that he had talked to a "very important partner" in the firm, and he was told that, given my track record of outlandish behavior, the firm was scared I was going to eventually sleep with Betty, or even do something worse than that, which would make me either a huge liability (if I, say, got drunk and set the building on fire) or invincible (if I slept with Betty). Why would it make me invincible? Because if she slept with me, and they didn't give me an offer, then they could be liable for a sexual harassment suit. Not that I would ever sue them if that happened, but considering my behavior that summer, I can understand why they viewed me as a liability. I was never able to verify these theories, but they made sense to me.

To me, the most delicious irony is that, ultimately, because I didn't sleep with Betty the firm was able to get me out. Can you believe that? Because I didn't fuck her, I fucked myself. But that's not all.

About a month later, my email started popping up. Everywhere. Paul had forwarded it to Linda Brewer, a Dukie at another Silicon Valley firm, who forwarded it to some other people . . . you get the picture. That email went around the world, several times, and at last count went through like 100+ firms.

The next thing I know, my Inbox is filled with these forwards, and my friends from all over the country are calling me, like, "Dude, what happened? Is that you?" My favorite random email I got was from some guy who wrote: "Mr. Max, with the hope of a six year old on the night before Christmas asking about Santa, I ask the same question: Do you really exist?"

I called John Steele a few months later for some reason, and the first thing he said to me was, "Man, you're famous. We've been collecting those emails, and have counted over 100 firms that they've been too. Hey, congrats, it was really well written." I swear to God, I had that conversation with him.

My mother even got that email. My uncle is a lawyer in DC and he got it and then forwarded it to her. Her only comment: "Well, I guess that's what happens when you can't hold your liquor."

I became a minor celebrity in the legal world after that. Every law student and lawyer in the country knew about me. Someone told me that some students at Columbia Law threw a "Save Tucker" party. I wish someone would have told me about it; I would have shown up. Of course, that probably would have been anti-climactic. When I got back to Duke, the Dean of Students wrote me a letter telling me that I should go into alcohol rehab. I thought that was pretty funny.

That is the whole true story, exactly as I remember it.

In the final analysis, I have almost nothing bad to say about Fenwick. Yes, they fired me, but I can understand their position: I acted like a drunk retard and they couldn't tolerate my potential liability. What could I expect them to do? Pat me on the back and get me a hooker and some beer? That would be pretty cool, though. Seriously, I hold no ill will towards them. I probably would have done the same thing had I been in their position, and some jerk-off had come in acting like me.

I often get asked if I regret what I did. I'm never exactly sure how to answer that; I mean, yes I would have liked to have kept making $2400 a week for the summer, but in the end, it was probably the best thing for me. I hated being a lawyer, but the money was so good, I don't know if I would have ultimately had the courage to quit on my own. I would have just languished in a job I hated, doing just enough to get by, and would become bitter and disillusioned, like almost every lawyer I know. So instead I did the immature thing and forced the issue, leaving the decision up to Fenwick, and they made it for me. Oh well . . . what can you do?

QUITE THE VACATION

Occurred—May 2000
Written—March 2005

I don't know exactly how many girls I've slept with, but it's well into the triple digits. You start to forget a few last names somewhere in the 30s, some first names around the 60s, and entire girls altogether somewhere around the 90s, but no matter how much or how many you fuck, some are just unforgettable.

This particular girl, "Candy," I met while working in Cancun. I was so busy fucking her sorority sisters, I didn't hit on her until the day before she left, but she was having none of me. I figured that she just respected herself and didn't want to fuck someone like me, so I was kinda surprised when she asked for my number the day she left. I gave it to her and didn't think twice about it, until two months later when Candy called and wanted to come visit.

By that time I had kinda forgotten what she looked like, so I was stoked when I picked her up at the airport and she was even hotter than I remembered. Short and Vietnamese but with just enough of the French rapist heritage coursing through her veins that she had that hybrid-vigor hotness that you really only see in mixed races.

I was 24 at the time and still didn't know as much as I thought that I did, so when on the ride back to my place she was very formal and quiet, I didn't understand what was going on. Why would this girl call me to come visit, knowing what I am like, and not be more into me?

One of my roommates was home when we got to my place, so we had a few beers in the living room and talked. Well, my roommate and I talked, and she just sat there and acted obsequious. Every time I tried to involve her in the conversation, she would briefly answer and then go back to her beer. I've seen kidnapping victims be more social with their captors.

Then my roommate left for the gym. As soon as the door closed behind him, I learned a very important lesson: sometimes the quietest and meekest in public are the loudest and wildest in private. I mean, I knew this about women in an intellectual way, but the reality of this proverb never hit home with me until I found myself being nearly sexually assaulted by this girl who had said no more than 10 words over the past hour.

Right after the front door clicked shut, she calmly put her beer down and then pounced on me like a jaguar. Since I have never had an Asian projectile fired at me, I wasn't sure what to do. She was literally jumping me, but I was so shocked and totally taken by surprise that I put my hands up and kinda hit her. Right in the face. I didn't mean to, but for a split second I thought she was trying to kill me. What would you think if some quiet Asian girl unexpectedly jumped at you?

She was fine, and I tried to apologize but couldn't talk because she was kissing me so hard. Fuck it; if she isn't hurt, I'm not going to worry about it.

Before that day, I thought I was aggressive and dominant in bed. That was before a 5'3" Vietnamese college girl turned me out.

She wanted everything and she wanted it hard. I hit it from the front, the back, the side, from underneath, on top, diagonally, every way I thought possible and then learned some new positions. I honestly didn't even think the pile driver was possible for normal people. I was wrong.

And no matter what I did, she wanted it harder and faster. So I put my dick in her ass. Not hard enough. I hit harder. And harder. And harder. I hit it so hard I was hurting myself. It got to the point where I was fucking with so much force her booty was clapping like Madison Square Garden, the bed was chipping the paint off the wall, my hips were bruising as they slammed against her ass bones and I was sweating like a migrant worker in a strawberry field, but it still wasn't enough.

I fucked her in the ass with so much force it started to bleed. Not much blood, but enough that I had to get new sheets. She didn't care, she just took my cock out, put a new condom on, and threw it in her pussy.

Then in her mouth, then back in the ass again when it stopped bleeding. Unreal.

I needed a few more dicks that weekend, because mine was not enough. It got to the point where I had to schedule rest breaks, because she was shredding me. It was emasculating in a way; this little docile girl totally out-fucked me. By the end of the weekend, after we had had sex some ridiculous number of times and my balls were aching and my cock was raw, she was still horny and would go down on my limp penis for like five minutes to get me hard, then she'd mount me and impale herself on my cock like a jackhammer. I think I could have gone to sleep and as long as I stayed hard, I doubt she would have cared.

I didn't fuck for like a week after she left I was so tired. My dick was raw. That normally only happens when I am black out drunk and try to jack off (which is a supremely bad idea). I still have scars on my back from her nails and rug burn on my knees from two days of violent sex with her.

She left and I told myself that was it. I couldn't handle another weekend of that, especially when it appeared that she was just fine.

Then I got the email. I still talked to one of her sorority sisters I had slept with in Cancun, and like a week later, she sent me this:

"Do you remember that girl [her name]? The quiet Asian girl in my sorority? She supposedly went home to visit her parents last week, but the day after she got back she had to go to student health with "female problems." Well, she always told us that she's never had sex, and she wouldn't tell us what was wrong, but my friend is a resident there, and he said that she had impacted bowels AND a urinary tract infection! Can you believe that? How could that happen if she doesn't have sex?"

BITCH, I'LL TELL YOU HOW IT HAPPENED—I AM AWESOME!

Truthfully though, I can't really take much credit. Whatever damage was done, she pretty much did to herself. I'm not going to sit here and write some lie about how big my dick is; it is exactly average for a white guy. I've measured and compared to numerous studies, and no matter how much I wish it hung to my knees, it sits right on the top of the bell curve. Her UTI was from going directly from anal to vaginal, which even with a new condom isn't a good idea, and the impacted bowels . . . well, she was a tiny Asian girl. My dick may not be huge, but it is probably bigger than her colon.

Nevertheless, to whoever is dating that girl now: You are a better man than me, and I wish you luck.

TUCKER GOES TO VEGAS

Occurred—October 1999
Written—April 2005

There are certain defining events in every man's life: the first time he has sex, the first time he gets drunk, the first time he gets in a fight. . . . and his first trip to Vegas.

During my 2nd year of law school I had to fly to LA for call back interviews, and I planned to stay with my good friend "Junior" while there. Junior is 5'9", well built, half-Italian half-Arabic, with light green eyes and olive skin. He's got that "dark with light eyes" look that that women lose their shit over. I knew Junior from Florida, where he used to work for my father. We became friends because he is one of the few people I've ever met in my life who not only does better with women than I do—WAY better, actually—but simply put, he can not only keep up with me, he can exceed me at times. Not many people can.

He lived in Santa Monica and was attending UCLA at the time. I arrived in LAX around 8pm on a Thursday, intending to party all weekend and go to my interviews on Monday. Junior was there to pick me up.

Junior "Hey, what's up man?"
Tucker "Not much, what's up with you?"
Junior "Nothing. Let's go to Vegas."
Tucker "Well . . . OK."

By about 8:15, Junior and I were on our way. I didn't even drop my bags off at his place.

Halfway there, in some shit-bag cow town called Barstow, Junior tells me to exit the highway and pull into a place called "In-N-Out." I was not impressed:

"Dude, where are we going? This place looks like shit."

Junior glared at me like I had turned down sex with Penelope Cruz and said nothing. He insisted that we go inside, as he said that one couldn't properly drive and give these burgers the attention necessary at the same time. He ordered me the Double-Double, and looking at it, I was still unimpressed. It's just a fucking hamburger.

I have only fallen in love three times in my life, and the first bite of that Double-Double was one of those times. The crispy bun complimenting the cool lettuce, the special sauce accentuating the fresh tomato, the sweet meat mixing with the salty cheese, all of it coming together in a harmonious medley of flavor thus far unseen on the American fast food landscape—I was smitten. It was the single greatest fast food meal in the history of civilization. Even though I was full, I immediately ate another Double-Double. I was nearly in tears at this meal, it was so transcendently excellent. Those fuckers should hire me as a spokesman.

This is me eating an In-N-Out burger—from the looks of it, my second of the day. I look pissed because pausing to pose for the picture is keeping me from my Double-Double.

Junior insisted that he drive for the second half of the trip. I didn't understand why until we pulled onto the strip; had I been behind the wheel, I would have wrecked. I am not a big fan of the movie *Swingers*, but I have to give it to Favreau, he really nailed the scene where they come over the mountain and see the lights of Vegas. I was like a child, I was so completely fixated by the flashing bright lights and shiny things everywhere. Times Square has nothing on driving into Vegas.

We pull into the Bellagio around 1am and immediately sit at the $25 blackjack tables and start playing. And drinking. And winning. Before I realize it, I am drunk, Junior and I are screaming, and we have collected quite the crowd around our table. We were "that table."

Everyone who has been to Vegas, or really any casino, knows the table I'm talking about: The one with the guys standing up, cheering at every winning hand, cursing at every losing hand, making ludicrous bets that pay off, yelling at everyone within earshot, ordering drinks for the entire floor, telling random onlookers to bring us food, grabbing the asses of cocktail waitresses, demanding the pit boss comp a room and some whores—that was us. There were many aspects to The Tucker and Junior Gambling Show:

We called every dealer, no matter what his or her name, "Slappy." We would routinely threaten every Slappy with bodily injury:

Junior "If you beat my 20, I'm gonna kick you right in the crotch."
Tucker "I swear on my grandmother's dried up decomposing corpse, if you draw a five card 21, I'll punt your tits across this casino floor."

One dealer nearly cleaned us out, so we threatened and cursed her and called her "The Angel of Death," to the point where she left the table nearly in tears. This didn't stop us:

Junior "You better not leave this casino alone! I'll find you!"
Tucker "I hope your children get lupus!"

One of the Slappys was quite the Puritan:
Tucker "Look at that card. FUCK ME IN THE EAR."
Dealer "Quiet. You can't say 'fuck' here."
Junior "We can't say 'fuck' in this casino, but prostitutes can run around selling themselves all over Vegas."
Dealer "Prostitution is legal in Vegas. Saying 'fuck' isn't."
Tucker "THAT'S HORSESHIT."
Junior "Can he say 'horseshit?' Is it legal for horses to shit in Vegas?"

I honestly have no idea how we didn't get kicked out.

As much fun as messing with Slappy was, you can only have so much fun with a dealer. What was more fun was the people who either gambled at our table or watched us. These two women stood near the table, one very young, and the other old and obviously her mother. Junior has the sex drive of a bull elephant in mating season, so he immediately perked up.

Junior "I'm going to go hit on her."
Tucker "Dude, what are you talking about? She's not even old enough to have seen all the episodes of *Seinfeld*."
Junior "I have to compliment you, because you obviously did a great job raising your daughter." [As he says this, he is facing the mother but ogling the daughter.]
Mother "My daughter is 15."
Junior "Well . . . I'm rich. I'll give you a large dowry."
Tucker "HOW MUCH FOR THE LITTLE GIRL! HOW MUCH FOR THE WOMAN!!"
Mother "Goodbye."

We got so carried away with the gambling and attention, the next time I took notice of my watch, it was 9am Friday morning, and I was feeling a bit tipsy. I casually ask the cocktail waitress how many beers I've had:

"I don't know sweetie. I work the 2am to 10am shift, and you were rolling along when I got here. I'd guess you've had at least 20 or 25 since I've been working."

Like when a young child doesn't know he's hurt until he actually sees the blood oozing out of the cut, I didn't realize how drunk I was until I realized how much I'd had to drink. I grabbed Junior,

Junior "You OK man?"
Tucker "Get me a fucking bed . . . I am about to hit a wall."

Junior laughed at me, told the pit boss and dealer to watch me, gave me about twenty $5 chips, and ran off. I went from 'Fun Tucker' to 'Comatose Tucker' in only five minutes. I am not sure what happened over the next half hour, but when Junior came back my head was on the table, I was randomly pushing chips forward, and the dealer was playing my hand for me. People were gawking and laughing like I was some sort of street performer. The best part: I was up $20.

Junior "We can't get a room, they are completely booked up, but I just met this girl, you can stay in her room. Tucker, meet [Charlene]."

Junior is amazing with women, but even for him this was something special. He not only picked a girl up in twenty minutes in Vegas—a hot girl no less—he got her to agree to let a complete stranger, me, pass out in her room while he gambled with her. Golf clap for Junior.

Too drunk at that exact moment to recognize this feat, I grunted a response, took her room key, and headed upstairs. I don't remember the trip to her room, or taking off my pants, or pissing on the bathroom floor instead of the toilet, or knocking over a side table, or laying on a bed or anything else that I did. I still deny responsibility for those incidents. That's the beauty of alcohol: if you don't remember it, it didn't happen.

My next clear memory is waking up to the sound of skin slapping against skin. I was so dehydrated, I couldn't even blink my eyes. Rubbing them, I saw Junior on the other bed humping that girl so hard that through my fogged vision, I thought he was trying to dig his way to China. A real pleasant scene. I passed back out.

When I woke up, they had showered and cleaned the stench of stranger sex off themselves. Junior and I left her room to go gamble some more, but not before Junior gave her a fake cell number, because he is a bad person. About two hours later, I realized that I had left my glasses in her room:

Junior "How could you leave your glasses? Are you so drunk you forgot that you couldn't see?"

I went back up to her room and knocked on the door. I think she thought that Junior was coming back for more sex, because she answered the door only in her towel with this seductive smile. When she saw me, her expression shifted to confused, then quickly moved to sly.

Charlene "What can I do for you?"
Tucker [confused by the palpable sexual tension] "Uhh . . . I, uhhh . . . I left my glasses here. Really."
Charlene "Come in."

I looked around and found my glasses under the bed. Then it just got weird. She was leaning up against the wall between me and the door with this look on her face I had never seen before. Well, I had seen it before, but only in porn movies where the lonely wife fucks the muscular plumber in the cut off jean shorts, and that just couldn't be happening here, could it? I mean, this is real life, and real life is never like porn . . . is it? Women don't randomly fuck strange men they just met . . . do they?

You have to understand, I was only twenty-three at the time, and didn't quite understand what I do now: While there are many wonderful women in the world who should be treated with respect, some are just filthy whores. Even though I was inexperienced I relied on my sixth sense about this and decided to roll the dice. Besides, what's the worst thing that could happen? She kicks me out? I'm leaving anyway:

Tucker "You aren't dry yet? Why are you still in a towel?"
Great line Tucker, real smooth. Apparently, it didn't matter:
Charlene "Why don't you finish drying me off?"

Twenty-three and naive, even I couldn't miss that one.

Now that I think about what I actually did, I am kinda disgusted. I followed one of my best friends not even two hours after he was done. She did shower though, so I guess that's good. Whatever; nothing counts in Vegas, right? The best part: I've never even told him about that. He's going to find out when he reads this story.

Afterwards, back down at the tables:

Junior "What took you so long?"
Tucker "I got stuck in something. That girl is pretty hot."
Junior "No shit. She's incredible in bed."
Tucker "I bet."

By this time it was around 5pm on Friday. We had an awesome roll the night before, but this day luck was not with us, and I ended up losing like $500. Whatever, I had at least 12 drinks, so I clearly came out on top. Stupid Vegas, they don't know anything.

The hemorrhaging stopped at 8pm, because my buddy SlingBlade was coming in on a flight. At the airport, I see him come out of baggage claim, and lean out the car window and yell:

Tucker "SLINGBLADE—THIS PLACE IS GREAT! WE DON'T EVEN HAVE A HOTEL ROOM! JUNIOR FUCKED SOME WHORE AND I WON LOTS OF MONEY! WOOOOOOO-HOOOOO!!!"
SlingBlade "I am getting back on the plane."

We ate dinner at the In-N-Out right off the Strip (yes, I am obsessive-compulsive), gambled and drank for awhile, and then went to the big club inside of The Venetian. Junior and I rounded up two women, and of course because they had vaginas SlingBlade hated them and spent the whole time grousing about "whores" and "wanton filth." At some point, the five of us noticed this hilarious scene on the dance floor:

A stunningly hot girl was casually dancing with one of her female friends, when this disgusting bald old man came up and started grinding her. Not just dancing next to her mind you; he was freaking her 6th grade negro style. It was ridiculous. She kept turning away, and he kept following, and we kept laughing at him. All of the sudden SlingBlade walked over to the old man as he was trying to wheedle his way between the girls, pulled him aside, pointed to the exit and said:

"You sir are a failure in dancing and in life. Please move away from the hot girl."

The expression on the hot girl's face was amazing; it was the personification of true love. She was almost in tears laughing, and immediately draped herself all over SlingBlade and gave him a big kiss on his cheek. In fact, so many people were laughing that the old man actually did leave the club.

The night progresses, and things start going really well with my girl. Her hands are down my pants, her tongue is in my ear at the bar and she whispers to me:

Girl "Is it true nothing counts in Vegas?"
Tucker "It only counts if you live here."
Girl "I am from Cincinnati."
Tucker "It counts even less if it's not in a bed."
Girl "That is so hot. I've never done that."

I immediately pull her into the bathroom hallway, where we start making out so intensely we could have been giving each other CPR. This club, instead of separate men's and women's bathrooms, has four unisex bathrooms. And the bathrooms have those really cool type of doors that are totally clear glass when unlocked, but frost up when you lock the door.

Cool bathroom doors aside, I have to find a solution to my dilemma: I am drunk and horny with a drunk and horny girl who wants to fuck, but there are 20 people in front of me waiting to use the bathrooms. I decide that since I am clearly a more important person and have greater immediate need, I can cut the line. I just have to give everyone something in return.

A door opens and I rush towards it, pulling the girl with me. A douchebag guido tries to say something, but I stop him, "TRUST ME—I'll make it worth your while." Before he can protest I push her in and lock the door, and the clear glass immediately frosts up. She grabs me and plants a sloppy drunken kiss on me:

"Fuck me so hard I forget my name."

You don't have to tell me twice. I spin her around and bend her over the sink, rip her Victoria's Secret panties as I pull them down her legs, and slam into her like Dale Earnhardt into the wall at Daytona. But as I thrust back and forth, my subconscious takes me out of the moment:

"Tucker, you have a promise to a guido to fulfill." Stupid fucking subconscious. I look around and try to think of something.

The way the bathroom is set up, the toilet is on the back wall directly across from the door, and the sink is on the wall to the left, so as she is bent over the sink and I fuck her from behind, I am positioned between the toilet and the frosted glass door. Then it hits me: Right there, in front of my face, is the lock for the door. Hello, payback.

I turn it open and the door immediately goes from frosted to clear. A few of the people in line turn to look at the door expecting it to open . . . but instead see me hammering away at this girl. I smile and lock it back.

No way. Did I just give all those people a shot of me having sex?

A few more thrusts, and I click it open again. The glass clears, but this time there are four people standing there. They all stare in shock. I give them a smile and a pump and lock it back again.

Unlock the door.
Eight people standing there. I start spanking her. They cheer loudly.
HOLY SHIT! HOW COOL IS THIS!
Lock it back.
Unlock the door.

A dozen people standing there. I do the 'look ma, no hands.' They cheer rowdily. WHO'S THE MAN NOW?
Lock it back.

Unlock the door.
More than a dozen people standing there. I grab her hair and spank her like a rented mule. They cheer wildly. I AM A SUPERSTAR! THIS IS AWESOME!
Lock it back.

I start to wonder: what do I like more, the sex or audience? I don't care. I should go into porn. After all, it's not the size of the dick that's important, it's the size of the crowd that the dick attracts.

I unlock it and lock it back over and over, giving them some different variation of the show each time; pulling her hair, putting my finger in her ass, pushing her clothes off, throwing toilet paper on her. Everything I do gets me more cheers from more people there each time. God I love being on stage. The best part is that the girl doesn't even notice; the only part that unfrosts is the door, and except for her ass she wasn't in front of the door. She could have just been an ass sticking out of the wall for all the crowd could tell.

By the tenth time I unlocked the door, there were at least 30 people crowded around watching me fire my cock into this girl. I'm getting close to cumming and I decide that for my big finish, I am going to shoot my load on the glass right as I unlock the door. I start pumping harder and harder, and right before I cum I pinch the bottom of my cock (to stop the cum from shooting before I am ready), turn towards the door and simultaneously splooge on it as I unlock the door, giving the crowd my best O face. WHAT A FINISH!

I didn't see him at first because I was caught up in the effect of my orgasm, but he came into my vision pretty quickly.

Instead of 30 people shocked to see me shooting a five-roper on the door . . . there was a huge 6'5" black bouncer, arms crossed on his chest, with a 12-inch Mag-Lite in his hand.

His eyes met mine, then he glanced down at the load shooting onto the door, and his eyes came back to mine. We shared a moment. A moment of complete and utter shock.

That shared moment ended quickly. I think the precise second it ended can be pinpointed to when he slammed his shoulder into the door, flinging it open and smashing it right into my face. Dick in my hand and pants still at my ankles, seeing stars, I stumble backwards . . . and land right in the toilet.

In case you were wondering, toilet water feels exceptionally cold against a bare ass.

The bouncer storms in, "WHAT THE FUCK ARE YOU DOING?"

He had the Mag-Lite half raised and I am convinced that had the girl not been there, he would have introduced it to my head in a violent and ferocious collision. Thankfully, she came to my rescue:

"AAAAAAAAAAAAAAHHHHHHHHHHHHHHHHHHHHHHHHH"

I guess he hadn't seen her in his rush to hurt me, because the bouncer jumped in shock. I took this opportunity to pull myself out of the toilet, and ass still wet, put my pants back on.

I tried to run, but I doubt Barry Sanders in his prime could have shook this guy. He was not only big and athletic, but his tackle showed perfect form, even despite the fact that he nearly slipped on the girl's torn panties laying on the floor. I would have complimented his flawless technique, but I had problems breathing through what felt like broken ribs and a collapsed lung.

He grabbed me by the shirt and basically dragged me across the dance floor. All I could do was muster a weak, "Help!" but thankfully SlingBlade and Junior saw me and came to my rescue. Well, they didn't stop the bouncer from dragging me out of the bar, so it wasn't really a rescue. It was more of a "We'll just watch and hope they don't beat Tucker any worse" type of rescue. I get kicked out of bars all the time, but this was the first time that I was actually thrown—physically thrown through the air—out of a place. And people say old school Vegas is dead.

Even though the seat of my pants was still soaked from my wet ass, we went to another casino and drank at the center bar for an hour or so, just to decompress and digest the events that just happened. SlingBlade has the intestinal fortitude of a premature newborn, and he was not handling the combination of alcohol, In-N-Out and stress very well, so we decided to go to a diner-type place in the casino to get him some coffee.

It was about 4am Saturday at this point, and this place already had its breakfast buffet out. Junior and I immediately got plates and sat down. Greasy eggs and pork fat spilling over the edges of the plates. When the smell caught SlingBlade, he winced and turned grey. I thought I was being funny at the time:

"That's not a good smell if you're feeling queasy. Well, whatever you do, don't think about greasy, fatty barbecue sandwiches with gobs of melting butter on top. And a full ashtray dumped on it."

SlingBlade immediately leaned over and vomited all over the booth.

Tucker "OH SHIT!"
Junior "WHY DID YOU SAY THAT!"
Tucker "I DON'T KNOW!"

Still reeling from falling in a toilet and getting my ass kicked by a bouncer, I just sat there. It was Junior who saved this day. He immediately jumped into action:

"Get up SlingBlade, get up. Alright, Tucker, hold him up. Just stay here, I'll be right back."

He ran off to the front of the restaurant and got the manager. She was a well-dressed woman, probably in her late thirties, who looked unhappy that, at her age, she was still pulling late shifts in a Vegas restaurant.

Manager "Hi. What can I do for you?"
Junior "Yeah, we were just seated, and, well, I don't want to get anyone in trouble for this, it's not a big deal at all, but it appears that someone left something in our booth, and nobody cleaned it up before we were seated."

He pointed to the booth SlingBlade had been sitting in.

Manager "What is that . . . Oh my lord! I am SO sorry. Oh my! Is that vomit? Please, oh, I am so sorry. I can't believe this. Please go to the front, we'll get you a new table and take care of everything right away. I am so sorry. JULIO, GET OVER HERE!"

SlingBlade and I went to the front of the restaurant, SlingBlade still holding his stomach in agony. They quickly seated us at another booth in a separate part of the restaurant. SlingBlade wasn't looking much better.

Tucker "Can you hold it together? Are you going to be alright?"

SlingBlade nodded. I was ordering him some coffee as the manager and Junior came over to our new table.

Manager "Please let me apologize again for that. I am really sorry, that has never happened before. Let me buy your meal, whatever you want. Again, I am really sorry."
Junior "That's really nice, but honestly, it's not necessary. Really. It's not a big deal."
Manager "No, please, I want to, I feel so bad about . . ."

I heard it before I saw it, but the noise was enough. By the time I actually looked at him, SlingBlade only had a small dribble of vomit coming out of his mouth, but there was chunky liquid was all over the carpet . . . right next to the manager's shoes.

She stood completely still, in total shock, except for her head which tilted downwards to see the damage. When SlingBlade started retching again, she jumped out of the way of his second wave of vomit. She waited for him to stop regurgitating before she spoke:

"I think all of you should leave now."

Junior and I were still wired from all the Red Bull we drank at the club, so we decided to gamble. SlingBlade was done, but the casino we were at didn't have any rooms either, so we had to travel all the way down the strip to Circus-Circus to find a room. Once we had the key we sent him up to the room, and started in on more blackjack. This was about 5am on Saturday morning.

Junior left the table at 10am. I kept playing and drinking Vodka Red Bulls until I looked up and it was 3pm (still Saturday). SlingBlade and Junior had come back down to the table:

SlingBlade "Jesus Christ. How are you still awake? Are you on coke?"
Tucker "NoDude,RedBullisAmazingStuff,PlusIThinkTheyReallyDoPump OxygenIntoTheseCasinos.VegasIsGreatILoveItHere!DoYouThinkIShould

SplitTheseTensAgainstAn8? BookSaysNo,ButImOnARoll! HITME! HITME! COMEONPICTURE!"
SlingBlade "Should I just call Gamblers Anonymous now, or wait till you pass out?"
Junior "What's wrong with your eyes? They are shaking."
Tucker "ImHungry, LetsGoToInNOutandThenGoToAStripClub! Double-DoublesOnMe!!"

We left the casino in Junior's car, and as soon as I sat down in the back seat I hit a wall. I passed out in the car and they just left me there. I woke up at 8pm, five hours later, still in the car, in some parking lot I didn't recognize. Whatever; this is Vegas, it's time to rally.

I look around and see Bellagio signs. I know why we are here. Yesterday—at least I think it was yesterday—we had been playing blackjack at the Bellagio in the early evening while we waited for SlingBlade to fly in. Junior, who has an amazing radar for big-titted girls with low self-esteem, was drawn like a tractor beam to the center casino bar. It was crawling with his exact type of women. Seriously, it looked like a Playboy shoot or something. He tried to pick up some of the girls but was continually and unceremoniously shot down. I found him and SlingBlade at the bar. Both were sipping drinks but not talking to any of the women.

Tucker "So what's up Junior? I've never seen you give up on pussy before, especially not pussy that looks like this."
Junior just shook his head as SlingBlade broke out laughing, "I can't believe you two idiots didn't recognize this yesterday. THEY ARE ALL PROSTITUTES! You don't hit on them, you negotiate price!"

That was the bad news. The good news was that Junior and Sling-Blade had not wasted their time. Even though Junior may not be able to pick up working prostitutes, he did get a Bellagio cocktail waitress to agree to come to dinner with us, and to bring two of her friends who went to UNLV with her. They met us at the bar and took us to this amazing local Thai place. Making small talk, the girls asked us what we do. I considered telling them the truth, but hey, this is Vegas. You can be anything you want here:

Tucker "We are in a band."
Girl 1 "No way really? Anything I've ever heard of?"

Tucker "I don't know—do you listen to Christian Rap?"
Girl 2 "I love Christian Rap!"
Tucker "Well, I am Big Baby Jesus, and [pointing to Junior] this is The Beat Boxin' Prophet, and he [pointing to SlingBlade] is DJ Orthodoxy. Together, we call ourselves Tha Last Suppa."

I wish I could have recorded the look on SlingBlade's face. There isn't a word strong enough for the look he gave me; "contempt" doesn't cut it, and "hatred" isn't rich enough. I fully expected the girls to laugh and ask us what we really did . . . and that is what I get for underestimating the stupidity of UNLV students.

Girl 2 "OH MY GOD! I totally think I have heard of you guys!"
Girl 1 "Were you on the radio today? I think I heard you!"

Now, I want to pause here and point something out. People always email me asking how it is I get into the ridiculous situations I seem to constantly find myself in. Well people, this is a how I do it: Where most anyone else would stop the joke here, I just dropped it into 5th gear and zoomed past the speed limit.

Tucker "Yeah! I can't believe you heard us. We aren't that big yet, but we're getting there. I'm glad that you two are fans."
Girl 3 "I'm a fan too!"
Tucker "Of course you are."
SlingBlade "And here I was thinking that Larry Johnson was the stupidest person to ever go to UNLV."

Junior played along great, but SlingBlade was not happy. Not only did he not like being "DJ Orthodoxy," but he could not stand the idiot girl he was talking to.

Girl 3 "So where are you from?"
SlingBlade "I don't care."
Girl 3 "Did you say 'here?' Like Vegas? Me too!"
SlingBlade "Yeah here. I'm from right here."
Girl 3 "This neighborhood?"
SlingBlade "No, this Thai restaurant. I was lost in a rather high stakes game of Omaha Hold'em by my degenerate gambler father, but luckily escaped from the glue factory and lived as a street urchin until this nice Thai family adopted me. I lived out the rest of my childhood scam-

pering amongst the chair legs, bussing tables for a cot and eating floor scraps for subsistence. This is like a home coming party for me."
Girl 3 "You don't have to be a jerk."
SlingBlade "Quite the contrary, my sloppy penile scholar. Order me another drink and be quick about it."

SlingBlade got up and went to the bathroom. Girl 3 turns to the table:

Girl 3 "You guys are really nice, but . . . DJ Orthodoxy is a jerk."
Tucker "Sometimes he has problems with the 'love thy neighbor' part."

To really solidify the Christian rapper shtick, at one point I took my beer, held it up and motioned to Junior and SlingBlade:

Tucker "Beat Boxin' Prophet, DJ Orthodoxy . . . I think it's time we tipped one out to our fallen lord. Hmm? Some beer for Jesus?"
Junior "WE'LL SEE YOU AT THE CROSSROADS, JESUS!"

I poured a little drop on the ground. Junior laughed hysterically and followed me, then the girls actually did the same thing. SlingBlade just glared at me.

SlingBlade "I hate both of you with a nearly unspeakable hatred."

This Thai place was fucking awesome. We couldn't finish a drink before they had another one in front of us. We got so drunk even SlingBlade started being nice. At one point, the topic of anal sex came up. As we were talking about the finer points of ass sex, Junior, who was very drunk by this point, stood up at his seat and yelled out,

"No girl's butt can take this dick."

As he said this, Junior takes his cock out and slams it on the table with a thud. And it does make an audible thud—the dude is hung like Tommy Lee. I think a few glasses even clinked. I distinctly heard one of the girls gasp. The table gets completely silent for what seems like a minute, but was probably closer to a second. He then belts out:

Junior "I've never had buttsex because no girl's ass can take this dick. Look at this thing; I have a black man's penis. Show me an ass that can handle this! Look at this dick! It's huge!"
Tucker "Now, now Beat Boxin' Prophet; you are being prideful."

As soon as my words were out of my mouth, all the women were immediately jarred out of a trance. They readjusted themselves and turned away from Junior as he put his cock back in, and some normalcy returned to the table. Well, as much normalcy as is possible after a fucking elephant cock was slammed in the middle of a dinner table.

After dinner we decide to go back to the house that two of the girls share. SlingBlade claims that he is tired and wants to leave. We know the truth: He freaks out at the prospect of having to sleep with a girl that he isn't in love with. The kid has problems. He gets in a cab back to Circus-Circus.

When we get to their house, the girls all go to the bathroom, and Junior asks me:

Junior "I can't believe they think we are Christian rappers. Do you think what we're doing is wrong?"
Tucker "Junior, I don't think anything I've ever done is wrong."

We all go into the basement, which has the TV and all the couches and what not. I pick one couch and Junior takes the other, but the three girls head upstairs, "we'll be right back."

I had to piss really bad, so I start wandering around the basement looking for a bathroom. I couldn't find one, and didn't feel like going upstairs to deal with whatever it was those three were planning, so I took the next best option, and started pissing in a cat box I found on the floor.

Junior "Dude, what are you doing?"
Tucker "Meow . . . meow."

All we could hear from upstairs was muffled arguing. Then a loud crash. Girl 2 came downstairs and told Junior that Girl 1 was waiting for him upstairs. She then explains to me:

"Yeah, I wish DJ Orthodoxy had stayed. We just had a big fight about who was going to fuck who. I don't actually live here, it's the other two girls' place, so even though I get to fuck you, we have to do it on the sofa down here."

We fuck and fuck and pass out and the next morning, I am awakened to a scratching noise and a cat bawling incessantly. I look over the sofa and see why: The fucking cat box is CEMENT. Totally hardened over. Wow—that was quite the piss I took. I threw the remote at the cat and it screeched and ran off, and I rolled the girl over and fucked her again.

Junior and I left a few hours later to go back to LA, having never changed our clothes or even showered, the girls wishing our band luck and saying they'd come see our next concert.

We ended up having to pull over on the drive back to LA to sleep. The weekend wasted us. We started at 1am Thursday night, and went almost straight through until Sunday morning.

The bad part about that story is that it ruined me on Vegas. Every trip back since then has been anti-climactic and shitty. I guess it's hard to top something like that. Plus, the way that weekend worked out, we really didn't run into or have to deal with the legions of douche bags and tools that now seem to infect every aspect of Vegas. Maybe we were just lucky, maybe it was a different time, but the city just doesn't seem the same place that it was during that trip.

And yes, I made it to all my interviews on Monday.

Floss

Occurred—April 2001
Written—March 2005

Don't let anyone tell you different: The only good part about Duke is that it is 15 minutes from Chapel Hill. That school was awesome; it was 65% girls, most of them hot, and the 35% guys were, for the most part, complete fucking tools and no real competition. Plus, once you got in with a girl, you were in with all her friends and her sorority. This effectively meant that meeting one girl who wanted to fuck you was like meeting 15 who wanted to fuck you, simply because there was such a shortage of good guys. There may have been no better pick-up line on earth than meeting a female UNC undergrad and saying "Yeah, I go to Duke Law School." God I miss that place sometimes.

One time I went to a sorority function with a UNC girl and quickly ignored her in favor of the hotter girls in her sorority. This one girl was particularly into me, but she was just a little too skinny for my taste; I don't like girls to look like concentration camp victims, and this girl was straight out of grainy Buchholz liberation footage. She noticed that I was giving more attention to another girl, so she pulled me aside.

Skinny girl "Why do you keep talking to her instead of me?"
Tucker "I like her."
Skinny girl "But I am so much better than she is."
Tucker "But I think I kinda like your friend."
Skinny girl "I bet she can't give head like me."

Don't you just love UNC sorority girls?

Tucker "Yeah, maybe, but you are too skinny. I like girls to have some meat on them. I am pretty aggressive in bed; if we fucked, I'm afraid one of us would get injured. Either I would split you in half, or I'd get my eye poked out by your sharp elbows. Plus, I'd spend the whole time thinking about how I should be getting you a burger instead of fucking you."

I figured this would be enough to get her to leave me alone. That was before I truly understood how desperate most UNC girls are for men.

Skinny girl "Trust me, you want me. Bulimic girls give better head. We don't have a gag reflex."

I almost choked. What girl says this? The ones that are attracted to me, apparently.

Since we were in a hotel and the sorority had a bunch of rooms rented, we immediately went to one of them and she nearly broke my zipper getting my pants off. She wasn't fucking around: The girl took every inch of me without even flinching. Granted, my dick is only average sized, but she forced so much of it in I am pretty sure the tip of it was tickling her small intestine.

But she didn't stop with my penis. She took just about my entire crotch area in her mouth. On every down stroke the girl seemed to take in more and more flesh. At one point I am pretty sure she had my cock and balls in her mouth at once. I didn't even think that was possible until little Miss Sorority Python came along and unhinged her jaw.

The most comical part was what was going through my mind; here is this girl sucking me off like my cock is the fountain of youth, and all I could think was that this was probably the most she had eaten in months without throwing up. I finished, she swallowed, and I started laughing, wondering if later she was going to purge my cum.

Ignoring my laughs, she stayed down and slurped me until I was dry, and then she looked up at me, smiled seductively and said, "I told you that you wanted head from me."

I looked down at her and couldn't speak. Not because of the blowjob—it was good, but it wasn't so good that I lost control of my faculties. It was something else:

In her smile . . . curled across her two front teeth and wrapped around the left canine . . . was the longest, nastiest looking pubic hair I had ever seen. And it was mine, directly off of my crotch.

It's weird how your brain works at moments like this. I wasn't really thinking about how nasty my pubes are, or whether this means that I should start trimming my pubes or whether or not I should tell her, or even wonder how she didn't feel a huge pubic hair in her mouth; no, the first thought through my mind was, "This is going to be someone's mom someday? Wow. Those poor kids; they are going to kiss that mouth." Then my next thought was, "I wonder how many calories my pubes have?"

I still have never shaved my balls or groin area, but I now trim my pubes on a regular basis. I don't trust myself with a razor near my best friends (plus I don't want to have shaved balls like a porn star) so instead I just use a groomer and trim the area. All because of a slutty UNC sorority girl. I guess they do have a use besides hooking up.

The Foxfield Weekend

Occurred—April 2000
Written—April 2005

I have never attended the University of Virginia, but I still feel like I have a bond with the school. I applied and got in for college, and to my mild regret chose to attend the University of Chicago instead. I got in again for law school, and chose Duke because UVa didn't give me an academic scholarship (Duke did). I have four cousins that attended UVa and I've probably visited that school more than any other. But it was one incredible event in April of 2000 that really cemented my unofficial tie to that school: Foxfield.

Foxfield is the name for the spring horse races they have on some farm near UVa. Everyone loads up their car or truck or RV with food and booze, parks in this massive field and tailgates all day. Allegedly there are actual horses and they race each other around the track, but no one I know has ever seen them.

I was a 2L at Duke Law School that year. GoldenBoy and his girlfriend (who would later become his wife) both went to UVa for undergrad, and she was still at UVa when we were at law school. The Friday night before Foxfield, GoldenBoy, Hate and I were out drinking in Durham. This is the rest of the story:

11:00pm: We are eating Mexican food and drinking beer. GoldenBoy regales us with wistful tales of Foxfield. He describes a weekend of virtually unlimited alcohol, raucous drinking, food spreads to rival great medieval halls, and girls in sun dresses with negotiable morals.

11:15: Hate and I ask him why we aren't going. He doesn't have a satisfactory answer. We demand to leave immediately. He balks. We call him out. Doubt his manhood. Inquire as to his sexual preference and conjecture that he is of bastard French origin.

11:16: GoldenBoy is on the phone with his girlfriend [GoldenWife], telling her that we are coming, and requesting that she go out and buy beer. GoldenBoy is easily manipulated.

12:00am: We are on the road to Charlottesville. I have a personal 12 pack to make the three hours go by faster.

1:12: My beer is spilling on GoldenBoy's car. I don't notice because I am passed out.

3:00: We arrive at GoldenWife's apartment. We ask her where the parties are. She doesn't know. This pleases GoldenBoy. He sees it as a sign she is true to him. Couples like that make me sick.

8:00: Hate and I wake up from a comfortable night sleeping on the hardwood floor. We bang on the bedroom door until GoldenBoy wakes up. "TIME TO DRINK!" He looks at us like we are rabid wild animals trying to eat his children. He slams the door and goes back to sleep.

8:03: Hate and I crack our first beer.

8:05: Hate and I crack our second beer.

8:08: Hate and I crack our third beer. I tell Hate that I can out drink him. He laughs, "So it begins, Max."

8:30: After we shotgun our 3rd beer in a row, I can feel the beer sloshing around in my stomach. Drinking in the morning = bad decisions.

9:17: I am on my 8th beer of the morning, and am already starting to look for places I can vomit. Hate is not slowing down. I decide that Hate can indeed out drink me.

10:00: Hate doesn't care that I have stopped trying, and keeps furiously pouring alcohol down his throat. He is stomping around the apartment, calling everyone out. "COME ON MAX—WHERE THE HELL ARE YOU AT? YEEEEAAAAAHHH . . . GoldenBoy, get your ass out here. Bloody Mary's, one-for-one, YOU AND ME. Max already tapped out. You can even get GoldenWife to help you. YEEEEEEEEEEEEAAAAAAAAAAAAAHHH. MAX YOU PUSSY!"

11:00: We get in the car and pick up GoldenBoy's undergrad friends who are in town for Foxfield. Hate has moved from Aggressive Drinking to Combative Drinking. He is attacking the beer. Hate sticks his entire upper body out the back window of the car screaming at every female he sees, "WOOOOOOOOOOOHHHHHHH . . . SHOW US YOUR TITS!!!"

11:15: GoldenBoy tells me that although there are lots of hot girls at Foxfield, no one actually hooks up there. It's more of a social drinking event, he says. I ask him if he knows who he is talking to. He rolls his eyes and condescendingly wishes me luck, "OK, Tucker . . . no one hooks up at Foxfield, they hook-up afterwards." GoldenBoy has thrown down the gauntlet. I pick it up and bitch slap him with it, "Motherfucker! How dare you besmirch my whore-attraction abilities. I'm going to hook up with a girl right in front of you, and then make you smell my finger."

12:00pm: We arrive. The field stretches beyond sight, an endless expanse of bushy-haired frat boy fuckwits in striped shirts and red pants, their cold beer and underage women ripe for the plundering. This is almost unfair.

12:01: I see my first hot girl in a sun dress and nearly break my neck staring at her. This scene will replay itself approximately 1,200 times this day.

12:13: We arrive at GoldenBoy's friend's tent. He starts to introduce us, but Hate pushes everyone out of the way and dives into the fried chicken. He looks up momentarily to greet them with a barely decipherable mumble about "less talking, more eating," before turning his full attention to the potato salad, pushing it into his mouth by the handful.

12:14: GoldenBoy tells me that he is a little surprised. He had been sure I would be the one who ruined the afternoon. I remind him that it's still early in the race.

12:38: One girl, trying to be nice to Hate, points to the cooler and offers him a drink. He examines the selections, "I will not drink light beer or diet soda as both have been found to cause cancer in lab rats and have not really helped fat Americans that much anyway. Do I see Hooch in that cooler? OHHH LORD! MAX, COME LOOK AT THIS! WHAT THE HELL IS WRONG WITH YOU PEOPLE?" I decide that it's time for Hate to walk around Foxfield with me.

12:50: Hate is not pleased, "Dude, they had beer. Why are we leaving?" I explain, "You already pissed all of them off, we have to find new victims. We'll just steal beer from people smaller than us." This pleases Hate, "SHOW ME THE WAY!"

12:54: We find our first victims. A tailgate with small kids. Hate storms up and starts rummaging through their cooler. "JACKPOT MAX! THEY HAVE BUD TALL BOYS!"

1:04: We go to another tailgate. Some sorority. Hot girls everywhere. Hate walks right in the middle, "HELLLLO LADIES! WHO WANTS TO DO A SHOT!!" He grabs a tequila bottle and starts recklessly waving it around, sloshing the contents on several people.

1:05: We are asked to leave the sorority tailgate area.

1:09: We find another sorority tailgate. Hate walks right into the middle of them, "I HEAR UVA GIRLS CAN DRINK! HORSESHIT! I CAN OUT DRINK ALL YOU SKIRTS!"

1:10: We are asked to leave our second sorority tailgate.

1:20: We find another tailgate of girls. I decide on a different course of action for us, "Hate, do not speak unless spoken to." These girls are athletes. My cousin rows at UVa. I ask them if they know her. They do, and I'm in. For college girls, common friends = the guy is safe = I want to have sex with him.

1:55: Things are going great. Hate is talking to a girl taller than him, so he is calm. Then it happens. Some girl decides to flirt with me by calling me out, "You don't look like much of a drinker."

1:56: This will not go unanswered, "Who are you talking to? Bitch, you couldn't even tie my drinking shoes." She challenges me to a shot contest. This makes me laugh, "Line'em up. And no girly shit either. Straight liquor. Anything except whiskey."

1:58: She raises the first shot and gives a toast, "Give me chastity and give me continence—but not yet . . . St. Augustine!" All her little friends laugh and cheer. Amateurs.

1:59: I raise my shot, "This is for all the bitches, ho's and tricks, I'd wouldn't talk to any of you, if I didn't have a dick . . . Tucker Max." Everyone laughs.

2:00: One of the girls asks me, "Who is Tucker Max?"

2:10: Two shots later, my female opponent bows out of the shot contest. I taunt her mercilessly, "You may be able to vote and drive, but you'll never be equal!" I am not a gracious winner.

2:11: One of her little friends comes up to me. She is cute with short hair and thick black framed glasses. She is pissed:

Girl "That was really sexist."
Tucker "No it wasn't, it was a joke. If I had said that women are nothing but life support for a pussy, now THAT would be sexist."
Girl "Excuse me?"
Tucker "If I had called her a hot mouth, that would be sexist too. Or, if I said that the only thing going for her is that she's 98.6 degrees and has two wet holes, that would be very sexist. But I didn't say those things, did I?"
Girl "WHAT?"
Tucker "Uh oh! Did I piss you off? Are you going to write angsty poetry?!?"

She is looking at me like I'm a toilet full of used condoms. Hate pulls me away from her before she recovers, "Max, I think you have caused enough damage here." It takes me a second to register it, but I realize that Hate is now the voice of reason. This does not bode well.

2:25: Using the same "Do you know my cousin" line, we get in with another tailgate. These girls think that drunk, sarcastic assholes are funny. Hello wheelhouse. I decide to mock people for their amusement.

2:27: Some redneck doofus walks by: "Look at yourself—does the carnival have the day off? If you can guess my weight, I'll give you a free beer."

2:31: To a slutty looking girl: "Is that a cross on your chest? Just because you spend most of your time in the missionary position doesn't make you religious."

2:33: An old woman walks by who looks remarkably like Ethel Merman. I bust out in verse, "You'll be swell, you'll be great, you'll have the whole world on a plate, starting here, starting now, baby everything's coooming up roooooses!"

2:34: One of the girls cracks up laughing, "OH MY GOD! AIRPLANE IS MY FAVORITE MOVIE EVER!" I walk over to her, "My name is Tucker and I am going to law school at Duke so I can be really rich and buy shiny things for my wife. What's your name?"

3:15: I am ruthlessly flirting with her. Hate saunters up, looks at her and then looks at me, "Do I even need to know this one's name?" I decide it is time to get this girl away from Captain Cockblock and find someplace private.

3:30: I am having difficulty finding privacy at an outdoor race course.

3:40: A stroke of genius hits me—I find the open grass area on the small hill behind GoldenBoy's tailgate, and suggest that we sit there, "to be alone."

3:42: I look around and realize that at least 2000 people can see us. One of those people is GoldenBoy. I wave.

3:45: I tell her that she is really pretty. She blushes. She tells me I am funny.

3:50: I tell her that she is exactly what I am looking for in a girlfriend. She blushes more. She tells me I am nice.

3:55: We are making out. In front of everyone.

4:00: Not satisfied with just kissing, I start exploring. She doesn't have any underwear on. Gold-digging sluts are awesome.

4:05: I've got two fingers in her vagina and one in her butt. I am giving this girl The Shocker. No one hooks up at Foxfield? Fuck you, GoldenBoy.

4:15: I try to climb on top of her, but she stops me. Prudes suck.

4:16: She grabs my hand and gets up, "Let's go somewhere else; we are on a hill in front of everyone." Oh . . . right, I forgot about that.

4:30: We walk past a Port-a-Potty. I consider the possibility, open the door, and immediately change my mind. No pussy is worth enduring that smell.

4:55: We come across an RV tailgate that is empty. The people next to it say that everyone is off watching the alleged horse races.

5:01: They left the door to the RV open. Whoops. I throw her on the bed and we start fucking. I don't even have to take her clothes off, as her sun dress without panties doesn't require it. Sluts are awesome.

5:04: Drunk sex is great.

5:08: I decide that drunk, transgressive sex in someone else's RV with a girl you don't know is even better.

5:10: I start hitting it hard. Every time I thrust in, she yelps. It sounds like a yelp of enjoyment, and she isn't asking me to stop, so I hit it even harder.

5:14: I hit it harder. She yelps louder.

5:15: I can feel it coming. This is going to be a great cum shot.

5:17: My eyes start burning. I ignore it.

5:18: HOLY SHIT I CANNOT BREATHE—WHAT THE FUCK IS GOING ON??

5:18: The girl and I stumble out of the RV, in tears, both coughing and barely able to breathe. I am very confused. My throat feels like I ate a handful of habanero peppers. We start gulping down water and beer to get rid of this awful burning.

5:23: She screams. "OH MY GOD! I KNOW WHAT THAT WAS!" She covers her face and runs back into the RV. She emerges, coughing again, with her purse held as far away from her as possible. "I was laying on my purse, and I guess my pepper spray went off accidentally. Everything inside it is ruined!"

5:25: I don't know whether to laugh or cry at this. Still processing this info, I reach down and adjust my sticky crotch. I learn the hard way that capsaicin (the active ingredient in pepper spray) works on any moist skin, not just the throat and eyes. I start screaming and hopping around the tailgate.

5:27: THIS SUCKS.

5:30: I find a hose by the Port-A-Potties, pull my pants down, and start spraying water all over my exposed genitals.

5:32: The water is Arctic cold. My balls have retreated so far up into my torso that I could pull them out of my throat. I look like a eunuch. Everyone is laughing at me. I don't care. Stopping the pain is all that matters.

5:35: The numbness has taken the edge off the pain. I stop spraying myself and cover up my genitals. My pants are completely soaked.

5:40: I can't find the RV or the girl. I am totally lost.

5:45: I stop and consider what just happened. I cannot believe it. I just got accidentally pepper sprayed during sex, then burned up my crotch, then had a crowd of people laugh at me as I hosed off my balls. What the fuck?

6:00: I am still lost. I can't even find GoldenBoy's tailgate. I try to call him on my cell, but it won't work. I remember that electronics do not mix well with water.

6:30: I finally find GoldenBoy's tailgate area. Everyone is gone. This is not good. A passerby lets me use his phone to call Hate.

6:31: He answers, but I can barely hear him. It sounds like he is in a wind tunnel. There are dogs barking in the background. This is too much for me. I just hang up.

6:37: I call GoldenBoy. He is back at GoldenWife's apartment. He tells me to meet him at her place. Am I supposed to walk? "Hey, you hooked up at Foxfield, apparently you can do anything." Jerk.

6:55: I walk about a mile before an old couple picks me up. They are nice and agree to take me to GoldenWife's apartment. There is a cooler in the back seat. I ask if I can have a beer. "Uh yeah, son, go ahead. You kids sure do like to drink a lot. You'd think a whole day of it would be enough." I disagree, "Sir, when you are an alcoholic, there is no such thing as enough."

7:30: I get to the apartment. Hate is not there. GoldenBoy thought he was with me. I thought he was with him. Uh oh. GoldenBoy calls Hate.

Hate "I'm not going to lie to you, I am lit up."
GoldenBoy "Where are you?"
Hate "I'm not sure. These guys gave me a ride in the back of their truck with their dogs, but they dropped me off on campus. Weren't you a SigEp at UVa? I think that's where I am."

7:45: We get to the SigEp house. Hate is asleep in a chair in the living room. No one else is there. I tell Hate to wake up and find his dignity.

7:46: Hate stumbles out the front door of the fraternity, "HAS ANYBODY SEEN MY GODDAMN DIGNITY?"

8:00: We go to a bar. The Biltmore. It is crowded. Hate decides that the service sucks and that as a result he is going to stand on our table and yell at people, "SOMEONE GET ME A GODDAMN BEER!"

8:32: Hate does not have good balance when he is drunk, and proceeds to tumble off the table, in the process crashing it into another table and flinging all the drinks on a guy sitting there quietly with his girlfriend.

8:33: The couple is completely covered in beer and vodka. I prepare myself to fight, but the guy just sits there. I ask "Are you not going to whip his ass?" He just sits there. His girlfriend gets pissed and storms off. Then he gets pissed at Hate. I point out the obvious, "No reason to fight now, your bitch already left."

10:30: GoldenBoy decides he'd rather be at home with the woman he loves rather than drinking his 20th beer of the day with his drunk, obnoxious friends. Pussy.

10:45: The line to piss is way too long. I walk outside and pee on the wall.

10:46: A cop walks up.

Cop "Son, you need to stop that and come over here."
Tucker "I can't stop; it'll burn. I have to finish."

10:47: As the cop pulls out his handcuffs he sees a fight break out 20 yards away. He runs off. Tonight, the Drinking Gods are on my side. Well, sort of.

10:48: As I zip up my pants, I run to another bar. Just in case.

10:55: At the new bar, I get a drink. Uncoordinated from my inebriation I spill the drink on myself. I get mad at it, "You naughty liquor, you drunken me."

10:56: Much to my surprise, my drink starts talking back to me. It tells me not to blame it, that I am a clumsy drunk. I believe I may have discovered a new level of drunkenness beyond 'Tucker Max Drunk'. It is called 'When Inanimate Objects Talk To You Drunk.'

11:15: I see a girl standing in line for the bathroom. I'm not sure why, but I am drawn to her.

11:16: I approach her. I tell her not to be sad. She tells me that she failed the bar. I tell her that's OK, she'll pass next time. She tells me that I am nice. 16 hours of continuous drinking and my Lonely Slut Radar is still sharp.

1:30am: Many drinks and lots of flirting later, we go to her place.

1:35: She is trying to convince me that she never does this and is not that type of girl. It was difficult for me to understand. Her enunciation isn't very good with my dick in her mouth. This thought is my last clear memory.

11:00am: I wake up in GoldenWife's apartment. Hate is passed out on the sofa. I reek of vomit and stale sweat. I am confused as to how I got there.

11:01am: GoldenBoy hands me his phone, and tells me to listen to the voice message. It is my voice, recorded around 2:45am. I am out of breath, and sound like I am running:

> "GoldenBoy, what is your address? Where are you? I just fucked some random chick I met outside The Biltmore. Apparently she didn't pass the Bar, so she liked me. The condom broke and I got the fuck out of there as soon as I could. I'm fucked. My illegitimate kids are going to be ugly and stupid. HELP!!"

The Austin Road Trip

Occurred—October 2000
Written—September 2003

The Steak & Shake Bond

Early in my third year of law school, I was sitting in the library with my crew of friends, skipping class and trading stories about our summers. At first, I was the center of attention, having just come off the summer of *The Infamous Tucker Max Charity Auction Debacle*, but PWJ quickly trumped me.

He told us a story about a gentlemens' club he frequented in Dallas, a place far different than the common strip club:

"The first time I got a lap dance there, I was kinda reticent about touching her, but the stripper grabbed my hands and put them on her tits. During the second dance, she turned around and basically dry humped me for the entire song. I didn't get a third dance, but if I did, I could have all but have had sex with the girl. She was SMOKING HOT and wasn't even close to being the best one there. And the very best part: $5 cover charge and $2 bottles and wells."

After we initially called bullshit, PWJ finally convinced us that this Lost City of Cibola did exist. We were greatly excited. JonBenet summed it up, "And I used to think there was a bright line between a gentleman's club and a brothel. Now you're telling me it's just gray . . ."

This place was called Baby Dolls, and it became our Holy Grail. We immediately planned a trip to Dallas. At the outset, all ten of us were in. But as the departure date loomed closer, various friends started taking dives.

- GoldenBoy bailed because he had just returned from a week long trip to Russia and didn't want to be apart from his fiancée for so much time. I won't say anything bad about this, because he married her, and I really like her, so I guess this turned out to be a good decision. If you're into the "responsibility" and "love" things.

- Hate decided to go on an interview. Unlike me, he was upset about not having a job.
- Brownhole is basically a pussy and a sycophant and was afraid that being arrested with us would ruin his political career. None of us are sure how he even got in the group.
- Credit was dating a girl who SlingBlade once referred to as "The most evil demon-slut in the long history of female chicanery and deception." Credit is a spineless coward and wanted to keep dating her, so he begged off the trip.
- JoJo made the same decision he makes whenever he sees a bunch of crazy white boys run off to get in trouble—he went the opposite way.
- JonBenet had the most ridiculous excuse. Instead of going on the trip, he flew to Boston with his girlfriend, a friend of Credit's evil demon-slut girlfriend, to look at apartments. TO LOOK AT APARTMENTS . . . not withstanding the fact that he wasn't moving there FOR AN ENTIRE YEAR. There is a reason he is now out of the group.

That left only four travelers:

- Because he was on law review, PWJ had lots of important and uppity legal talkin' to do. Luckily, he follows his penis around like a divining rod, so he promptly cleared his schedule.
- SlingBlade's busy schedule included drinking alone in the dark and jacking off to his Star Trek Limited Edition Seven of Nine poster. He was solidly in.
- El Bingeroso had already planned a trip to visit a friend in Austin so he combined his trip with ours, and then got his fiancée some sort of shiny trinket to distract her from his new plans.
- I was able to squeeze the trip in between outings to Chapel Hill involving sex and drinking, interspersed with some drinking and sex.

On a crisp Thursday night in early October, SlingBlade, PWJ, El Bingeroso and I began our journey to Dallas. We would soon become known to the State of Texas by our biblical names: Pestilence, Plague, Hunger, and Death.

Our first stop was a Steak & Shake somewhere outside of Charlotte, where we bonded with each other by recounting tales of our fucked up youths. I recalled a childhood colored by parental instability, multiple divorces, re-marriages (seven between my two biological parents), step-parents, constant relocation, loneliness and emotional pain. No one cared about my problems, because they had already read about my father's most recent divorce (it was in Time magazine), and didn't need any more details to know I was fucked up.

PWJ told us of an awkward youth being the son of an Army Colonel, where his Styx jean jacket and obsession with all things vehicular could not make the Kansas yokels overlook his abnormally misshapen egghead and triple digit IQ. Popular he was not, but since none of us are his normal dim-witted naïve teenage girl prey, we didn't care. While his age (3 years older than us) gave him a wisdom and maturity that none of us yet possessed, under this composed and compassionate exterior, PWJ could be the biggest snake of the group. The fact that he grew up smart, but a social outsider, forced him to learn game the hard way and also planted a retributive mean streak. Even though he is more often than not the voice of reason in the group, he is also the one who will manipulate an innocent eighteen-year-old into sex with lies and deception (whereas the rest of us just find the slutty girls and let them do what comes natural).

SlingBlade regaled us with tales of his emotionally distant, risk-averse and over-protective parents, who split time yelling at him and cloistering him in his room. His was a youth spent with action figures as his friends and a Nintendo as his baby-sitter. He also told us perhaps the most defining story of his life: He and his high school girlfriend, the love of his life, went to different undergrads. He spent the first semester of college passing up on sex with every girl who approached him (and there were many), because he was naïve and in love and didn't want to cheat on his girlfriend. She did not possess the same integrity, so she cheated on him. A lot. And didn't tell him until he went down to visit her and noticed that guys kept coming by her room, asking what she was up to later that night. SlingBlade does not deal well with emotional pain, and as such he is now bitter and imputes her cuckoldry on all women.

But it was El Bingeroso who stole the show. He grew up in a very small town in Nebraska, with about 700 people, one Dairy Queen and one gas station. He remembered his father making his brother and him run timed 100-meter races against each other. At age 6. When he got to elementary school he was fat and would constantly eat paste, so the teachers just assumed he was retarded and put him in the Special Ed class. He was in the Special Education program until age 8 when they finally gave him an IQ test, realized he was a genius, and moved him to the gifted class. He was actually upset about leaving the sped class, because he liked the coloring and frequent snack times. He also told us about the time he and his brother, then aged 9 and 11, watched from the locked car while their dad beat up a mugger, nearly killing him by repeatedly smashing his head into the hood and fender, spraying blood all over the car [I have subsequently met El Bingeroso's father, and believe me—he is not a man to cross. I have a robust fear of him].

But what really distinguished him from the rest of us was that he was truly in love and actually had a stable life. Even though he was a partier like the rest of us, he loved his fiancée, was totally committed to her, and was very excited that he had finally convinced her to wear a French maid outfit to the Duke Law Halloween party.

Day One: Baby Dolls

We arrived in Dallas on Friday afternoon. After a quick nap, we went to an early dinner at some Mexican place in Deep Ellum, then across the street to a roadhouse-type bar designed for yuppies. Both Pabst and Guinness on tap. Metrosexuals dressed in brown Lycra as far as the eye could see. I immediately hated everyone.

We get two pitchers and decide to play table shuffleboard. Barely into our first pitcher, I notice two girls checking us out. A hot blonde [Blonde] and a decent red-head [Redhead]. They stare at us for about ten minutes. I want to have sex with the blonde, so I start things off:

"You gonna come talk to us or just stand there and stare?"

They accept my invitation. I stare at the tits on the blonde. They are nearly flawless, and quite seductively exposed. The girl knows what she's doing. Despite my nearly forensic examination (she doesn't notice—I am a pro at this), I keep the conversation moving along nicely until dumbass El Bingeroso decides to fuck everything up:

Blonde "So, what brings you guys to Dallas?"

El Bingeroso "We came to go to a strip club." El Bingeroso is an engaged cock-blocking jerk. Thanks asshole, I didn't want to fuck her or anything.
Redhead [kinda pulling me aside as El Bingeroso keeps talking to Blonde] "Did you really come to Dallas to go to a strip club?"
Tucker "No, no. We had a week off from law school, so we came to visit some friends, hang out, that sort of thing. El Bingeroso just wants to go to a strip club he heard about."
Redhead "Do you like strip clubs? Those places are gross."
Tucker "Yeah, they are kinda gross. But my friends really want to go, so what can I do? I don't know anyone in Dallas. Besides, I like naked breasts."
Redhead "You can stay here . . . hang out with me."
Tucker "Yeah, maybe." And maybe I'll watch reruns of *Alf* on Telemundo.
El Bingeroso tugs on me, "Dude, you might want to get in on this." [He turns back to the blonde] "So, you think you want to come to Baby Dolls with us?"
Blonde "I'll come to the strip club with you guys; I want to see some big titties."
Tucker "Have you ever been to Baby Dolls before?"
Blonde "Yeah, I auditioned there once."

DING DING DING DING!!! JACKPOT!!! Call the pit boss, we have a big winner!

El Bing "Do you like girls?"
Blonde "Of course."

Excellent. All we need is 70's music to start playing and we've got a porno in the making.

I glance at the other end of the table. It's our turn, but El Bingeroso and I haven't thrown the pucks for ten minutes. SlingBlade is glaring at me with his standard half-bored, half-disdainful, "Another whore?" expression that he always gives me when I start talking to random girls. I motion for him to come down to our end of the table . . . and then I see PWJ.

Great Holy Jesus—it looks like he fell into *Kentucky Fried Movie*. He is talking to a woman with a leopard cowboy hat on over platinum bouffant hair. Her make-up looks like it was applied with a shotgun. She has on tight orange hot-pants, which she obviously brought from her last job at Hooters. Around her waist is a belt, and there appears to be a toy gun holstered to it. She was probably very attractive in, say, 1986. Now, she's in the death throes of a losing battle against time and fashion irrelevance.

Tucker "Dude, what is PWJ talking to?"
SlingBlade "I don't know . . . some whore. She squirted him with her water gun, and off he went. She has big tits . . . Cupid has spoken."

Fifteen more minutes of bullshitting, and the Blonde is sealed up. Unfortunately, she wants Redhead to come with us, who is not at all enthused at the prospect of going to "one of those places." I am presented with a logistical nightmare: I want to fuck Blonde, who is throwing her cooch at El Bingeroso. The only way she is going to Baby Dolls is if Redhead comes. Redhead is in love with me, but does not want to come to Baby Dolls. El Bingeroso is drunk and no help. So what do I do?

Here is where taking econ classes at the University of Chicago helps out with real-life game. This is a classic example of the Prisoner's Dilemma; if I keep paying attention to the Blonde and try to capture my small chance to fuck her, I will probably fail and then I get no pussy, and the group gets no lesbian action at the strip club, because neither will come with us. Everyone loses. But, if I take one for the team, ignore the Blonde and instead seal up the Redhead, I can get both to come with us to Baby Dolls. This means that I probably won't fuck the Blonde, which decreases my chance at personal happiness, but I will give the group the best chance to maximize the situation, by getting two girls to come to a strip club with us. See—even Tucker Max can be altruistic. If it benefits him.

Tucker "Redhead, come on, let's all go to the strip club. It'll be a good time."
Redhead "Don't go to a strip club. You know those girls don't care about you."
SlingBlade "That's not true. They sit on my lap and tell me they love me." SlingBlade usually chooses the funny joke over the smart play. And this, folks, is why he gets no pussy. Well . . . that, and he has no confidence, and is scared of emotional commitment to a woman because he thinks they are all cheating sluts.

Tucker "Thanks asshole. Why don't you go watch Deep Space Nine and leave this to me. Dick."

I pull Redhead away from Captain No Pussy, "Come on sweetie. It'll be fun. Your friend wants to go."

Redhead "I don't want to go to that place. It's gross."

Tucker "Yeah, I know. But I'll be there, we can hang out together. We'll let them," waving dismissively at my friends, "look at naked women, and you and I can just hang out. Together." I actually reach out and put her hands in mine.

Redhead "Why don't you just stay here. With me?"

Tucker "Yes, let's stay together . . . at the club."

Redhead "But I don't want to go to a strip club."

Tucker "But I want to go. With you . . . us . . . together."

Redhead "I don't like it there."

Tucker "Have you ever been?"

Redhead "No . . ."

Tucker "I tell you what: If you and Blonde come with us, I promise that you and I can sit in a corner somewhere and stare into each other's eyes, completely ignoring everything around us. It'll be romantic. We'll be so busy staring into each other's eyes, we won't even see what's going on."

Hearing these words, I nearly threw up in my mouth. She paused and contemplated.

Redhead "No . . . I don't want to go to a strip club. I . . . I just can't."

This is just fucking great. Even I have my limit, and that 'staring into each others eyes' bullshit was it. SlingBlade and El Bingeroso tire of this, go fetch PWJ away from his water-pistol packing cow-whore, and start to leave. Redhead is trying to convince me to stay at the bar with her. She is almost pleading with me. Before I know it, my friends are already walking out the door.

I make my way to the door, Redhead still attached to my arm like a lamprey. I try to make a cost benefit analysis: Probable hook-up and possible sexual activity with Redhead, or definite nakedness but little chance of a hook-up at Baby Dolls. I need to pin Redhead down on our late-night activities.

Tucker "Are you going to hang out with me later tonight. I mean, are

we going to *hang out* after we leave here, like at *your* place?" My tone of voice is not subtle.
Redhead "I don't know if I can; I have to be up at 7am."
Tucker "7am? For what?"
Redhead "A Young Life meeting."
Tucker "I have to go catch up with my friends."

I streak out of the bar before she can even change her facial expression.

[Aside: Young Life is a fundamentalist Christian youth group that preaches abstinence and all sorts of other ridiculous pablum. I got blue-balls so many times in middle and high school dealing with those girls—NEVER AGAIN.]

In the car on the way to Baby Dolls, PWJ explains his little adventure:

Tucker "Dude, who the fuck was that woman you were talking to, and where did she get her uniform, at a Whores-R-Us closeout sale?"
PWJ "I don't know. She works there. She had a toy water pistol in her belt . . . is it wrong that that turned me on?"
Tucker "She WORKS there? I guess no one cares if she spends thirty minutes talking to you. Apparently her job is to degrade herself and chat up pasty thimble-headed geeks."
PWJ "You don't understand . . . that's not the best part. I learned her philosophy of dating: 'Don't fish off the company pier, and don't fuck your friends. I've tried both plenty of times and it never works' . . . OH YEAH . . . I nearly spat out my drink when she told me that she has cats rather than kids because, and I quote, 'you don't go to jail when you get your cats high.'"

We decide that we are starting to like Texas. Baby Dolls does nothing to derail our crazy train.

Baby Dolls should be the model from which all strip clubs are cast. The neon glow from its trim-molding and signage can be seen from miles away. A huge pink one-story stand-alone building rising out of a sea of asphalt with pictures of nearly naked girls on the 4-story billboard looming over it from the parking lot. The entrance is two huge wooden doors adorned with brass fixtures and two NFL linebacker-sized bouncers. It is covered by a pink awning that extends up the walk about ten feet. The huge oval main stage is flanked by an enfilade of four smaller side stages, each with a brass pole reaching from floor to ceiling. Mirrors cover every wall and extend to every ceiling. Two full bars, and two beer bars are staffed by a phalanx of female bartenders and cocktail waitresses. And MOST importantly: it's all nude. No pasties. No g-strings. No crotch tape. Nothing between you and the naked, nubile flesh of attractive women . . . except dollar bills. The girls were hot beyond hot. Dozens of incredibly beautiful and sexy women, each giving smiles that convey the sincerity of a single mother with rent due.

At age 24, this was my Elysium.

Two dancers come over almost immediately after we sit down. The hot one is at least 5'10", blonde bobbed hair, smooth, almost creamy skin, and gorgeous fake breasts. Perfectly round and sitting high on her chest. She sits on PWJ's lap.

Stripper "So what do you do?"
PWJ "I'm a law student."
Stripper "Wow . . . so do you go to SMU?"
PWJ "Not exactly . . . I go to Duke."
She gives him a blank stare. A few seconds later, one can almost see the flicker of candlelight in the thought bubble above her head.
Stripper "You mean Duke Duke?"
PWJ pauses and chuckles, "Yeah, Duke Duke."
She gives him a doubtful face, "Oh, like I've never heard this one before. Let me guess, you went to Harvard for college."
PWJ "Well, no, not exactly . . ."

PWJ went to Princeton for undergrad. I stop paying attention because as much as I love beauty, I hate stupidity, and seeing the two combined pisses me off. Plus, I need to start drinking and her nipples aren't spouting vodka.

I find a cocktail waitress and begin drinking. Combatively. I've driven 16 hours for the specific purpose of going to this strip club, and I'll be damned if I get here and nothing happens. To help achieve this end—getting drunk and making something happen—I make friends with our cocktail waitress, Liz. Gentle readers, let me explain something to you:

It is an almost universal rule of gentlemen's clubs that the cocktail waitresses are more fun to talk to, and more apt to fuck customers, than the strippers. They are not as pressed for time, so they will banter more. The limp-dicks that overtip the strippers usually don't tip the cocktail waitresses at all, so attention to a cocktail waitress will get you much further than attention to a stripper. Plus, they tend not to be high or drunk on duty, whereas strippers are almost always in some altered state, so conversation with them can actually accomplish something. The funniest thing is that they always think they are better than the strippers; in their mind there is a bright line separating them from the women who actually take their clothes off, thus it is usually much easier to get a cocktail waitress to go home with you. Strippers are jaded, abused, used-up; they hate men, and usually for good reason. The cocktail waitresses are far less defensive. They are so used to being ignored or looked through, that when you do pay attention to them, they respond to it. Some innocuous flirting and a good first tip to Liz gets my friends and me a constant, uninterrupted stream of drinks and a flirtatious hottie hanging around us. Read and learn fellas. Back to the action:

SlingBlade gets one of the hottest girls in the club to give him a dance. Before she takes his money, she tries to talk to him, and actually seems genuinely interested, not just stripper interested. This probably has something to do with the happy confluence of his sarcastic, standoffish sense of humor and the inability of her step-father to show her any affection growing up. So what does SlingBlade do? Does he flirt with her? Does he at least try to exploit this situation? Of course not. He places his finger on her lips, patiently explains that he, "would rather mainline Drano" than listen to her for another second, and commands, "Less talkie, more boobie." The kid has problems.

Apparently, something about PWJ just says "sucker," because another stripper comes up and puts her hands over PWJ's eyes, coyly whispering something erotic in his ear. She is UGLY. Her face looks like it lost a frantic battle with a Roto-Tiller. The woman is literally missing some teeth. I can't tell for sure, but I think she has a tattoo tear on her left eye. I motion to him by making a cutting gesture across my throat and yelling,

"Dude—she is unattractive. Bottom of the barrel. Needs to put her clothes on and learn how to type. Don't do it! YOU'RE A YOUNG MAN!"

He doesn't get my warnings in time. She sits on his lap. PWJ tells her he doesn't want a dance, but she says it's okay, and remains on his lap talking to him. I wonder, out loud for everyone to hear, if the zoo knows they are missing their three-toed sloth. She is not pleased. Fuck her, it's not my fault she looks like Adrian Brody with saggy tits.

PWJ ignores me and continues engaging her in conversation. When I hear her say, "Yeah, I had two hearts tattooed on my hips, but then I got pregnant and carried my son on my left side. Now this one looks like a tomato," I get up. I'd rather rip my penis out by the root than listen to another minute of her stripper-ramble.

I saunter around flirting with waitresses and bartenders and strippers, double-fisting vodka and sodas . . . and then it happens: I see El Bingeroso's future wife. It's not actually her; THAT would be a story, but she looks exactly like El Bingeroso's fiancée. It's spooky. I immediately walk over to where she is and stand there, waiting for her to finish the dance she's giving to some random guy. He's less than pleased. Whatever buddy, you're wearing a Detroit Red Wings jersey to a strip club, you obviously suck.

I give her enough to pay for two dances for El Bingeroso, and then an additional ten dollars. I tell her that she has to tell him her name is "Kristy" [his fiancée's name], and to answer to nothing else. I point him out, and she walks over, and introduces herself.

"Hi, I'm Kristy. Dinner is on the stove, baby."

After what seems like only ten minutes, I glance over, and she's just sitting there talking to him. Fine, maybe she's just warming him up. A few more minutes, same scene. I'll be damned if El Bingeroso doesn't get my money's worth. He's the type that would pay her more not to dance, thinking it would violate his relationship or some such bullshit. I walk over and interrupt El Bingeroso in the middle of a story I had heard the day before:

El Bingeroso "Yeah, I was fat when I was a kid. You know how kids jeans at K-Mart came in three different sizes, Small, Medium, and 'Husky'? I had to buy Husky."
Tucker "El Bingeroso, what the fuck? Is stripper-fiancée going to dance for you?"

El Bingeroso looks confused. "What are you talking about? Dude, she already did both dances, she's just hanging out now."

Maybe I'm drunker than I realize.

I find Liz and ask her how many drinks I've had. She looks at me with the same look El Bingeroso gave me, "Tucker sweetie, what are you saying? I can't understand you."

I guess I am fucked up.

I try to stagger back to my seat when a very hot, voluptuous stripper grabs me by the belt loops and pulls me towards her. She has a skin tight tiger-stripe body suit that is virtually painted on her. To say that her breasts were spilling out would be to imply that this outfit covered them at some point. Her J-Lo booty smiles at me, and I smile back. It takes me a few seconds to find her eyes. I have to shade my eyes, because the gobs of silver glitter eye shadow smeared on her face are reflecting an inordinate amount of light. She says something to me, but I don't understand it. I pretend to listen for about 3 minutes, then I interrupt her:

"If I were dating you, I'd never leave the house. I'd never even leave your general vaginal area. Unless it were to cum on your face."

She thinks I am funny. She really wants to give me a dance. I tell her I am a starving lawyer, and can't afford one. But there is something about her. Maybe it's the lighting, maybe it's her aggressive attitude, maybe it's her ghetto booty, maybe it's her 36 DD fake breasts pressing against me . . . maybe it's the 3 margaritas, 6 beers and 15 vodka clubs, but she just strikes me in that right way.

I guess she saw the acquiescence in my eyes, because without any further deliberation, at least that I can remember, she drags me back to a secluded booth in the rear of the club and starts dancing. By this time, I'm so drunk I even know I'm drunk.

Another great feature of Baby Dolls: The strippers encourage you to touch their boobies. I exploit this privilege ruthlessly. I grabbed both her beautifully fake breasts full on. I was kneading her tits so hard all I needed was a little water and some active dry yeast and I could have made bread. Towards the end of the dance, I was actually trying to pop the saline implants. Those things are pretty durable.

Finished, she snuggles herself up against me, breasts right under my chin,

Big Tits "Do you want to go somewhere . . . more private?"
Tucker "Yeah . . . sure . . . for what . . . ?"
Big Tits "If we get a champagne room, we can do anything we want."
Tucker "Anything?"
Big Tits "*Anything*."
Tucker "OK."
Big Tits "It's 300 for the room, plus usually about 100 dollars more. Depending . . . but you're cute."
Tucker "So . . . 400 total?"
Big Tits "Uh huh."

I pause and contemplate. I can vaguely recall a moral dilemma I might have had with this situation milling somewhere around my frontal lobes . . . provided I were sober enough to recall what exactly the tenets of my ethical system were. Or even what an ethical system was.

This drunk, I could only consider price. Thank you, University of Chicago economics classes.

Tucker "I'll give you 20 dollars."
Big Tits laughed. "No. It's 400, baby."
Tucker "Okay . . . 22 dollars."
Big Tits "Well, you're cute and funny; I'll do it for 350."
Tucker "25."
Big Tits "325?"
Tucker "No, just 25."
Big Tits "I have to give the club 100 to get the room for an hour."
Tucker "I can't last an hour . . . I'll give you 28."

This went on for at least 10 more minutes before we finally settled on a price.

$55. For a half hour.

I could write a book on negotiation. And as drunk as I was, you can believe she earned her $5.

When I found my friends, two hours and $55 wisely spent dollars later, they were out in the parking lot eating sloppy joe's they bought from a guy selling them out of the back of his Chevette. Needless to say, they were aghast. But in my vodka-addled brain, I had a defensible position:

"Dude, I had to. How could I pass up a bargain like that? IT'S A MATTER OF PRINCIPLE!"

Day Two: The Texas State Fair and The Embassy Suites Story

The next day we woke up scattered across our hotel room, still clothed and reeking of hairspray and bar smoke. We pack up and head to Austin. On the way there, we see a huge sign on the road:

"This way to the Texas State Fair!"

El Bingeroso nearly has a fucking aneurysm, "OH OH OH OH!!! WE HAVE TO GO, WE HAVE TO GO! Guys, The TEXAS-STATE-FAIR!!!"

It is the most insane morass of trucks and rednecks and cheap carnival trinkets I have ever seen. SlingBlade gets a funnel cake, I get a Slushee, PWJ falls in love with the "classic" (read: penis) cars, but it was El Bingeroso who really tapped into the essence of the Texas State Fair. He made friends with a fat, brown-toothed teenage redneck wearing a WWF Mankind t-shirt covered in mustard stains. The poor kid looked like he had the cultural I.Q. of someone who just staggered out of a sheep orgy. We see them standing over by some video game thing, and he waves us over.

El Bing "Guys, you see this thing? [pointing to the game] It is called 'The Shocker.' You hold these metal handles here, and it sends an ever increasing charge of electricity through you. As the wattage increases, so does your score, and if you can hold it all the way to the end, you win . . . something. And this guy, [Jethro], thinks he can do it."
Tucker "What do you win?"
SlingBlade "A free electroshock treatment, apparently."
PWJ "You can't hold that for more than a few seconds."
Jethro "Fuck dat; ike'an duit."
El Bing "OK man, give it your best shot. Here, we'll even put the money in."

As PWJ put the dollar in the machine and the redneck rubbed his hands together and mentally prepared himself, I pulled El Bingeroso aside. He was giggling like a Japanese schoolgirl in a Hello Kitty store.

Tucker "Dude, who is this kid? What the hell is going on?"
El Bing "I saw him staring at this thing and I bet him he couldn't do it. He got all worked up. Dude—I've seen this thing knock out 250 pound guys before. They were outlawed in the state of Nebraska! THIS IS AWESOME!"

The young redneck firmly planted his feet, rubbed his face, spit into his hands, rubbed them together and wiped them on his shirt. We started cheering him on:

El Bingeroso "YEAAAAHHHH!"
Tucker "Eye of the tiger!"
PWJ "What does not kill you makes you stronger!"
SlingBlade "There is no spoon!"

He muttered some inspirational phrases to himself, pressed the start button and grabbed the two metal handles. For the first few seconds he was fine . . .

Then his arms started shaking.
Then his shoulders.
Then his torso.
Then his head.
Then his mouth began frothing and spitting saliva everywhere.
Then this strange, guttural, animalistic groan emerged from him. Still gripping the handles, his whole body was in violent convulsions when an older woman pulled him off of the machine. He fell to the ground and she yelled at him,

"Jethro, git away from that'n thang. Thar makin funna YEW!"

I don't know if I have ever laughed so hard in my life. I was laying on the hot asphalt of the Texas State Fair, curled up in a ball, tears streaming down my face as I held my stomach muscles and convulsed with laughter. I was able to look up and see the confused, blank look on Jethro's face as his mother led him off, wiping the spit off of his face, his arms still twitching slightly.

I really hope that God has the capacity for forgiveness that Christians claim, because I am going to test the absolute outer limits.

We get to Austin and check in at The Embassy Suites. After a nap, El

Bingeroso calls his friends, and we all meet up at a place called Cheers Shot Bar on 6th street. It was me, PWJ, SlingBlade, El Bingeroso, and three of his college friends, "Thomas" (from the story The Night We Almost Died), "Dirty," and "Mermaid."

It was around 8pm when we rolled in there, and the bar was nearly empty. Not a problem, this crew can make its own party. Mermaid told the bartender, "Seven Flaming Dr. Peppers."

At the time, I had no idea what a Flaming Dr Pepper was. The bartender set up 7 pint glasses, each about half full with light beer, in a sort of pyramid formation on the bar. He filled 7 shot glasses about 90% full with Amaretto, then topped off each with Bacardi 151, and set them on the lips of the pint glasses. He then took a huge swig of Bacardi 151, put a lighter up to his face, and blew the alcohol in his mouth through the flame, sending a massive fireball over the shot glasses, each catching fire. While they were still on fire, he hit one of the shot glasses, starting a domino effect, each shot glass falling into a pint glass, putting out the flames and fizzing the beer up. We each grabbed a glass and chugged it, and I'll be damned if it didn't taste exactly like Dr Pepper.

It was the coolest thing involving alcohol I had ever seen. Being OCD, I had to see it again. And again. And again. 6 rounds of Flaming Dr Peppers later, I was fucked up, and we had nearly set the bar on fire.

People, heed my warning: That stuff is Special Olympics in a pint glass. You think they are harmless and not very strong, and the next thing you know it is an hour later and you are in the bathroom of the bar with your pants off, surrounded by five girls, giving your boxers to a bachlorette party because one of the girls is cute and told you that you had a nice butt. Be forewarned.

After that little fiasco, we head across the street to a dueling piano bar. We discover that one of the two piano players is blind. We are basically jackals who walk on two legs, so true to our nature, we focus on the weak one.

We must have given him about 20 notes with song titles on them. Finally, the blind piano player stopped his music and said, "HEY IDIOTS! Stop giving me written song suggestions. I AM BLIND! BLIND! I CAN'T READ THEM!"

One of the helpers came over and took the song suggestions over to the piano player who could see, and he broke out laughing so hard he couldn't even keep playing. He kinda stopped the music and said into his mike,

"Well, I would love to play these songs, but unfortunately I don't know any of them. Let's see if you know them Phil. They are:

- Please Kill Yourself
- Isn't Ray Charles supposed to be black?
- I'm gonna steal your wallet because you can't see who I am
- Have you ever fucked a goat by accident?
- You are blind because you masturbated too much as a child
- I'm gonna set your hair on fire
- Come to the bathroom so I can fellate you
- I bet you fuck ugly girls because you can't see their faces
- I pissed on your shoes when you were at the urinal

And so on. Phil, you know any of these? I'm stumped."

It was awesome. The irony was that while most of the crowd was aghast, the blind guy was laughing his ass off right along with us. I guess crippled people can be useful sometimes.

After a few more beers, we went on to another bar, and another bar, and another bar, ad infinitum. The night was very funny . . . for us . . . because we are not nice people. Here are some selections of our behavior at the various bars on 6th street that night:

At one point, I went up to some deaf people who were signing to each other and began signing with them. I actually know ASL because I took sign language for my foreign language requirement at the University of Chicago, and as I was asking them where the hot sluts are, in sign language, PWJ comes up to me and says, "Tucker, I didn't know you spoke deaf."

- While traveling from one bar to the next, PWJ saw a low rider El Camino with hydraulics that was bouncing up and down on 6th street. He ran next to the car and started jumping up and down with the car and yells at the driver, "NICE CAR MAN!," to which the driver, a male of obvious Hispanic descent, gives him a look of disgust and yells back, "Get away from my car, ese, or I'll fucking bust a cap in you mane."

- Of course, there were women. Countless women, thousands it seemed like, most of them were hot, and all of them drunk. Some of the interactions I caught on my voice recorder:

Tucker "Hey, what's your name?"
Girl "My name is Pocahontas."
Tucker "Right bitch, and my fucking name is John Smith."
SlingBlade [In a bar whisper] "Tucker, that's not good game."
Tucker "Are you married?"
Girl "Yes."
Tucker "How good is the marriage?"
Girl "Very good."
Tucker "So there is no chance of us hooking up?"
Girl "No."
Tucker "Well, do you have any hot friends who aren't fucking prudes? Hey—where are you going? I was only kidding! I respect the sanctity of the monogamous relationship! WHORE!"

- PWJ made me be his wingman at one point, but the friend was a hideously ugly fat girl. I tried to end it quickly with this, "You don't want to talk to me, I have festering sores on my scrotum." She thought I was hilarious, so I had to bring out the heavy artillery, "So that spare tire you're carrying, is it for a car or a truck?" I plead ignorance when PWJ asked me what happened, "I don't know man, I was trying to help you out, she just wasn't into me. What can I do, not all girls like me."
- Dirty took a picture of me and some girl, and then said to her, "You can see these pictures of yourself on Poopsex.com." She quickly scurried away.
- SlingBlade was his usual charming gin-drunk self. His lines that night ran the gamut from awful to patently offensive to nearly criminal. His standard pick-up line that night was—I swear to Christ—"Pursuant to Megan's Law, I am obligated to tell you that I am a convicted sex offender. What's your name?" After I made him stop talking about molesting children, he moved on to these gems, "Oh good, you smoke. When you're done sucking down that death stick I want your advice on which brand of vodka to chase my Percocet

with," or this one, "Hi, can we just skip the pleasantries and go straight to the part where you call me Captain Kirk and give me a handjob in the backseat of my car?" Quite the wingman he was.

- This was my personal favorite interaction of the night:

  Tucker "Do you mind if I flirt with you for a while?"
  Girl "Please zip up your pants first. Thank you."
  Tucker "Oh, sorry. So, what's your name?"
  Girl "[Blah, blah, blah . . . .]"
  Tucker "You have an underbite! Wait . . . COME BACK HERE, I THINK THAT'S SEXY!"

- SlingBlade somehow managed to get a hot girl that he didn't think was a whore interested in him. Fascinated by this rare event, I talk to her and immediately discover the reason: The girl was not a day over 16. Well, maybe 17. He whispered to me, "This is what lawyers in Texas call, 'the age of consent.' " There was only one barrier to SlingBlade sealing the deal—She didn't believe that he went to Austin High with her. She asked him what the mascot was. He accused her of not knowing herself, and trying to steal that information from him. I came upon a plan that could solve this dilemma: I told him to whisper his answer to me, and then she can tell me what the mascot is, and I'll tell her if he got it right. She agrees. He pretends to whisper something in my ear, and I tell her, "Unless the mascot is 'I'm going to knock this girl unconscious and anally-fist her,' he didn't go to Austin High." He still hasn't forgiven me.
- PWJ and I were talking to some girls, and PWJ seemed to be doing well with the ring leader, when she saw through his bullshit,

  Girl "Do you remember what my name is?"
  PWJ "No."
  Girl "That's attractive."
  PWJ [Turning to me] "Tucker, these girls are sleeping with us on the 7th of never. Time to move on."

These fun little games were all well and good, but it was getting near closing time and we had no prospects, so Tucker had to get serious and do what Tucker does best: Pick up some women. By this time we had gotten separated, and it was only me, SlingBlade and PWJ. I found a group of three girls, bought all of us a round of shots, made a few jokes, and the crew was set. The way it worked out, I got the hot one, SlingBlade got the good-looking one, and PWJ got the fat one. I assigned the plump one to him because big tits are his kryptonite, and hers were individually each as large as his planet-sized cranium. When he gets a few beers in him, large breasts block out any other physical consideration: fatness, facial features, lack of personal hygiene, etc.

After a round or two, they agree to come with us to get some food at Kerbey Lane, a late night diner. As we walk to the car, we see about a dozen cops, some of them on horseback, chasing after some random drunk guy, beating him senseless with batons and what not. I laugh at this scene. The girls gasp in horror. SlingBlade offers to help the police beat him. What does PWJ do? He runs after the cops yelling—and I am quoting him VERBATIM:

"I'M A LAWYER, AND I SWEAR TO GOD THAT I WILL FILE A SECTION 1983 SUIT VINDICATING THE 4TH AMENDMENT RIGHTS OF THAT MAN!!!"

Yeah, my friend is a closet dork. Except without the closet.

It ended up working out well, because I convinced the girls that PWJ was a big time criminal defense lawyer, and we had gone to law school with him. I save my friends more than Goose Gossage.

Anyway, we get into the car, and on the way to Kerbey Lane I look in the rear view mirror and see PWJ doing his best to eat the face of the fat girl. Then I make the unfortunate mistake of looking down, and I see his hand in her crotch. When I say "in her crotch" I mean it. I couldn't see anything below the elbow. It was almost enough to make me lose my appetite.

In spite of that scene, I am still starving when we get to the restaurant. I know the hot one is going to fuck me, so I want to hurry up and eat so I can get this pony in his stable. I take the hot girl by the hand and kinda pull her towards the entrance as I power walk there. She has her head turned and is yelling something back to one of her friends behind us as I walk by a light post, hear a dull thud, then a scream, "OW! MY FACE!"

I turn to see the hot girl crumpled in a ball on the ground, holding her face and moaning in agony. I accidentally walked her face-first right into a light pole. As her friends ran up to see if she was OK, I just stood there, watching my best shot of the night evaporate, said, "Well, I guess I'm not getting laid," and walked into the restaurant.

I hope my daughters date guys like me.

After this, of course *I'm* the bad guy. All the girls at the table are scowling at me. SlingBlade is not happy either; apparently the girl he was assigned has had sex with another guy at some point in her life, so he thinks she is a shameless prostitute. He has issues with women. PWJ is drunker than all of us and happier than a pig in shit. I glance at SlingBlade. He and I have been picking up women together so long that we don't even have to speak—he has found these girls to be wholly worthless and wants to leave now without even acknowledging them. I do too, but I have to make sure my other friend is taken care of,

Tucker "PWJ, I'm going to piss, you want to come with me?"
PWJ "No dude, I'm fine."

I kick him several times very hard and in rapid succession until he gets the picture. Once in the bathroom, I lay it out for him,

Tucker "Dude, SlingBlade and I are leaving. You want to come with us or you want to fuck the girl you're with?"
PWJ "I don't know man; she's kinda fat. What do you think I should do?"

PWJ is so drunk his eyes are crossed and he is swaying in his place. Whatever I tell him to do, he'll do . . . so of course I throw him under the bus. Literally:

Tucker "Dude—You should TOTALLY go home with her. She's not that fat. She has huge tits. Shit—I'd fuck her."
PWJ "Yeah, she does have big tits, doesn't she? I love big tits. OK, OK, I'm going with her. Thanks man . . . you're a good friend."

We go back out to the table, I sit down for about 30 seconds, catch SlingBlade's eye, and we both simultaneously rise and head for the door. The hot girl says, "Where are you two going." I call back to her, "The bathroom," to which she yells out, as we leave the restaurant, "The bathroom is the opposite direction!"

I hadn't realized how supremely shit-housed I was until we stumbled into our room at the Embassy Suites. You ever been so drunk you forgot that you have to shit until the last minute? Well I was at that stage. I nearly had my pants completely off when SlingBlade snaked past me and got into the toilet first. Fine, I go get out of my bar clothes and change into a t-shirt and pink Gap boxers to sleep in. I wait patiently for about three minutes, then I start pounding on the door, screaming at him that I am going to shit on his bed if he doesn't get out of there.

A short time later he opens the door laughing his ass off, and says, "That was perhaps the most prodigious shit ever. I just put that toilet into therapy."

I take a gander into the bathroom. It looks like Revelations. The toilet is overflowing, brown shit water is spilling out all over the bathroom floor, and the tank is making demonic gurgling noises.

THE MOTHERFUCKER CLOGGED UP A HOTEL TOILET!

Hotel toilets are industrial size; they are designed to be able to accommodate repeated elephant-sized dumps, and their ram-jet engine flushes generate enough force to suck down a human infant, yet skinny-ass, 165-pound SlingBlade completely killed ours.

I nearly panic. I let loose a flurry of unintelligible curse words at SlingBlade, punctuated by a "WHAT THE HELL IS WRONG WITH YOU?!," and knock over the lamp in my dash out of the room. The turtle is sticking his head out, and he is coming whether I am on a toilet or not.

I figure that there must be a bathroom somewhere in the lobby, so I shoot down the hall and hop in the elevator. Once in the lobby I can't seem to spot a bathroom anywhere. So, I head around the corner to the front desk, which doesn't face the lobby. It's about 4am, and no one is at the desk. I furiously hit the bell for at least a minute—CLANG CLANG CLANG CLANG CLANG CLANG CLANG CLANG CLANG—until some poor lady comes out with sleep lines all over her face and tells me that the bathroom is in the corner of the lobby.

It is hard to describe, so let me give you an aerial picture of what the lobby looks like:

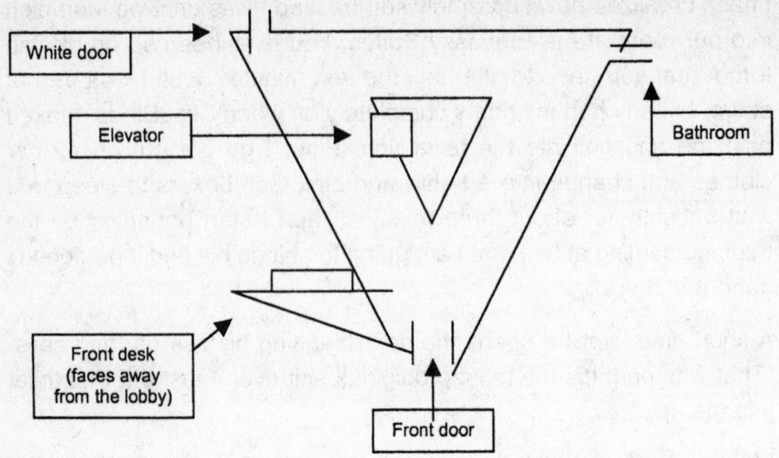

I turn the corner from the front desk into the lobby and realize I don't know which side of the triangular lobby she is talking about. I don't have time to go back and ask her, and I see a white door at the end of the left-hand side, so I quickly waddle towards it. Why am I waddling? Because I have to physically hold my butt cheeks together to prevent myself from crapping all over my pink Gap boxers. I am literally pressing my ass cheeks together with my hands. One of the prouder moments of my life.

I nearly bust the door off its hinges as I plow through it. I hear a loud, "AYYYY!!," that almost literally scares the shit out of me. I jump back to see that this is a janitor's closet, complete with a small Mexican lady janitor. I momentarily contemplate taking a dump in the janitor's bucket, but decide against that, mainly because of the presence of said female janitor.

I try to be as diplomatic as possible, considering that I am about to crap my pants:

Tucker "WHERE IS THE BATHROOM?"
Janitor "No, no hablo Ingles."
Tucker "WHAT?!? Huh, uh . . . DONDE ESTA FUCKING BANO?"
Janitor "AYA, AYA!"

She points across the lobby. About 60 yards from where I am standing, at the complete other end of the lobby, there is a set of doors that have a large "Restroom" sign over them. Right where the front desk lady said it would be, except on the opposite side of the lobby.

I have about half a second to make a crucial decision: I can either sprint and hope I make it there before I shit in my boxers, or I can stick my thumb up into my ass and shuffle the 60 yards to lavatory freedom. The decision is simple: I break into a full-on sprint.

I played football, baseball and basketball in high school, and I stay in good shape. I have run from cops before, I have run from guard dogs, from a legitimate drive-by shooting once while in Kentucky, but I don't think I have ever run that fast in my life. Nothing motivates like the prospect of being covered in human excrement.

Unfortunately, I was not fast enough. It went something like this:

- 20 yards into the run I feel my boxers start to sag.
- 30 yards into the run, about halfway, I feel my ass crack and legs get noticeably wet.
- 40 yards into the run, my boxers have slid down to mid thigh. I am struggling to keep it together.
- 50 yards into the run, I can feel wetness all over me and little specs of something hitting the back of my head and ears.

By the time I get to the bathroom door, the end of the 60 yards, I have completely lost it. I am shitting myself. Full on crapping in my pink Gap boxers.

I crash through the door as I step out of my boxers, shit already puddled in the seat. I blindly hurl them away from me, and nearly break the door to the first stall. I plop down on the seat and immediately slip off, because my ass is covered in slimy, runny feces. All the while, my butt hole is spouting forth waste. I finally get situated on the toilet and lose perhaps 20 pounds in the next 2 minutes.

During a short respite in my nearly superhuman flow of crap, I notice that the toilet is almost completely full of shit, so I flush. Predictably, the toilet overflows. Great. I move to the next stall, and continue my little adventure, except this time I courtesy flush every few seconds.

By the time I finish, I am physically exhausted, completely dehydrated, and my eyes are tearing up from shitting so hard. I laugh at the inadequacy of toilet paper to clean my body. I take my shirt off and see that the back of it is completely covered in little specks of shit that my heels kicked up from the diarrhea that ran down my legs as I ran. I throw the shirt in the trash, and then see the mirror. A thick black streak leads from the top of the mirror down to my pink Gap boxers, which are crumpled in a ball on the sink countertop. This is their final resting place.

Completely naked and covered in my own poop, I chuckle. At this point if I don't laugh I have to cry. As I open the bathroom door to the lobby, I think to myself, "Who else on earth could be having a worse night than me?"

My question is immediately answered.

I see a trail of shit, starting very wide at my feet, getting progressively smaller until it apexes at the chunky white shoes of none other than the small Mexican lady janitor.

Her eyes met mine. We may have been separated by numerous religious, linguistic, cultural and socioeconomic barriers, but the expression on her face crosses all boundaries.

Now really—picture this scene: I am butt-ass naked, crap plastered all over my ass, legs, back and head, standing about 20 yards away from a Mexican maid, with a trail of black liquid shit leading from her directly to me. What would you do? I don't think there is any established etiquette for this situation.

I shrug my shoulders, say, "Uhh, sorry. I mean, uh . . . *lo siento.* Good night. *Buenos noche* . . . or whatever," and calmly walk to the elevator.

From the glass window in the elevator, I can see her openly weeping. The rest of the lobby tells me why: Not only had my legs kicked shit up on the back of my ears and head, they had sprayed little specs of poop all over EVERYTHING. The couches, the walls, everywhere.

Whoops. Oh well, someone has to clean up my messes, and it sure as shit isn't going to be me.

When I get back to the room, SlingBlade is already in bed. He rolls over, takes one look at me and, never one for sympathy, begins laughing uncontrollably. He literally has to stop laughing because he strains his abdominal muscle. It takes him five full minutes before he can get the words out:

SlingBlade "Where . . . where the fuck are your pants?"
Tucker "FUCK YOU ASSHOLE. This is all your fault, Mr. Rhino Dump. If you hadn't had that miscarriage in our toilet I wouldn't be COVERED IN SHIT!"

He couldn't stop laughing long enough to respond. I took what remained of my dignity and got in the shower. He was still laughing when I got out, and in between giggle fits, managed to get this out:

"This is clear proof that there is a God, and that he is just!"

Day Three: The Yellow Rose and The Arrest

I awoke the next day to PWJ coming back into the room around 10am. I recounted my shit-in-the-lobby story, and after he collected himself, he told us about his night:

PWJ "Yeah, thanks a lot Tucker, you fucking asshole."
Tucker "Hey, it's not my fault that you are into manatees."
SlingBlade "Did she give a whale call when you were tubing her?"
PWJ "Fuck you."
Tucker "So, did you actually fuck her?"
PWJ "Yeah."
Tucker "I can't wait until one day The Manatee shows up with fat genius children with thimble heads and claims they're yours."
SlingBlade "WAIT—You fucked her? What about her promise ring?"
PWJ "She had a promise ring?"
SlingBlade "What a whore."

Of course, this sent us into eruptions of laughter. Apparently, The Manatee had told SlingBlade (but not PWJ) that she was nearly engaged to her boyfriend, who was out of town that weekend. It turns out SlingBlade is right for once: This one really is a cheating slut. PWJ went on,

PWJ "Now I know why she made me fuck her on the floor—her bed creaks and she didn't want her roommates to know she was cheating on her boyfriend."
SlingBlade "I hate women."
PWJ "You should have been there this morning when she dropped me off. She pulled up to the hotel and said, 'Thanks. It was nice to meet you.' I said, 'Yes it was,' got out and came up here. That was it."

Tucker "You mean you didn't take her to breakfast?"
PWJ "Fuck you."
SlingBlade "He can't afford it. He's on financial aid as it is."

I made SlingBlade call down to the front desk to get our toilet unclogged. About 30 minutes later, the door flung open and a woman who could have been Pootie Tang's mother started to scream at us:

Maid "Who kilt my toilet?"
SlingBlade "That was me. I'm sorry; I'll have a written apology to you in the morning."
Maid "Iz aight. At least it didn' flood the seelin so's da people down stairs'all 'Why da hell shit comin' down from ma seelin'?'"

She quickly and efficiently went to work, every few minutes yelling something barely intelligible out of the bathroom, "DAMN BOY, what'chu been eatin'? You be needin some Mylanta. Hehehehe."

We spent the day resting up, and eventually met up with the rest of the crew at Mermaid's apartment. We pre-partied there for a few hours, and went back out in Austin, except this time we went out on 4th street, which is less of a college crowd and more of a young professional crowd. We started at a place called Lavaca Street because they had table shuffleboard, and El Bingeroso is addicted to that game.

Dirty and I played El Bingeroso and Mermaid, and we spent the next 2 hours beating them like Gitmo detainees. This absolutely incensed El Bingeroso. He is very proud of his ability at table shuffleboard, so me beating him was beyond the pale for his ego.

He started drinking . . . but not happy drinking. It was like he was trying to douse his anger with alcohol. Every game we won would make him drink faster. After 2 hours of losing, he was fuming mad and very drunk. Being a good friend, I was a gracious winner:

Tucker "I thought you were good at this game? You are a failure. Dirty and I aren't even trying anymore. Beating you is like teasing fat people; it's just too easy. You aren't even a man. Did Kristy forget to let you bring your sack with you on this trip?"
El Bing "FUCK YOU ASSHOLE. I'LL BEAT YOUR ASS."
Tucker "You can't even beat me at table shuffleboard. Do you have fucking palsy or something? Why can't you throw the puck straight?

I'm shit-faced and I'm better than you. You are fucked up . . . you can't even out drink me."

El Bing "WHAT? YOU ARE THE WORST DRINKER I HAVE EVER SEEN. YOU DRINK LIKE A FUCKING SEVEN YEAR OLD." Then El Bingeroso made the bet that would cause a Butterfly Effect on both our lives, "MOTHERFUCKER, I'LL OUT DRINK YOU THREE-TO-ONE. ANYTHING! YOU PICK IT, I'LL DO THREE FOR EVERY ONE YOU DO, YOU FUCKING KINDERGARTEN DRINKER!"

I'd done it now . . . I'd finally pushed El Bingeroso too far. Almost immediately, Mermaid appeared with four shots of tequila. Mr. Tequila does not get along with Tucker. In fact, Mr. Tequila turns Tucker from normal-happy-drunk Tucker into violently-hurl-all-over-everything Tucker.

Tucker "I'd rather eat out a bull's ass than take a shot of tequila."
Mermaid [Sniff, sniff] "I smell a pussy."

I throw my shot back, and barely keep myself from throwing up. Isn't alcohol fun? This is one of the few times I can remember where someone successfully manipulated me into something.

El Bingeroso gets through the first three shots relatively easy. Mermaid shows up five minutes later with four more shots. El Bingeroso and I stare at each other. Even though we are holding it together, we both know that if we do these shots, it's over. I know I'm going to vomit, and he knows he's going to go into a drunken violent rage and black out. But come on, we're 24-year-old guys, do you really think either of us are going to back down?

I do my shot first because I figure that I have less to lose, as I am not engaged, nor do I even like myself very much. El Bingeroso does two of his shots. I run to the trash can and vomit my guts out.

Of course, El Bingeroso leads the rest of the bar in merciless taunts. I deserve it, as I have just vomited from two tequila shots (and the 15 or so beers I already had in my stomach). My only solace came when I saw El Bingeroso do his sixth and final tequila shot. It was like watching one of those NFL's Greatest Hits videos where they show the moment of impact in slow motion, and you can actually watch the receiver go from conscious to unconsciousness or see the quarterback's leg bones penetrate his sock as they compound fracture. I could see El

Bingeroso go over the edge. His eyes started moving independently like a chameleon's, his knees buckled, and he had to catch himself on the table. His fate was sealed. He quickly recovered and stood up straight again, but I've been drinking with him enough to know the result of that little sequence: He's going to jail.

SlingBlade goes to the bar to get us a round of beers. While there, he starts up a conversation with an older lady who was sitting on a bar stool by herself with a poodle in her lap:

Woman "I wish I were young again, and full of piss and vinegar like you guys."
SlingBlade "We're just full of alcohol and Mexican food. You could do that."
Woman "Oh my! You are funny."

As SlingBlade chatted her up, he surreptitiously fed her dog beer. When she discovered this, it did not please her.

Woman "WHAT ARE YOU DOING! Oh my goodness, Pookie, are you OK?"
SlingBlade "Your dog has a drinking problem, you might want to look into that. Take him to doggie AA or something."
Woman "WHY DID YOU GIVE BEER TO MY DOG!"
SlingBlade "Your dog drank my beer. There is a difference."

The bartender stepped in.

Bartender "You and your friends are cut off."
SlingBlade "WHAT? I am 165 pounds of pure athleticism. I can recycle alcohol with impunity. Bring me more beer woman, and be quick about it."
Bartender "Don't make me call the police."

That was pretty much it for us. Mermaid took us to some other bar that was located in an alley, and before any of us even knew what was happening, El Bingeroso was tossing trash cans around, knocking over dumpsters and kicking doors down. He was in full-on El Bingeroso Destroy Mode. He's the type of drunk that makes you wonder why alcohol is classified as a depressant.

It was clear we had to get him off the street. While deciding what to do, we came across one of the numerous street musicians that swarm 6th street. Some guy was playing "Friends in Low Places" on his guitar, and next thing we know, El Bingeroso has his arm around him, crooning at the top of his lungs:

El Bing "CAUUUUSE I GOT FRIENDS IN LOW PLACES, WHERE THE WHISKEY DROWNS AND THE BEER CHASES . . . MY BLUES AWAY . . . AND TUCKER IS GAY . . ."

The guitar guy stops playing, and tries to help El Bingeroso out:

Guy "Man, you need to put that beer down, there are open container laws in Texas."
El Bing "YOU WANNA GO?"
Tucker "EL BINGEROSO, STOP IT—he's trying to help you."
El Bing "YOU WANNA FIGHT TOO? Come on jackass, gimme some more Garth before I kick your teeth in. I'LL DO IT!"
Guy "You need to get your friend away from me."

If I had a nickel for every time I've heard that said about me or my friends, I'd be driving a Bugatti.

While this went down, SlingBlade was making friends with one of the numerous homeless denizens of Austin. One beggar sparked this exchange:

Beggar "Hey man, do you like, have any change man?"
SlingBlade "Hahahhahahaha. He talks like you, El Bingeroso! I bet he was a promising law student once, before the huff-huff and all. Come here El Bingeroso, take a look into your future!"
Beggar "Do I get some change, man?"
SlingBlade "Tell you what—I will give you all my change if you give me that can of beer in your pocket."
Beggar "But . . . it's all I have. I live on the streets, man."
SlingBlade "IT ACCEPTS THE DEAL OR IT DOESN'T GET MY CHANGE."
Beggar "OK, man, OK. Here you go."
SlingBlade "Very nice. I don't have any change, but thanks for the beer."
Beggar "But . . . but . . . man, that beer was all I had. I live on the streets, man."
SlingBlade "And do you think that perhaps your poor negotiation skills had something to do with this? Hmmm?"

Beggar "No man, my ex-wife kicked me out man, I got nowhere to go."
SlingBlade "You just said the magic words. Here's your beer back."
Beggar "How about some change?"
SlingBlade "Don't push it. You're lucky I haven't knocked out your tooth."

We decide to go to a strip club, The Yellow Rose. To this day, I still laugh recalling our thought process: El Bingeroso is too drunk and violent to walk around the streets, so let's take him to a place with naked women and large angry bouncers! Sounds great! It'll be all sunshine and kittens from there!

There are six of us, so we split into two cabs. Cab 1 is me, Mermaid and Dirty. Cab 2 is PWJ, SlingBlade and El Bingeroso. It's only like ten minutes to the Rose, and Cab 1 arrives with no problem. The three of us go inside, and immediately Mermaid says to me, "We are in Gomorrah."

If you go out a lot, you know that you can never try too hard to make a party; you just have to kinda see where the night takes you. You do that enough, and every now and then you stumble into one of those absolutely perfect situations, where it seems like everything just falls into place. It was that kind of night at the Yellow Rose.

It was a Sunday night, so the place was not crowded, but for some reason there were lots of dancers on shift. We were dressed well, had lots of cash on us, and all three of us have good game, so before we realized it there were about 5 or 6 girls hanging with us at our table.

Dirty assesses the situation, looks up at me, gives his devious smile and then pulls a classic Dirty maneuver, "Ladies, do you know who that guy is?" He points to me. "That is Tucker Max. He looks like a humble guy, but in reality he is one of the creators of, and the fourth largest stockholder in, Yahoo. I'm sure I don't need to tell you ladies what Yahoo is, do I?" Of course, two of them did require explanation, but the other four knew what it was, and one said she owned stock in Yahoo.

Now, obviously this is not even remotely true. I was dirt poor and didn't even own the car I drove. But Dirty went to the PT Barnum School of Marketing, and learned the most important lesson very well: The bigger the lie, the more likely people are to believe it.

I pretended to be unassuming and nonchalant as he kept talking me up. All six couldn't have been hooked more if we'd landed them with tackle and a line. The best part was the dancer who owned stock in Yahoo seemed to know a little bit about the stock market, and tested me by asking who the CEO was. I had worked for Fenwick & West that summer, and one of their main clients was Yahoo, so I knew quite a bit about them. The look on her face when I said, "Are you kidding? I helped hire Tim Koogle," was fucking priceless. I thought she might go down on me right there at the table.

Playing the part, I ordered bottle service for the table, and before we knew it, there was free lap dances and gratuitous groping all around. It was great. One of the strippers had done some porn before, so I asked her about something I had always wondered about:

Tucker "I understand how female porn stars are selected, but if you are a guy, and you don't have a huge cock or shoot 8-ropers, how do you get into the porn industry?"
Mermaid "Networking, dude, networking."
Stripper "I don't know. I just fucked whoever they told me to. It paid good."
Tucker "Well isn't that pleasant? I bet your parents are beaming with pride."

We had all six convinced to come back to our hotel with us, when all of the sudden Mermaid looks up at us and goes, "Where the fuck is El Bingeroso?"

In our eagerness to exploit strippers, we had totally forgotten about the other three guys. I checked my phone—4 missed calls, all from PWJ. I wondered what was vibrating in my pocket.

Mermaid grabbed my phone and went outside to make some calls. He came back five minutes later with a look of complete exasperation on his face, "Dudes—El Bingeroso is in jail. We need to get out of here."

Leaving the strippers and what should have been a night of carnal ecstasy that would have made Caligula blush, we return to Embassy Suites. PWJ fills us in on the story of Cab 2:

As soon as they got in the cab, PWJ and SlingBlade realized that El Bingeroso was in trouble. He was passed the Violent Drunk Stage, and was now barreling towards the Comatose Drunk Stage. In order to keep him awake, they asked him questions.

PWJ "So, El Bingeroso, how did you meet Kristy [his fiancée]?"
El Bingeroso "Dude, I met her in a bar, man. It was in college. I worked there."
PWJ "Was she in a sorority?"
El Bingeroso "Yeah man, I met her in a bar."
PWJ "I know this, you already told me that. What did you do on your first date? Something special?"
El Bingeroso "I met her in a bar, man. I met her in a bar."

It went on like this until he basically collapsed in SlingBlade's lap. About two minutes later, and only about 3 blocks from the strip club, El Bingeroso shoots upright and says, "We need to pull over!"

Assuming that he is going to throw up, the cab immediately pulls over into the parking lot of a convenience store. El Bingeroso gets out, stumbles around for a second, unzips his pants, drops them to his feet, and starts pissing. Right in the middle of the parking lot.

He is still weaving, and PWJ doesn't want him to piss on his pants, so he gets behind El Bingeroso, wraps his arms around his chest, and holds him up while he pisses.

Now picture this scene in your mind: It's Texas, midnight on a Sunday, and in the middle of a convenience store parking lot is a guy with his pants around his ankles, and another guy behind him with his arms wrapped around his chest. What would you think?

Me too. And that is exactly what the cop that drove by at that moment thought.

PWJ said all he heard was the screeching of tires before he looked up and saw a large Austin City Police officer hop out of his car and yell (in a good-ol-boy Texas accent):

"WHAT IN THE FUCK ARE YEW TWO DOIN'?!?"

SlingBlade tried to get out of the cab to explain, but the cop put his hand on his gun and barked, "GET BACK IN THE CAB!" SlingBlade immediately complied, because this is what a childhood of risk aversion does to a man.

PWJ stepped in front of El Bingeroso, "Officer, I'm sorry, please let me explain. My friend got very drunk tonight, and we pulled over because we thought he was going to vomit, but he started to pee, so I got behind him to hold him up. He is very drunk, he just needs to go back to the hotel and lay down."

The cop was the stereotypical idiot meathead Austin Cop, "So you think you can just piss here, right on the road, right here in this parking lot? There's a hospital two blocks away, we're trying to keep this neighborhood pristine, and you're over here pissing all over the place."

PWJ is money under pressure, and for once being the son of a domineering military officer paid off—he stayed calm, and after about 5 minutes of very lucid, reasoned and submissive explanation, he reassured the cop that everything was OK and got the situation under control. It looked like he was going to get El Bingeroso off the hook.

Then a second cop car pulled up, and the second cop pulled El Bingeroso aside and talked to him separately. PWJ said he looked over about 2 minutes later, saw El Bingeroso gesticulating wildly and pointing in the cop's face, heard him yell something about "Mr. Plastic Badge," and then watched him get thrown on the hood of the cop car, hand-cuffed, and taken away, kicking the rear windows as it pulled off. This is when the phone calls started.

Now back to the hotel room. We decide to send PWJ and Mermaid to bail out El Bingeroso, and the rest of us go to sleep. It's about 3am at this point. I wake up at 8am, and PWJ, Mermaid and El Bingeroso still aren't in. I realize that my phone was turned off, so I turn it on, and see that I have 3 new messages. I listen to them, break down laughing, and wake up everyone else to listen to them also. Here they are, copied absolutely fucking verbatim off my voicemail:

Message # 1, 1:32am: "Jackass, I am in jail . . . um, I am in, uh, jail dude. I am in Austin County Jail. Umm . . . you need to call me man. You need to fucking come bail me out. I'm in jail dude, it's not cool."

Message # 2, 2:44am: "Hey dude man, I'm in jail. This is El Bingeroso. You need to come get me. Uhhh . . . PWJ called . . . it's not cool man. Come get me."

Message # 3, 7:48am: "Tucker, this is El Bingeroso man. I'm at the police headquarters in Austin. And I just got out of jail. I don't know who posted bond, but you know, whatever. Like, uhhh, I'm looking for a ride, so hopefully I'll run into you guys, and uhh, get a ride. If I don't, have a good time in Dallas."

As El Bingeroso was making that last call, PWJ and Mermaid were waiting for him outside on the steps of the Austin County Courthouse. He was finally released a few hours later:

El Bingeroso "PWJ, let me ask you one question: What did I do to get thrown in jail?"

They bring El Bingeroso to the hotel, and he is in bad shape. He looks like a Johnny Cash song. In addition to his rank smell and disgusting clothes, he has a huge shiner above his right eye.

Mermaid "El Bingeroso, dude, what's wrong with your eye? Did the cop hit you?"
El Bingeroso "Probably."
Mermaid "Why did he hit you?"
El Bingeroso "I said horrible things about his grandma in Spanish . . . apparently he spoke it."
Mermaid "What was going on? How did it happen?"
El Bingeroso "I was in a cell with all these Mexican guys, and you know, I was pissed, so I was organizing a prison riot with the bendejos, when all of the sudden the door opened and WHACK. It is not fun waking up on the floor of the drunk tank, covered in vomit and piss."
Mermaid "Are you OK?"
El Bingeroso "Yeah, I guess . . . Guys, seriously, how did I end up in jail?"

We recounted the entire night to him. He lost memory somewhere around the 6th tequila shot. After we finished telling him the story, he was quiet for second, then looked at us with the most pitiful expression I have ever seen on his face,

"Dude . . . I am not a good drunk."

Day Four: The Trip Home

This was not the end of El Bingeroso's problems. He made the catastrophic mistake of calling his fiancée while in the drunk tank, waking her up at 3am, and then calling her parents. Let me reiterate: HE CALLED HER PARENTS FROM JAIL. He was in quite the shit storm of trouble with her, plus he had a drunk and disorderly charge to deal with, so he had to stay in Austin a few more days.

The other three of us decided to head back to Dallas, and then Durham. I believe I put it as such, "We might as well go back to Dallas; there is nothing left to do in Austin. What else could we do that would top the last two nights? Burn down the city? Kill the governor?"

As I am checking out of the Embassy Suites, the manager comes out of the office and asks to speak to me. "Mr. Max, were you the one who had, ahem, 'an accident,' in the lobby two nights ago?" I told her it was me indeed, and that I was sorry, that I was not accustomed to the effects of the drink and I would seek help as soon as I returned to Durham. She did not smile. "I have to inform you that you will no longer be able to stay at this, or any other Embassy Suites, ever again."

What?

"Sir, we have a national 'Do not accommodate' database that your name has been added to. After your incident, we would prefer you not stay at any of our hotels again."

I was permanently banned from ALL Embassy Suites. Forever.

Well . . . I guess sometimes actions do have consequences.

When we got to Dallas, we checked back into the same Radisson, and slept until dinner time, then went out in Deep Ellum.

Fast forward to the next morning. I had been up all night drinking and fornicating with some girl when I walk into the hotel room at 8am and find vomit all over the floor. Apparently the Reuben sandwich SlingBlade ordered last night at the bar wasn't the best of ideas. He was in full-on SlingBlade time-to-go-to-the-ER mode. The kid has the constitution of a six-year-old lupus victim, and after four nights of raucous drinking and corporeal abuse, his frail Bubble-boy immune system had shut down.

He crawled into the backseat of his eggplant purple Saturn, curled up into the fetal position and let out moans every few minutes, as PWJ and I drove back to Durham. We were somewhere in Arkansas when SlingBlade shot up and started hitting the back of my seat. I freaked out, swerved all over the road, but before I could get to the shoulder I heard it come loose,

"BLAAAAHHHHHH."

SlingBlade opened the door, leaned halfway out and just let loose, vomiting all over his own car. He eventually got out of the car and started vomiting again in the grass.

After a good solid five minute puke-session, he crawled back in the car and we took off. Not even a minute later, he starts slapping at his legs and yelling in pain. The idiot stepped in a red ant nest while vomiting, then tracked a bunch of them into the car. Before we knew it, all three of us where swatting angry red ants off of us. We had to pull off at the next exit.

SlingBlade found himself at some redneck roadside gas station in Arkansas, cleaning vomit and red ants out of his car . . . using newspaper, because this gas station didn't have a vacuum.

He nearly lost it, "This is pretty much the worst day of my life, and I have only been awake for three hours. I refuse to believe this is happening."

The rest of the trip was rather uneventful; while PWJ and I discussed all order of semantics and philosophy and other nerd topics, SlingBlade slept and moaned and cried. Somewhere around Chattanooga, he woke up, scribbled something on a scrap of paper, handed it to us, and passed back out. It read:

"Please kill me."

The Epilogue

Texas hasn't been the same since that October. Unfortunately, the Baby Dolls that I wrote about no longer exists. Dallas zoning laws have changed the club, and though it still stands, it's no longer the bastion of debauchery it once was.

A few weeks after we were on 6th street, Cheers Shot Bar caught fire from Flaming Dr Peppers and though it was fine, the drink was banned after that in Austin. You can still get them at some bars, but officially they are illegal.

And much to my dismay, I have heard that The Shocker is now banned in Texas.

As far as I know, I am still banned from all Embassy Suites. I had forgotten about this until about two years later when I tried to register at an Embassy Suites in Atlanta. Lo and behold, my name was still in the database and "Tucker Max" was not allowed to register as a guest. A small price to pay for what is probably the funniest story of my life.

For the four Duke Law School friends who went on the trip, things were also never the same.

For El Bingeroso, it marked the last true balls-out drink-and-destroy weekend he had as a (nearly) single man. After waking up in the Austin City Jail covered in piss and vomit with a huge black eye, he really had to check himself, realize that he is engaged and in love and needs to stop acting like Colin Farrell. He married Kristy that next summer. He still drinks, sometimes to excess, but the El Bingeroso we saw that night is dead. He wasn't even like that during his bachelor party when we hired a bunch of strippers and a midget.

The reforms that El Bingeroso implemented began at the Duke Law Halloween Party. Before he left for the road trip, he had convinced Kristy to wear a French maid outfit to the party. He even bought it a month ahead of time he was so excited. Kristy was predictably unhappy about El Bingeroso's antics in Austin, and as his first public act of contrition, *he* wore her French maid outfit to the Halloween party, while she wore an orange prison jumpsuit. Quite the couple they were . . . and still are.

For SlingBlade and PWJ, pretty much nothing changed because they never grow as people. SlingBlade is still bitter, utterly lonely, risk-averse and continues to have issues with women. PWJ is still a bad person who is unable to resist any girl with big tits.

Much to our amusement, his dealings with The Manatee did not end that night. She never told PWJ her name or address, yet she knew his name, found out his address, and a few weeks later sent him a thank-you note, with no return address, along with a check for her share of the cab fare from 6th street to her apartment. The check was for $3.64. It was a Muppet Show check.

In true Chinese Zen flow of life style, from the ashes of El Bingeroso rose the phoenix that you know as Tucker Max. I'd done plenty of crazy and out of control shit in my life, but that was the first weekend I consciously took a voice recorder out with me, and that was the first weekend I ever really understood how truly insane and funny my life is. I returned to Durham with 10 pages of quotes and thought to myself, "This would make a great movie." It was the flap of the butterfly wings at the exact right place at the exact right time that eventually led to Hurricane Max. I didn't realize it then, and I fought it for another three years, but after that weekend my life arc was irreversibly redirected away from law and towards writing.

My Key West Trip

Occurred—July 2001
Written—February 2005

When I lived in Boca, I was seeing a girl who had more money than she knew what to do with. Daddy was a big real estate developer in South Florida and loved his little girl, and Tucker loved his little girl's fake tits and black AMEX [for the poor people: A black Centurion American Express card is reserved for those who spend more than $150,000 a year on other AMEX cards].

One day I told her that I had never been to Key West. The next day we were on a chartered jet from West Palm Beach to Key West, had a limo meet us at the airport and take us to a really nice hotel on Duval Street. The plane, the limo and the hotel room all had bars in them, so by the time we got settled in our room, like 11pm, we were pretty tanked. I can get used to this.

Now, even though Daddy'sGirl had lots of money, sadly she couldn't seem to afford any brains. She was 18 and had left Florida State two months into her freshman year because it was too difficult. Seriously—that's not "too difficult" as a euphemism for "sucked 100 dicks in a month;" she was literally just too stupid for Florida State. TOO STUPID FOR FREE SHOE UNIVERSITY! If this seems hard to believe, it's because you don't know any Florida girls. After a year there, you stop being shocked at these things.

Daddy'sGirl wanted to go to some bars, but she neglected to bring her fake ID . . . or even realize that she NEEDED A FAKE ID TO GET INTO A BAR.

Tucker "How do you get into bars?"
Daddy'sGirl "I don't know. In Palm Beach they just let us in. Everyone

knows my daddy. Or we drink at The Breakers or one of the other country clubs. No one has ever asked me for an ID."

Tucker "Did it occur to you that we aren't in Palm Beach anymore?"
Daddy'sGirl "But I thought EVERYBODY knew my daddy!"
Tucker [blank stare]
Daddy'sGirl "This is so unfair!"
Tucker "It's a good thing you are rich, otherwise you'd have already have been spit out the bottom of the porn industry."
Daddy'sGirl "What? I told you that I don't like porn. It's gross."

I just walked off.

We get back to the hotel and decide to order champagne and strawberries and go down to the hot tub. Cliché, I know, but look at the girl I was working with. You can't make chardonnay out of shit.

I know that Cristal gets all the press because rappers have discovered it, but let me tell you something: Cristal is overrated and rappers are stupid. If I want to slang dope or steal a car, I am going straight to DMX to get advice, but for insanely expensive limited edition vintage alcohols, I think I'll get my counsel elsewhere, thank you.

I made the mistake of asking Daddy'sGirl what she wanted:

Daddy'sGirl "Ohh—let's get Cristal!"
Tucker "What's your favorite TV show?"
Daddy'sGirl "I don't know. I guess *TRL*. Or *The Real World*."
Tucker "Let's leave the ordering to me."

The hotel had a great selection, so I got us a bottle of 90 Bollinger Grande Annee. I think it was $450. It's not every day I have access to an unlimited credit line.

We head down to the hot tub, and it is a really nice set up. Half hidden from the rest of the pool area by foliage, super hot water with lots of shallow places to sit. It took a glass and a half of champagne for her to loosen up, but after that, it was easy. Top off, panties off . . . full-on sex in the hot tub, here we come.

We finished off and put our robes on. As we walked back toward the lobby, I glanced up at the balcony overlooking the pool area and noticed this guy staring at us. He was zipping up his pants, breathing heavily and sweating. He muttered:

"Thanks. You just saved me $9.95."

Daddy'sGirl looks up, and even though she is dumber than a burlap sack, she is not stupid enough to miss this. She immediately busts out in tears, "OH MY GOD!!! AHHHHHHH!!!," and runs back into the hotel. I just start laughing.

Tucker "No problem. We've all been there."

I don't know why I said that. I have never in my life jacked off while watching other people fuck. Well, not in person. Of course I jack off to porn all the time, but come on, porn stars are only objects for our sexual gratification, not real people.

Daddy'sGirl was so shook up and upset about this she took two Valium to sleep and made us leave at like 6am the next day, insisting that we go out the back door.

Daddy'sGirl "WHAT IF WE SEE HIM AGAIN??!"
Tucker "I don't know. Charge him for the show this time."

When we got back to Palm Beach, she didn't call me for like three days. I called her, and she was not happy to hear from me.

Tucker "What is wrong with you?"
Daddy'sGirl "Well, TUCKER, you gave me an STD!"
Tucker "What? Which one?"
Daddy'sGirl "A urinary tract infection! I can't believe it!!"

I couldn't stop laughing. For like two minutes, she was screaming at me on the phone as I teared up with laughter. I tried to make her understand that UTI's aren't really STD's and that she got the UTI from the bacteria in the hot tub and not from me, but that concept was far too hard for her to wrap her head around. She hung up on me.

In a fun turn of events, about 4 months later I got this voicemail from her:

"Hey Tucker . . . uh, I am sorry . . . I guess you didn't give me an STD. I had sex last week with my boyfriend in my parents' hot tub, and the same thing happened . . . he got tested and didn't have a UTI . . . so I guess you were right . . . anyway, I broke up with him before he found out and now he won't call me anymore . . . what are you doing this weekend?"

Girl beats Tucker at his own game

Occurred—October 2001
Written—June 2004

I met Rachel at some ill-conceived fundraiser for infant amputees with swollen spinal cords. It was thrown by the Junior League or some sort of similar organization dedicated to finding rich husbands for vacuous single women. She was one of the organizers, very good looking, and seemed normal, which is very significant in Florida. We talked about the wine, I pretended to listen to her, she loved that I came from a "prominent Florida family"—a quote that still sends me into fits of laughter—so we went on a date later that week.

The first date she only reaffirmed my initial impression: not dumb, but not bright, not interesting, but not totally repellant. This girl was there as a human being, but that's about it. There seemed to be nothing compelling about her aside from her looks. Despite this, and the fact that she refused to hook up, something about her kept me into the first date enough to go on a second. I couldn't quite put my finger on it, it was just a feeling that I got, but there was something there that I wanted to see more of. Besides, I hadn't had sex in like a week and she was my best option, so I agreed to a second date.

Date Two started out boring as well, until I figured out why I had a subconscious interest despite Rachel's inability to hold a conversation. I made a totally innocuous joke about having to pay more when you beat up Cuban hookers during sex, and the girl instantly went from polite-but-distant to clearly-into-me. The conversation turned to sex and it was like a switch was thrown; everything about her lit up, she became totally engaged in the conversation and actually became slightly interesting. At one point, she got a Cheshire cat grin on her face, her eyes narrowed and she coyly asked me,

Rachel "Are you naughty, Tucker Max?"
Tucker "Who are you talking to? You can't think up anything that I haven't done already. Twice."

I didn't know it then, but that exchange would soon have a place of honor in the Couldn't-Have-Been-More-Wrong Hall of Fame.

Remember when I said she seemed normal? Yeah . . . I was quickly disabused of that notion when we got back to my place and she took my hands, placed them around her neck and told me:

"I want you to strangle me as you fuck me. Not too hard, don't choke me and don't leave bruises, but make sure I can feel it."

It was a bit awkward at first. Not really strangling her; there are plenty of girls I've wanted to choke to death, but more coordinating the act while also sexually penetrating her. It's not easy to fuck with both your hands around a girl's neck, especially if you've never done it before. You're so accustomed to your hands being used for other things—balance, hair-pulling, using the remote—that it takes you awhile to get a rhythm going. But once I got acclimated, it was kinda fun, choking this girl as I fucked her.

The next date, we moved from my hands to my belt. Around her neck, pulling on it as I fucked her from behind. The best part was when she was putting the belt around her neck, and asked me,

"Do you have a t-shirt or washcloth I can use? I need to put something soft between the belt and my neck or it'll leave marks."

This girl was straight out of an HBO *Real Sex* episode (except not ugly). If it was sexual, she wanted it do it, and she wanted it to include pain and humiliation. Over the next three weeks, we ran the entire gamut of sexual deviance:

First was erotic asphyxiation.

Next we added dominance role playing, name calling, and brutally violent ass sex.

Then we acted out her mock rape fantasies.

Then it just avalanched from there . . . tossing my salad, comfy cuffs, kitchen utensils, whips, chains. Pain. Torture. Everything you can imagine and worse.

Hmmm . . . I wonder if her daddy used to spank her when she was bad?

At first, I kinda liked it. I got to beat her up during sex, call her whatever names I wanted, pull her hair, throw her around, fuck any hole I could get my dick in as hard as I wanted, and basically do anything I could think of whenever I felt like it; nothing was out of bounds. She was like my own personal sexual canvas to experiment on. Pain, torture and humiliation do not turn me on sexually, but I had never really done anything like this before, especially not to this extreme. The novelty was exciting.

But every night some variation of this thought would go through my head, "Am I really doing this to her? Did I just stick a carrot in her ass as I fucked her doggy-style?" After about three weeks of this, every time pushing it further and further, I was at the point where I was doing shit to this girl that could have literally gotten me thrown in jail. I was thinking about filming her consenting to this stuff, Tupac style, because when I dumped her I didn't want the blood on my spatula to be used as evidence against me in a domestic assault case.

The true irony was that in a way, these sorts of things were almost more debasing to me than to her. I pride myself on being so outlandish and outrageous that normal people don't know how to deal with me—but this girl, without realizing what she was doing, was flipping it on me. She was beating me at my own game. No matter what I did, she wanted more. If I spanked her, she wanted to be spanked until her ass was raw. If I spanked her ass till my hand prints were plastered on her glutes, she wanted to me to spank her till she bled. If I called her a "bitch" during sex, she wanted to be called a "whore." If I called her a "whore," she wanted to be called a "filthy cunt whore." I'm literally a professional at humiliating and debasing people, but this girl was absorbing my entire repertoire and then coming back and asking for seconds.

She was like Tyler Durden in *Fight Club*, in the scene where he lets the mobster beat him up after catching them using his bar basement for weekly fights. Tyler just lets the guy beat his ass. The mobster hits him and hits him—dropping fist after fist right on his face—but Tyler gets up, covered in blood, and laughs at him. That is so fucking demoralizing. When someone takes your absolute best shots and, instead of retaliating, simply gets back up and asks for more—what the fuck do you do then? That WAS my best shot!

Even though this girl's appetite for pain and degradation was outstripping my ability to hurt and humiliate her, I refused to let her beat me. It wasn't even about the sex or the experimentation anymore (and it was never about the relationship, because aside from the freaky sex, this girl was basically worthless). No, for me it was about seeing whose limits we could reach first. I HAD to get her to blink. Tyler Durden isn't having Fight Club in MY basement, goddamnit.

I started browsing S&M websites, emailing my friends asking for suggestions and even consulting dominatrixes for ideas. I was about to run out of ideas, when one night it all came to a head.

Like every other time she came over, Rachel showed up ready for abuse. I met her at the door, pulled her by the hair into my place (she loved that) and started forcing myself on her (another of her favorites; believe me, this is not my normal way of greeting people).

As I was ripping her blouse off, I realized I had to drop the kids off at the pool. I was about to excuse myself to take a dump when it came to me—something that had to be too much for her.

I took her by the hand into my bathroom, dropped my pants, sat on the toilet, pointed to my dick and looked up at her: "Start sucking."

Now, this has GOT to be the limit. There is no way this girl is going to give me head while I drop a fucking deuce. No way. NO girl would do this. NO FUCKING WAY.

What did she do? Say no? Leave in disgust? Storm out of my apartment in a rage? Nein, fraulein.

Without a moment's hesitation, she went right to work. Just when I thought I had won the race to the bottom with this girl, I was proven wrong. Again.

How absurd is this? Picture yourself in this situation: Sitting on a toilet in a relatively small residential bathroom, pushing feces out of your ass, with a girl on her knees in front of you, still fresh from work in her nice business casual blouse and linen pantsuit, lips wrapped around your cock, working it like a runaway. What would *you* do?

I started pushing harder. I didn't care if I popped a blood vessel in my head and died on the toilet from an aneurysm Elvis-style, I was determined to get her to quit. I thought to myself, "I bet this will be the only time in my life where I desperately wish for a disgusting flood of diarrhea."

The first turd (sadly, it was solid) plopped loudly into the toilet. No reaction. Nothing but continued enthusiasm for my cock.

The second turd . . . nothing. It was like she was just giving a normal blowjob. I kinda leaned back in the seat so the odor would have more room to waft up into her nostrils.

The third turd . . . she started to hit her stride, really working her hand on the shaft and slurping the head.

The fourth turd . . . aren't her knees at least hurting? This is a tile floor.

I pushed and pushed and pushed until I was on the brink of giving myself hemorrhoids when my colon finally just gave up, completely devoid of fecal matter . . . and Rachel was still going strong. No matter how bad the smell got, nor how loud I grunted, nor how disgusting the gas noises my ass made were, she would not stop. Nose full of fart, mouth full of cock, she never even paused. I don't know how she kept breathing. I damn near choked from the smell and I was a full two feet further above the poop than she was.

As I sat there on the uncomfortably warm toilet seat, unwiped, smelling my own shit, my ass sweating and falling asleep at the same time—about to come because she was so good she could bring me to orgasm in a coma—I gave up.

Fuck it. If I can beat her, choke her, shove things into her ass and get incredible head on the toilet, and STILL not find her limits, then she wins. I can't go any further.

Now, you may be thinking, "Dude, there are tons of things you could have done worse than that. Why not a Cleveland Steamer?" etc, etc.

That is a legitimate question, but even I have my limits. I'm not Chuck Berry and I'm not crossing into the world of defecation for sexual gratification. I know it turns some people on to take a dump on their partner or have them drink piss, but I'm sorry, that shit is just out of bounds for me . . . literally.

I mean, I was willing to race her to MY bottom, but not THE bottom. I was not willing to go beyond things that I was comfortable with. The fact that she EAGERLY sucked me off on a toilet seat as I took a dump really drove it home—this girl meant business. It almost makes my skin crawl thinking about what I would have had to do to hear a "No" out of her. Yeah, I could have brought a dog in and asked her to fellate it, but for fuck's sake—what if she said yes? Then what do I do? Watch her suck off a Dalmatian while I wait my turn? Hit it from behind as she slobs on Fido's bone? Thank you, but no.

I honestly thought I was beat. I even got a little depressed, and started moping around South Florida, unsure what to do next. But in a stroke of amazing Tucker Luck, I broke her totally by accident, in a way I never would have imagined. Three days later, she sat me down at dinner and said, in a very somber serious tone:

"Tucker, you need to get serious with me, or we can't keep seeing each other. It is humiliating to me that I am seeing a man that my friends know is also seeing other women."

I didn't even know what to say. I really didn't. I was totally stupefied by that sentence. Did this girl actually think I would seriously date her? Is this a joke? It may be a double standard and I may be an asshole, but how the fuck am I supposed to have any respect for a girl who would do the things she did? Especially with ME of all people?

At the time, I could only muster one response:

"HAHHAHHHAAHHAHAHHAHAHAHAHAHAHAH. Wait, wait . . . .HAHAHAHAHAHAHHAHAHA."

She got pissed and stormed out of the restaurant.

I know I should have said something like, "You mean when I double-penetrated you with produce, *that* wasn't humiliating, but what your friends think about us *is*?" but I just couldn't.

Though, to be honest, I may have gotten her to blink first, it was a hollow victory. I was like that Korean boxer who "beat" Roy Jones Jr. in the '88 Olympics. Yeah, I got the gold medal, but everyone in the world knows I didn't really win this contest.

Tucker Tries Buttsex; Hilarity Does Not Ensue

Occurred—Summer 1997
Written—June 2003

I spent the summer between my 2nd and 3rd year of college suckling on the parental teat in South Florida. It was the absolute prime of my "do anything to get laid" phase. Recently freed from a 4-year long-distance relationship that began in high school, I wanted nothing more than to have sex with as many girls as possible.

Most of the things I did that summer are not story-worthy; you can only tell the same, "I got drunk on Dom and fucked this hottie" story so many times before it gets annoying. That summer I experienced every random sex situation that a 20 year old can imagine: fucking on the beach, getting head from random girls in club bathrooms, sleeping with two or three different girls in a day, getting so drunk I passed out during sex, getting arrested for receiving fellatio in the pool at the Delano, blah, blah, blah . . . Jesus. What does it say about how fucked up my life is that I don't consider these stories to be extraordinary anymore?

Anyway, while most of my stories from that summer may not be extraordinary for me, there is one very notable exception. . . .

I was seeing one girl, "Jaime," about twice a week. She was a fresh arrival to South Beach, having moved there 5 months ago from Maine as a 19 year old with a modeling contract. We met through a mutual friend who befriended her while they were modeling. Five weeks and lots of sex later, she thought we were dating. I knew better, but she was way too hot to bother correcting her assumption.

The ex-girlfriend of 4 years I previously spoke about was very sexually conservative. It was missionary in the dark and then straight to sleep, with maybe a blowjob on the weekends if she'd had a few glasses of wine with dinner (it was a high school relationship, I didn't know any better). After four years of this, I was ready to experience all the things I'd missed out on (when I wasn't cheating on her, of course).

Buttsex, known in the biz as "anal," was one of these unknowns, and I decided that I wanted to try it. Jaime was the perfect partner: very hot and very sweet, but more importantly, very naïve and very open to suggestion.

She was reluctant at first, not understanding why we just couldn't keep having normal sex, so I had to employ my persuasive powers:

Jaime "But . . . I've never done it."
Tucker "I've never done it either; it can be *our* thing."
Jaime "But . . . I don't know if I'll like it."
Tucker "You won't have to worry about getting pregnant."
Jaime "But . . . I like normal sex."
Tucker "Everyone's doing anal. It's the 'in' thing."
Jaime "But . . . I don't know . . . it seems weird."
Tucker "It's the preferred method in Europe. Especially with the runway models. Don't you want to do runways in Europe?"

After a few weeks of this, she finally consented. Though she agreed to let me put my penis in her small hole, she extracted a promise in return:

"OK, we can try anal sex, but I want it to be special and romantic. You have to take me out to a nice place, like The Forge or Tantra, NOT one of your father's restaurants, and it has to be a weekend night, NOT a Monday. And you have to keep taking me out on weekends. I'm tired of being your Monday night girl."

I made reservations for the next Friday at Tantra. Aside from being insanely expensive, Tantra is famous for having grass floors. Really; they put in new sod every week. They also advertise their food as "aphrodisiac cuisine." Yes, at that point in my life, I thought these things worked.

Thanks to my father's connections, I got us a corner booth in the grass room. She was quite impressed. I ordered like it was the Last Supper. No expense was spared. Two $110 bottles of merlot, veal rack, stone crabs, the Tantra Love platter—it was lavish and decadent. I was 21, stupid, and wanted to fuck Jaime in the butt; I wasn't about to let a $400 tab get in my way.

By the time we left Tantra, this girl had doe eyes that would have made Bambi look like a heroin-chic CK model. She could not have been more in love with me. The entire drive back to my place she was rubbing my crotch, telling me how badly she wanted me to fuck her, how hot I made her, etc, etc. We get back to my place and our clothes are off before we even get in the door. We collapse on the bed and start fucking. Normal vaginal sex at first, just like always.

Now, what she did not know, and what I have not told you yet, was that I had a surprise waiting for her.

[Aside: Before I tell you what the surprise was, let me make this clear: As I stand right now, I am a bad person. At 21, I was possibly the worst person in existence. I had no regard for the feelings of others, I was narcissistic and self-absorbed to the point of psychotic delusion, and I saw other people only as a means to my happiness and not as humans worthy of respect and consideration. I have no excuse for what I did; it was wrong and I regret it. Even though I normally revel in my outlandish behavior, sometimes even I cross the line, and this is one of those situations. . . . but of course, I'm still going to write about it.]

This was going to be my first time foraging in the ass forest, and I wanted to have a reminder of my trip, a memento I could carry with me the rest of my life . . . so I decided to film us.

I planned this beforehand, but I was afraid she would decline, so instead of being mature and discussing this with Jaime, I just made the executive decision to get it on camera . . . without telling her.

That alone is pretty bad. But instead of just setting up a hidden camera . . . I got my friend to hide in my closet and film it.

No really—I know that I will burn in hell. At this point, I'm just hoping that my life can serve as a warning to others.

I left my door unlocked and we arranged it so that around midnight my friend would go over to my place and wait until my car pulled in, and then run into the closet and get the camera ready. The top half of the closet door was a French shutter, so it was easy to move the slats and give him a decent camera shot through the closed door.

By the time Jaime and I got to the bed, I was so drunk I had forgotten that he was filming this, and of course she had no idea he was there. After a few minutes of standard sex, she kinda stopped and said, all serious and in her best seductive soap opera voice, "I'm ready."

I quickly flipped her over and grabbed the brand new bottle of AstroGlide I had on my bedside table.

A week prior, after Jaime consented to buttsex, I realized that I didn't have any idea how to do it. How exactly do you fuck a girl in the ass? Luckily, I had the world's best anal sex informational resource at my disposal: The gay waiter. I consulted several gay waiters who worked at one of my father's restaurants about the mechanics of buttsex, and each one recommended AstroGlide as the lubricant of choice. Much to my dismay, I learned that spitting on your dick is not enough lube for buttsex. Stupid, lying porn movies.

The other important piece of advice I remembered was from Calvin, "Make sure you use enough, because if this is her first time, she'll be especially tight, and it might hurt her. Use enough to really loosen her up and go slow until she gets used to it. Then it's smooth sailing from there."

Well, since some is good, more is better, right? At 21, this seemed logical.

I opened the cap, crammed the bottle top into her asshole, and squeezed. I probably emptied half of the 4 ounces of AstroGlide into her. I have since learned from homosexuals that a 4-ounce bottle usually lasts them about 6 months. So yeah—I overdid it.

But Tucker Max wasn't done. Oh no, after depositing enough grease in her to run a Formula One racecar, I dumped half of what remained onto my cock and balls, really wanting to lube up because I didn't want her to be uncomfortable.

Really—consider my thought process: I was going to fuck her in the butt and film it without her consent, yet I was truly concerned about her personal comfort. Sometimes the contradictions in my personality even amuse me.

Predictably, I slid in with ease. She was a little tense at first, but with an Exxon Valdez size load spilled into her poop chute, she quickly loosened up and got into it. I liked it also; it had a different feel to it. Not as good as vaginal sex, a little grainy, kinda tight, but still very nice.

Before I knew it I was fucking her like the apocalypse was imminent, burying it to the hilt with impunity. After a few minutes I was ready to come. My urgency was expressed in my tempo, and I began really jackhammering her. As the excitement got the best of me, I pulled out too far and my dick came out of her ass. I kinda scrambled to grab my dick and put it back in so I could finish off inside of her, but before I could even get a hold of it and put it back in her ass, I heard a faint "psssst" sound and felt something wet and warm hit my crotch.

It was dark in the room (I was not smart or sober enough to leave the lights on for the camera), so after I looked down it took me a few seconds to realize that my dick, balls and groin area were covered in a viscous black liquid. I stopped moving and stared at my strangely colored crotch for a good 5 seconds, completely confused, until I realized what happened:

"Did you . . . did you just . . . shit on my dick?"

I reached down to touch the liquid feces, still in complete and utter disbelief that this girl shot explosive diarrhea on my penis, when, without warning, the smell hit me.

I have a very sensitive nose, and I have never been more repulsed by a smell in my life. The combination of synthetic AstroGlide and rancid stench of raw fecal matter combined to turn my stomach, which was full of seafood, veal and wine, completely over.

I tried to hold it back. I really did everything I could to stop myself, but there are certain physical reactions that are beyond conscious control. Before I knew what I was doing, it just came out:

"BBBBBBLLLLLLLLLLLLAAAAAAAAAAAAAAHHHHHHHH"

I vomited all over her ass. Into her crack. Into her asshole. On her ass cheeks. On the small of her back. Everywhere.

She turned her head, said, "Tucker, what are you doing?," saw me vomiting on her, screamed "Oh my God!," and immediately joined me:

"BBBBBBLLLLLLLLLLLLAAAAAAAAAAAAAAHHHHHHHH"

Watching her throw up on my bed made me vomit even more. Her vomiting all over my bed, me vomiting on her ass, the next step was almost inevitable.

I heard the loud CRASH first, turned to see my friend break through the shutters and rip the closet door off as he, the video camera, and the door tumbled out of the closet and crashed onto the floor next to us:

"BBBBBBLLLLLLLLLLLLAAAAAAAAAAAAAAAHHHHHHHHH"

The memory of the 2-second span where all three of us were vomiting at once is permanently seared into my brain. I have never heard anything like that symphony of sickness.

I think the crowning moment was when my eyes locked with Jaime's, I saw her moment of realization and then her quick shift from shock and surprise to complete and irreparable anger. Between bouts of hurling she flipped out:

"**OH MY GOD**—BBBLLLLAAAAHHHH—**YOU FILMED THIS, YOU ASSHOLE**—BBBLLLLAAAAHHHH—**HOW COULD YOU**—BBBLLLLAAAAHHHH—**I THOUGHT YOU LOVED ME**—BBBLLLLAAAAHHHH—**OH MY GOD**—BBBLLLLAAAAHHHH—**I LET YOU FUCK ME IN THE ASS**—BBBLLLLAAAAHHHH."

She tried to stand up, slipped on the huge puddle of backflow AstroGlide on the bed, and fell into both my pile and her pile of vomit, covering her body and hair in vomit, shit and anal lubricant. She flailed on the bed for a second, grabbed the top sheet, wrapped it around her, and started running out of my place. Still naked and retching, my dick covered in shit and lube, I followed her as far as my front door.

The last contact I ever had with her is the image I witnessed of her in a dead sprint, a shit, vomit and grease stained sheet stuck to her body, running from my apartment.

Postscript

The camera we used was one of those ancient fragile ones that filmed onto a VHS tape, and when he crashed out of the closet, the tape recorder and tape broke. It didn't occur to us at that the tape records the images magnetically, and we could take the actual tape itself and get someone to put it in another holster until after we had thrown it out. I know it seems stupid now, and believe me I kick myself about it everyday, but you should have seen the apartment afterwards—the tape was not a high priority. AstroGlide, shit and vomit covered EVERYTHING.

I had to rent one of those steam cleaners, buy a new mattress, and I STILL lost my deposit. It was impossible to get the smell out. The next month was like living in a sewer. Every girl I brought back to my place after that refused to stay there, and some even refused to sleep with me anywhere because of how my place smelled.

What I never found out, and I *still* want to know, is how the girl got home. I never heard from her again, and the mutual friend who introduced us called her but didn't get her calls returned. I never heard anything about her or from her again, even though she left her clothes and ID at my place (she wore a tight dress out that night, and didn't bring a purse or any money with her).

Can you picture that scene? What did she do, hop in a taxi? Wave down a passing car? Get on the bus? She lived at least 30 miles away, there is no way she walked home. It perplexes me to this day. I'm hoping she reads this. Maybe then I'll find out how she got home.

THIS'LL JUST HURT A LITTLE

Occurred—July 1998
Written—March 2005

Look, I know how bad some of these stories are. I know that in return for my youthful behavior, fate will give me five daughters and make them all vicious sluts who sleep with guys like me and then throw it in my face. I know that in any cosmically just afterlife, I deserve to have all order of awful punishments waiting for me, but in the corporeal interim one girl gave me a little bit of my own medicine. I normally like to focus my stories on how awesome I am, but it would be intellectually dishonest to leave this story out, because it really is funny to everyone but me:

I met "Stephanie" in South Beach. She was 19 at the time, smoking hot and still in college but was spending the summer in Miami doing modeling. Stephanie had the type of body you see on the cover of Maxim, except she was that hot in real life and not just airbrushed hot. Granted, she threw up a lot of dinners for that body, but considering that I wasn't paying for her food, I didn't care.

Like most super hot girls, she was incredibly insecure. She wore too much make up and not enough clothes, which is always a sign of despair in a woman. But she went beyond the normal female do-these-pants-make-me-look-fat insecurity, which is manageable, and graduated to full on, I-am-so-ugly-and-worthless, I-hate-myself, please-fuck-me-so-I-can-feel-close-to-someone insecurity. As a result of her severe and unquenchable insecurity, she was quite promiscuous, to the point where dating her was similar to the experience of sitting on a warm toilet seat: Even without seeing him walk out of the stall, you knew that someone else had been there only moments before you arrived.

I was 22 at the time and this sort of super-hot, super-insecure girl was right in my wheelhouse. It was my pattern at that time in my life; I would meet them, sense their insecurity, feed off it, play with it, and before I knew it the girl was in love with me. I would quickly dump her, and then there would be some sort of incident. I used to do this with pretty much every girl I met. My friends used to joke that my conversations with these girls would go like this:

Girl "Hi."
Tucker "Hi."
Girl "I'm lonely."
Tucker "Me too."
Girl "I love you."
Tucker "I love you too."

I honestly was NOT trying to fuck with these girls or hurt them, I was just too young to understand what I was doing, too stupid to figure it out, and too fucked up myself to stop. I have since learned how awful it was and now take pains to explain to women what I want and what I expect from them before we do anything, which is not only the right thing to do, it prevents the kind of issues that happened here from occurring later on.

So back to the story: We fucked and hung out and fucked some more, and I played the "great guy with an edge" part and let her totally fall for me. She told me she loved me, and I probably told her the same thing . . . but then I got bored, stopped calling, and left it at that. Another day, another hit, right? She wasn't ready to let go so easily.

She called and called and called, and I ignored and ignored and ignored, until one day she decided that she needed to take her anger out at me in person. I was drinking at a bar with some friends when she and her ugly friend (all hot girls have at least one ugly friend) came storming in.

Ugly friend "Why haven't you been calling her back?"
Tucker "Why haven't you been losing weight? Same reason."
Stephanie "SHE IS NOT FAT!"
Tucker "That's not what you say behind her back."

Her friend wasn't actually fat—only by ridiculous South Beach model standards—but the point was to undermine Stephanie's moral support, not to be factually correct.

Ugly friend "You called me fat?"
Stephanie "NO! TUCKER, YOU ASSHOLE! WHY DIDN'T YOU CALL ME BACK?"
Tucker "I didn't want to. Let it go, and just leave."
Stephanie "FUCK YOU! I DON'T CARE ANYWAY, YOU HAVE A SMALL DICK AND YOU SUCK IN BED AND YOU CUM QUICKLY!"

Oh, Steph . . . I wish you hadn't done that. Granted, I was a cowardly dickhead and I should have called you, but you called me out in front of other people . . . now I have to destroy you.

Tucker "Well, if that is the case, then why did you search me down to scream like a lunatic about getting dumped? Shouldn't you be happy about losing me instead of embarrassing yourself in public like this?"
Stephanie "I AM NOT EMBARRASSING MYSELF."
Tucker "Then why is everyone laughing at you? You want to know why I didn't call you back? Fine: you are insane and whorish. When you close that revolving man-door you call a vagina, come back and we'll see if I've gotten any better in bed."
Stephanie "FUCK YOU!"
Tucker "I'm sorry that you hate yourself and that no one loves you, but it's time to end this crazy show. Take the mountain troll and leave—we are trying to meet some women who are actually dateable."

She was utterly fucking speechless. At that moment, if she shitted a dictionary you couldn't have gotten a word from her. She turned to leave; if I was a good person I would have let it go there, but that's just not me:

Tucker "Didn't go as well as you thought it would, did it? I bet some random guy is getting pussy tonight! Female insecurity: It's the gift that keeps on giving!"

The whole little crowd that had gathered were laughing, even the bartenders. I am pretty sure by the time she hit the door Stephanie was in tears. Win the crowd and you always win the argument.

Tucker: 10
Stephanie: 0

I figured with that, it would be over, but two days later I got this voicemail:

"Tucker, it's Stephanie. I just got tested, and I have Chlamydia, and you need to get tested . . . jerk."

When I was young I was an idiot, but I wasn't stupid enough to blindly believe something an angry woman told me. She wouldn't give me the name of her doctor, so I demanded a copy of the test results. She mailed them to me a few days later, and well, there it was. A positive result for Chlamydia. Wow. I guess I have to get tested now. That sucks.

I had to go to one of the many free clinics in Florida, because I didn't want my father, whose insurance was covering me, to know that I might have Chlamydia. After fighting off the crack heads and prostitutes in the lobby, I tell the nurse I need a Chlamydia test. Do you know how they test for Chlamydia? Before going in, I didn't.

In the examination room, the nurse tells me to drop my pants and pulls out a 6 inch long thin metal rod and sticks a cotton swab on the end. No way . . . she can't be thinking . . . I mean, that can't go there . . . it won't fit . . . and besides, that would be inhumanly painful . . . well, then what is she going to do with it?

Nurse "OK, I am going to insert this into your urethra, and then—"
Tucker "WHAT?"
Nurse "I am going to insert this into your urethra, and—"
Tucker "NOPE! NOPE! NOT GOING TO HAPPEN! There is no way you are putting that massive metal Q-tip INTO MY DICK HOLE. No way."
Nurse "That's how we test for Chlamydia."
Tucker "No, there has to be another way. THERE HAS TO BE ANOTHER WAY. This is the 21st fucking century, there is never a need to stick metal into my dick. I'll pay—whatever, but THERE HAS TO BE ANOTHER WAY."
Nurse "Not to test for Chlamydia, there isn't."

I argued with her for 30 minutes, until she finally gave up and got a doctor. I argued with him for 20 minutes until he threatened to throw me out or call the police unless I got the test. Who knew the word "medieval quackery" could get someone so upset?

I wait for a week, making up bullshit reasons to turn down sex ("You can't come over tonight, I promised my grandmother I'd watch *Matlock* with her"), until my test result comes back, and much to my relief it was negative.

My first thought, being a naïve 22 year old was that she had just gotten it somewhere else, and I got lucky.

About a month later I saw her best friend out at a bar (not the ugly one, a different cute one). She saw me and started giggling and waving. At first I thought she was hitting on me, which made me laugh. Females are always fucking over their friends. So I went over and started talking to her, but she and all her friends kept giggling at me and kinda mocking me:

Tucker "What the fuck is so funny? Do I have a booger hanging out or something?"
Girl "Heehehehehhehehehehehhehehe—I can't tell you, you'll get mad."
Tucker "Just fucking tell me."
Girl "Well . . . Stephanie's friend is a nurse and she took someone else's positive test, whited out the name, put her name in there, photocopied it, and sent it to you! Heheheh!"
Tucker "What? She never had Chlamydia? So there was no chance that I had Chlamydia?"
Girl "Nope! Hehehhehehehehhehehe! Isn't that funny?!?"
Tucker "I GOT THAT AWFUL FUCKING TEST FOR NOTHING?"
Girl "Hehehhehehehehhehehe!"

Tucker: 10
Stephanie: 500

Winner: Stephanie

And that marked the last time in my life I ever underestimated the resourcefulness or motivation of a woman that I had wronged. Of course, if I was smarter I would have just stopped wronging women and instead been honest with both myself and them about who I was and what I wanted, but that didn't happen for another few years.

THE UT WEEKEND

Occurred—September 2002
Written—October 2002

Thursday

It's a typical Thursday in my life, noonish, I'm at the laundromat washing my filthy rags, when my cell phone buzzes. It's my cousin, TheCousin, who goes to the University of Tennessee.

"Dude—Tucker—I've got tickets to the UT-Miami game this weekend, AND it's Homecoming. You have to come down. It's going to be awesome."

I need no other persuasion. Check last minute flights to Knoxville: $1047. Looks like I'm driving.

The drive is no problem, until I get about 60 miles from the Kentucky-Tennessee border. I stop at some low-rent redneck place so I can pick up beer for the last hour of the drive. I want to arrive prepared.

I had heard about "dry" counties before, but they were still an abstract and foreign concept to me. I thought of them as silly anachronisms from a long distant prohibitionist past, something only found in the pages of National Geographic. I was wrong. Evidently, every county along I-75 from Richmond, KY to the Tennessee border is dry. THIS INFURIATED ME. I almost got into a fight with the redneck checkout woman when she told me I have 40 more miles to go before I could buy liquor.

"HOW AM I SUPPOSED TO ARRIVE DRUNK IF YOU WON'T SELL ME LIQUOR?? WHAT KIND OF BARBARISM IS THIS??"

I stopped right across the Tennessee border, excited by the sign that says "First Place to Buy Beer." But at the gas station, there didn't appear to be any alcohol for sale. I inquire:

Tucker "Don't you sell alcohol?"
Attendant "No, we're too close to a church."
Tucker "What? Didn't Jesus drink wine?"
Attendant "Yeah, well, 'round here, ya gotta go-on down da road bout'a half mile, to da bar."

Driven by my need for libation, I "go-on down da road bout'a half mile" and find, literally, a bar with a drive-thru liquor store attached. But apparently, this wasn't enough. They had firecrackers for sale, right there next to the beer, in the drive-thru liquor store. I'll just pause here and let everyone make up their own redneck jokes.

I arrive at my cousin's apartment, and it's a TV cliché of a college apartment; beer cans piled to the ceiling, pubic hairs all over the sink, filthy underwear hanging from the lamps. I go to get a beer from his fridge, and what does he have? Cans of "Country Club Malt Liquor." Sometimes, I really do think that God hates me.

After enduring a few cans of this ghetto swill, we head out to a line of bars that everyone in Knoxville calls "The Strip." Typical college town with typical college bars, we pick one and start the night.

Not ten minutes later, three girls walk in—two are attractive, one is fat. My cousin tells me that one of them has been sweating him for months. Which one? "The fat one."

I immediately walk over and point out my cousin to Fatty, and she almost knocks me and a random girl over to get to him and give him a hug. He gives me a look of, "I fucking hate you, and hope you immediately die an agonizing death."

The rest of the night saw two dramas play out simultaneously: While my cousin tried to fend off the obvious and painful advances of Fatty, on my side the two attractive girls were battling to decide which one was going to hook up with me. It wasn't that I was so incredibly charming. The 1st Law of Scarcity was at work; two of them plus one of me equals my desirability increasing substantially. It was awesome. They were being catty bitches to each other, each one trying to monopolize my attention and push the other one out. It was like a bad episode of *Elimidate*.

Apparently, I didn't have much of a say in the matter, but I was rooting for the short girl; she had the better face, and seemed somewhat intelligent. My cousin saw what was going on, knew I liked the short girl, knew I was drunk, and set the match to the gasoline:

TheCousin "Hey Tucker, you know she's French, don't you?"
Tucker "Oh hell no—You're French?"
Girl "My parents are, but I was born here. I want to move to France after graduation."
Tucker "You fucking cheese-eating surrender monkey. I thought someone stunk around here. So if I start speaking German can I push you around and take all your stuff? Those hairy fucking stink-bags would be speaking Kraut right now if it wasn't for us, and they aren't the least bit appreciative. I hope they all fucking die, and your frog-sympathizing ass with them."

That pretty much settled it: I am going home with the tall one. The four of us head back to her apartment, and as we walk in, she tells us to be quiet, because her roommate is sleeping, and she is bipolar and will flip out. Telling me this, especially when I'm drunk, is akin to letting a starving, rabid pit bull loose in a Montessori school.

"Give me and TheCousin ten minutes with her; she'll be trying to hang herself with her pantyhose. HEY—CRAZY! COME OUT HERE. I WANT TO POINT OUT YOUR FLAWS AND SHORTCOMINGS. I BET YOUR DAD DOESN'T LOVE YOU, DOES HE?"

The tall girl and I eventually go into the bedroom, leaving my cousin on the sofa to be devoured by Fatty. During foreplay banter, tall girl makes a request:

Girl "Massage my forearm. It's sore."
Tucker "Right. The only way I'm doing that is if it's a post-coital activity."
Girl "What? I don't speak Spanish."

Oh boy . . . it's a good thing I was drunk.

This girl had a nose job and told me that she has to use Q-tips to get the boogers out of her nose, because the surgery left her nostril holes too small for her fingers to get into. She got mad when I tested this by trying to stick my fingers into her nose. By god, she was right; I couldn't even get my pinky in there.

Ten minutes later she told me that she was so poor growing up that there were times when she and her mom ate only potatoes and peanut butter sandwiches. My response, "I guess stripping really does pay sometimes, doesn't it?" She got mad, but hey, if she can't take a joke, fuck her.

Friday

I wake up the next morning and find my cousin, naked, sheets wrapped clumsily around his torso, asleep on the floor next to the sofa. Why the floor? Because Fatty was so big that both of them couldn't fit on the sofa at the same time. I was in tears laughing at the scene. We eventually leave, telling the girls lies about how we'll call them later. As soon as we get outside, my cousin flips.

TheCousin "I cannot believe you made me do that. It was awful. She said I was only the second person she'd ever had sex with, which I don't doubt, because honestly—who would want to have sex with her? Except for people whose asshole cousin set them up with her, of course."
Tucker [I could barely get this out between fits of laughter] "She had a hot face."
TheCousin "Oh yeah, asshole, she'd be hot as hell if she wasn't fat as fuck. Eat shit and die, you cocksucker."
Tucker "Well, at least she had big tits."
TheCousin "Yeah, that was the best part. She thought she was hot because she had such big tits, but you didn't notice them because they were resting on her stomach. They were like bags of oatmeal."

I really hope his parents read this story.

TheCousin is currently finishing his undergraduate studies at the University of Tennessee because he was kicked out of the Merchant Marine Academy. Why? He was on restriction, and went off campus to get a sandwich. He'd gotten in so much trouble during his four years there, that this was enough to get him kicked out—THREE DAYS BEFORE HIS GRADUATION. Yes, he is obviously related to me.

TheCousin and I went back to his place, and he took a shower, scrubbing himself like a rape victim. He had a late English class that day, and I decided to tag along and see what it was like. I went to public school in Kentucky, and I say this now with full understanding of the meaning: That class, a 300-level class, was possibly the biggest farce of education I have ever seen. I've heard 14 year old meth-addicted Thai prostitutes say more prescient things than the woman that was supposedly a "professor." I had a hard time believing that this was a class. I wish I could give you a recap of the conversation, but that would be like trying to recount the disjointed ramblings of a senilic nursing home sewing circle. That "school" is a joke. I would have learned more watching a Special Olympics spelling bee.

After class, my cousin showed me around the campus. There were beautiful women everywhere. Wanting to test my cousin's game, I dared him to approach a random girl and invite her to the lacrosse party we were going to that night. He casually sauntered up to a beautiful girl, used some dumbshit line, and she looked at him with such shock and disgust I almost fell over laughing. She looked like a homeless person had asked her to wash his ass. Of course, I wasn't helping much. I came up right behind him and said, "Is he giving you that lacrosse party line? It doesn't exist. If you show up to that address, he's going to drag you into an alley and beat and rape you."

My cousin wasn't that upset, because he said that there would be plenty of lacrosse groupies at the party. He calls them "lacrosse-stitutes."

The highlight of the campus tour was when we came across this old guy standing on a corner with a megaphone, preaching to everyone about the Bible and Jesus and whatnot. He had serious mental problems, but was nonetheless hilarious. I loved him. He was castigating and vilifying every attractive girl that walked by. I stopped for awhile to provoke him. Some samples:

Me "What do you think about that girl?"
Him "She will burn in the fires of hell for her heresy! The Lord forbids such dress!"
Me "Hey man, what about her? Look at her skirt man, that's pretty tempting."
Him "HARLOT! JEZEBEL! She is a WHORE, WANTON IN HER DEBAUCHERY!!"
Me "Good Lord! Look at that blonde girl. I'd sell my soul for her."
Him "DO NOT FALL VICTIM TO HER TEMPTATION! She is a com-

mon prostitute, smeared with the paint of seduction, flaunting her wiles for Satan!"
Me "She owes us a rib, right?"
Him "MORE THAN A RIB! SHE OWES US OUR VIRTUE!! SHAMELESS STRUMPET!!

For my money, there is nothing funnier than provoking idiots. I could have hung out with that guy all day, but there was alcohol to be consumed and women to be exploited, so it was off to the party.

My cousin is also the assistant men's lacrosse coach at UT. He would play for UT, but he used up his four years of eligibility before he got kicked out of the academy. He is like a grad assistant, and hangs out with the team a lot, thus we went to their party that night at the lacrosse house. At one point in the night, I got to trading stories, and these three guys I met had some great ones:

Guy #1 told me that, "I'm not drinking in the shower anymore, because the last time I did that I woke up with no hair." Apparently, one time he passed out in the shower, slammed his head on the wall and got a concussion. His roommates, instead of helping him, came in and shaved all the hair off his body.

Guy #2 told me a story about how one time he got so drunk on Red Bull and vodka that when he woke up the next day, his mother came in his room and showed him the police report from the night before. He had NO MEMORY of this, but, according to the police report, he had driven his car into a house, fought the police when they came to the accident scene, spit on several cops at the police station, and got a DUI with a .25 blood alcohol level.

Guy #3 (actually TheCousin), told me a story about when he was in Europe and hooked with up a Swedish girl. She was giving him head when he started taking off her pants and said, "Alright, we have to have sex," to which she responded, "I don't know—I can't have another abortion." He said there is no quicker way to lose an erection. We all agreed.

At some point later, I drunk dialed a friend of mine. The conversation went like this:

Tucker "AAY, waz up?"
Friend "Tucker, what are you saying?"

Tucker "Am I slurrin' my speech?"
Friend "Are you what?"
Tucker "Yeaaa, everbuddies a comedian."

I was sitting in the kitchen trying to hit on this one girl, and it wasn't going well. So, in typical Tucker fashion I just swung for the fences:

Tucker "Why don't you come over here and sit on my lap."
Redhead "Why?"
Tucker "Because then your cooch will be up against my crotch."

It didn't work well.

People started doing keg stands, which led to perhaps the defining moment of the trip. This one girl, who was ugly and a bitch (thus, didn't have basic human rights) started doing one. Don't ask me why I did this, because I have no idea why, but when she was upside down, legs spread apart, I punched her right in the vagina. This caused her to violently spit up the beer she was trying to consume, and fall backwards into the two people holding her up, all of them splashing to the mud.

I ran off, laughing so hysterically I couldn't breathe. Thankfully in the alcohol-addled confusion, no one noticed who did it.

I ended up leaving the party with a girl who was an alumnus (remember, it was Homecoming). We'll call her "Melissa." The only problem was that she didn't live in Knoxville, and I couldn't find my cousin or his apartment, so we had to go to her friend's place where she was staying for the weekend. This wasn't that bad, except that we had to sleep on the sofa. I hook up in style.

Saturday

The next morning Melissa and I start catching up on everything we missed the night before. For instance, she didn't remember my name.

It turns out she is a Special Education teacher, and she told me some great stories about her students. Sometimes when she gets frustrated with them she'll start moaning and walking around all weird and say, "I'm not Miss Cochran anymore, I'M A MUMMY!" then they all freak out and run around the room screaming. Her school is by an Army base, and every time a helicopter flies over, she yells at her kids, "WAVE!

Wave to the people dying for your country!" and they all run to the window and wave at the helicopter.

She teaches kids in grades 2–4, and she often has them spell. Sometimes, even though she uses simple words, she has to use creative grammar to get them to understand what she wants them to spell, and even then it doesn't always work. One spelling exchange:

Melissa "Is . . . Is you my friend . . . Is"
Kid "Yes Miss Cochran, I am."
Melissa "No, I want you to spell 'is.'"

She said the hardest part of the job is the random and violent emotional outbursts of the kids. Many of them have severe behavioral problems, and sometimes they just flip out. She's had to learn several effective ways to "restrain them without leaving marks." One of the best ways to control them is with sugar. Her quote, "Retards will do anything for candy."

Some other random conversations:

Me "Do you actually call them 'retards.'"
Her "We're not supposed to."
Me "So that's a yes?"
Her "Well . . . not to their face."
Me "Do you ever mess with them in a mean way, like tell them that God hates them because they're retarded?"
Her "NO!"
Me "You ever put signs on their back that say 'Kick me, I'm Retarded?'"
Her "NO! TUCKER!"
Me "Or make them wear a dunce cap that has 'Retard' written on it."
Her "NO! You're mean! What would you do if you had a retarded child?"
Me "I'd bash its head against a rock, and have another kid."
Her "Oh my god!"

She loved it. Thought I was hilarious. We were still talking about tards when the girl she was staying with got up and started cleaning the apartment and talking to Melissa. Then she abruptly turned to me, and said, "I'm sorry, who are you?" Melissa cut in and explained, "Oh, this is Tucker. He was too drunk to find his apartment last night, so we came here." This explanation satisfied the girl. Later in their conversation something was said, not directly to me, that I commented on. Melissa turned to me and said, "Shhh. You can't talk—you're a random."

I got Melissa's cell phone number and eventually made it back to my cousin's place. I changed clothes and we headed out for the pre-game partying at the lacrosse house. On the way to the party, my cousin and I stopped at a liquor store to pick up some hard stuff. I go in while my cousin waits in the car, talking to someone on his cell phone. He later described the next scene as such,

"I knew it was going to be trouble when Tucker came out of the liquor store giggling like a 12-year old girl."

I had purchased Everclear, which is pure grain alcohol. 190 proof. The bottle has three prominently displayed warning labels:

"Caution: Extremely Flammable!"
"Caution: Over consumption may be dangerous to health!"
"Not Intended to Be Consumed Without Non-Alcoholic Mixers."

Sounds like a wager to me!

I bought a liter of Everclear, a quart of Gatorade, and a can of Red Bull, and poured all of it into my CamelBak. I come prepared.

We arrive at the lacrosse house, and I begin sucking back the Everclear/Gatorade/Red Bull mixture, which I will hereafter refer to as "Tucker Death Mix." It tasted like ghetto romance. It was awesome.

The lacrosse house sits in a busy corner on campus, and has a huge wraparound porch, where me, my cousin, and a bunch of lacrosse players and lacrosse-stitutes were hanging out. The only problem: Everclear doesn't get me drunk. It turns me into a raving lunatic. It has the same effect as a nail gun to my frontal lobes. I became Phinneus Gage; I lost what little social tact I have, and shouted anything rude I could think of. Starting with a 10 person audience, I started making fun of everyone that walked by the porch. I was too drunk and maniacal to remember everything that I said, but here is a sampling:

- An ugly guy: "Holy crap, looks like God screwed up. Don't worry you'll find an ugly girl that'll love you."

- A hot girl: "You have great tits; they'll get you a husband some day. If you don't fuck them floppy, that is."
- A guy with orange, black and white camouflage overalls (UT colors): "OH MY GOD! DID A BLIND PERSON WHO HATES YOU PICK OUT YOUR CLOTHES! LOOK AT YOURSELF!? LOOK AT WHAT YOU ARE WEARING!! YOU DEFINE THE WORDS "REDNECK LOSER" EXAMINE YOUR LIFE!!"
- A big fat black guy with cornrows: "HEY HEY HEEY! FAT ALBERT FUCKED LUDACRIS AND THEY HAD A SON!"
- A fat white guy in camouflage pants: "LOOK OUT! IT'S THE PILLSBURY COMMANDO! ALL YOU CAN EAT?!? THE JOKE'S ON THEM!!! Hmmm, steak or chicken, steak or chicken? WHY NOT BOTH? SAY GOODBYE TO ALL THE LEFTOVERS."
- A woman with the worst, most disheveled hair I have ever seen: "OH MY GOD! Where did you get your hair done? A wind tunnel? A bombing range? The "I Hate Myself Salon?" Hey grandma, the heroin chic look went out years ago. Do you realize that you are in public?"
- A guy with a mullet: "YEAAAAHHHH! My first mullet in Tennessee! WELL STOMP ON FROGS AND SHOVE A CROW BAR UP MY NOSE!! WELL PAINT ME RED AND NAIL ME TO THE BARN!! HEY MAN! LET'S DRINK SOME MOONSHINE AND SET SOME FIRES! COME ON BUDDY!!"

I was like this for a solid two hours. One girl had to go inside twice to fix her mascara, which had run all over her face from the tears she was crying while laughing. By the time we headed to the game, there were about 40 people hanging out on the porch listening to me rip everyone that walked by. I am convinced that the only reason no one tried to kick my ass is because there were several large guys hanging out with me.

Let me just say this: There is nothing better than college football Saturday in the South. The weather is warm, the liquor is bountiful, the barbecue is sumptuous, there are countless hot girls in sun dresses, and all of it is topped off with three hours of brutal, modern gladiatorial competition for your enjoyment. After the game, you go home, have drunk sex and pass out. What beats that?

We get to the game, and our seats are 20 rows up on the 40 yard line.

Awesome. The only problem: It's UT-Miami. I mean honestly, who do you root for, the rapists or the murderers? I hate both teams. I figured I would just root for myself to find a nice girl.

I got a free coke at the game by telling one of the black girls working the counter that she looked "like a Hallee Berry posta." Some guy at the game almost tried to kick my ass when he was looking for his girlfriend, and I told him, "Your girlfriend left with a bunch of black guys."

This one girl, after drinking deeply from my CamelBak, informs that she is not in a sorority. Why? Because she was kicked out for leaving dirty condoms outside her room. She got mad when I asked her why she didn't just save everyone the trouble and tattoo 'I'm a whore' on her forehead.

My idiot cousin had spent the entire pre-game, and game itself, trying to get laid by offering pulls from my CamelBak to every girl at the game. I thought this was no big deal since alcohol kills bacteria and germs. Yeah, well, apparently not these germs. Before halftime, I was carrying the entire plethora of viruses, germs and bacteria of every cocksmoking whore at UT. By the time I left the game I was so sick my lymph nodes looked like I had goiter.

My cousin, a friend and I find my car, which was parked on a side street, completely boxed in. The car behind us pulled up literally to the bumper. Still feeling the effects of the Tucker Death Mix, I get in my car and start alternately backing into the car behind me and bumping the car in front of me. This doesn't bother me because I got this car for free. After smashing into the car behind me a good five or six times, a couple girls come out of the house across the street, and start yelling at me from their porch.

"HEY!! THAT'S MY CAR!!"
"WELL WHY THE FUCK DID YOU PARK IT SO CLOSE TO MINE?"
"DON'T SMASH IT UP!"
"Alright, then come move it. I'll wait."
A reasonable request, I thought.

Instead, the girl just stood there for about 5 seconds, staring at me, and then raised a large piece of posterboard that had, "Not So Fast My Friend!" written on it. I hate Lee Corso, so I backed into her car a few more times just for spite, and drove off.

I was home at 6, and by 8, I was dead. Saturday night in Knoxville, and I couldn't make it out. Stupid poetic justice.

Did I just pack it in? Nope. I called Melissa, and she came over to my cousin's place, and we had a great time hanging out, eating pizza, and having lots of sex. She stayed there all night with me. I have to say this about the girl: she is awesome. I was a mess, blowing my nose, coughing like a TB patient, farting like Jim Belushi, making rude comments. She was fine with it. I guess working with retards is the perfect precursor to hanging out with me.

THE PEE BLAME

Occurred—July 2003
Written—July 2003

When I was visiting Austin, I met some frat guys at the University of Texas. They were pretty cool (read: they worshiped me), so one weekend I accepted an invite to a party they were throwing.

Let me explain something to all of you out there who didn't go to college: The easiest place to get laid on earth (without paying) is an American college campus. And the easiest place on a college campus to get laid is a frat party. You don't need ANY game to get laid at a frat party. You generally don't need much game to pick up 18-21 year old girls anyway, but college frat parties are ridiculous. It's like a clearance sale in the pussy aisle at the hook-up store; Everything Must Go! No Reasonable Offer Refused!

One girl in particular drove this point home for me. Towards the end of the night, I was walking to the bathroom to urinate, when I saw a girl I had been talking to earlier. I called her over to me and explained my problem, "I'm drunk and can't undo my jeans. I need to get them off or I'll pee in my pants."

I fully expected her to look at me like I had just told her to kick a kitten into a wood chipper. I mean come on—who would buy that stupid line?

A drunk college girl at a frat party, that's who.

She laughed, remembered my name from earlier, told me I was cute, and undid my jeans for me. Well . . . fuck me, it's time to push it. After all, the only way to see how far she'll go is to ask, "Will you hold it for me; I'm going to pee on my hands if I try to do it."

Laughing again, she led me into the bathroom, and though she declined to actually hold my penis while I pissed, she did stand behind me, hold my hips and say, "I'll stand here and be a spotter for you."

Tucker being Tucker, I decide to test her spotter skills. I pissed on the wall to the right side of the urinal, and she laughed and said, "Move left." I shifted all the way to the left, and pissed on the wall to the left of the urinal. She giggled and kind of nudged my hips so that I peed in the urinal. Meanwhile, she checked out my package the whole time; I guess this was our foreplay.

She then zipped my jeans back up, being considerate and observant enough to make sure not to catch my penis in the zipper, and we got another beer together. I honestly don't remember what I said to her over the next ten minutes, but it ended with, "Let's get out of here," and her following me home. I was only staying a block away from the frat house, so this worked out well, as my driving skills at this point would have been about equivalent to a narcoleptic chimp.

At my place, clothes come off and fucking starts. I am completely shit-housed drunk AND wearing a condom . . . yeeeah, Tucker is not coming tonight. I had a hard-on, but Jenna Jameson on prison-quality crystal meth wouldn't have had enough energy and skill to get me off.

I started to slow down because I wasn't going to cum and I was tired and drunk, but she was into it, and told me to keep going. What? Fine, I go for another 5 minutes, get bored and stop . . . and AGAIN she tells me to keep going because she is close.

Well thanks bitch—I'M NOT.

I start pumping again, but the situation quickly becomes intolerable: I can't feel anything, the latex is chafing and hot, and I am so drunk I am about to vomit. Without any other options, I do something I have never done before, and honestly didn't even think guys could do:

I faked it.

I swear to all I find holy (i.e. open bars, hot women and money I don't have to work for), I pumped real hard for ten seconds and then collapsed. She kind of let out a sigh, and said she wished I had kept going because she was almost there. I started laughing, "Yeah, well my penis has a mind of its own." We both pass out, me giggling to myself about how sneaky I am.

The next morning I wake up completely covered in urine. I know it's urine because it SMELLS. I know it's me because my side of the bed is soaked, and she is on the other side of the bed and only slightly wet on her side, not her crotch.

[The irony of this is revolting. Not even two months earlier, a girl peed in my bed and I made fun of her ruthlessly for it. Yes the gods of alcohol obviously have a sense of humor, and yes they are using it to mock me.]

My bed is completely fucked up. There is piss everywhere. What do I do? Do I just accept the fact that I am an incontinent buffoon who wets his bed?

No. I decide to stand against the gods, to deny them pleasure at my expense and to change their bankrupt prophecy. Tucker Max does not bow to fate.

I get up and change my clothes, throwing my piss stained t-shirt into the washer. I delicately roll her onto my side of the bed, the urine-soaked side, and then pour some lukewarm water on her crotch. As I do this, she starts waking up, so I shake her to confuse her and yell, "Wake up. WAKE UP!"

She slowly wakes up, looks around, and is obviously still drunk. Before she can even process what is going on I tell her to look down. She sees the massive dark stain and feels her wet shirt (We both had shirts on, as we were too drunk/horny to fully disrobe before fucking). I help her out in case she is still confused:

Tucker "You fucking pissed my bed. You PISSED in my BED."
Girl "What?" She reached down and touched the sheets, "OH MY GOD!"
Tucker "Why would you do this? Could you not find the toilet?"
Girl "No . . . I . . . this never . . . I've never . . . oh dear god!"
Tucker "God is not going to clean this piss up."
Girl "I'm so sorry, I've never . . . I can't believe I was that drunk. I am so embarrassed."
Tucker "No shit. I'd be embarrassed too if I pissed in someone's bed."

I got up and went to the bathroom because I just couldn't hold in my laughter anymore. I came back to my bedroom and she was standing there, in utter disbelief, staring at the bed, nearly in tears. She turns to me and says,

"I can't believe I drank that much last night . . . I still have to pee right now! How could I pee all that out in my sleep and still need to pee more in the morning???"

I almost lost it again. I had to leave the room, pretending to be in anger but nearly biting through my hand to suppress the laughter. I got into the shower and laughed for a good ten minutes while in there.

When I got out she had already stripped the sheets and put them in the washer, on top of my piss clothes that she didn't notice. She apologized about 100 times, wrote me a check for a new mattress, and then got out of my place as soon as she could. Predictably, she did not leave a number.

I nearly framed the check. I didn't cash it because even I have limits on how much I will exploit someone. I took all her dignity, I didn't need her money too.

TUCKER GOES TO A HOCKEY GAME

Occurred—October 2002
Written—November 2002

Sometimes even I need a night off, and after an intense Thursday and Friday I decided to spend a relaxing Saturday hanging out with a friend of mine from high school who happened to be in town that night, "Mark."

He shows up at my place around 4pm with a 30-pack of Old Style, which we manage to polish off rather quickly. As I am trying to decide how to steal some more beer from my neighbors, a commercial comes on for a regional minor league professional hockey team, which coincidentally has a game in two hours. Mark wants to go see hockey. He considers it the best idea of all time. I disagree. I want a relaxing night.

Somehow he manages to convince me that drinking 15 beers and then going to a hockey game can qualify as a "relaxing night." But not only does he want to go to the hockey game, he desperately wants to bring the CamelBak, having read about it in the UT Weekend story. I pause and consider my options. I can:

A) refuse to go anywhere, knowing myself well enough to see that this night is obviously on course to become a catastrophic trainwreck.
B) agree to go to the hockey game, but refuse to bring along the CamelBak, because it will quite obviously result in my early demise.
C) say "fuck it," throw all caution and temperance to the wind, go to the game with the CamelBak full of Tucker Death Mix, and dare the consequences of my actions to catch up with me.

You've read my other stories, what do you think I did?

I load up the CamelBak with Tucker Death Mix, but this time, instead of Everclear, I use real Kentucky moonshine. My mother lives in Kentucky, and one of her neighbors makes moonshine in his barn. Seriously.

We arrive at the arena fully shit-housed. We don't have tickets, and the only scalper we can find has got to be the dirtiest, poorest, shittiest looking crack addict in Chicago. He is trying to sell two ratty tickets. They look like he got them with a McDonald's Super Value meal. This does not stop me from bargaining with him. I am a master negotiator, especially when drunk:

Tucker "How much for the tickets?"
Crack fiend "40 each."
Tucker "Get the fuck outta here? Do we get a handjob too? Are you kidding? I'll give 20. Total."
Crack fiend "Awww, come'on man. Deez is good seaats, yo."
Tucker "You know . . . scalping is illegal."
Crack fiend "Man, don gimme dat shit. Deez is 8th row, at the co'na."
Tucker "40 is steep. After all, you're just going to spend the money on crack."
Crack fiend "Man, fuck you."

We settle on $40 total, find our seats right before the game starts, and much to my displeasure, there are about 10 women total in the entire arena. Not that we came to the game to pick up girls, but there is always that hope. I loudly say to Mark, "Jesus H Christ. What the fuck is this, Gay Hockey Night?" These two dorks on the left look at me horrified, while the old guys on the right start laughing. Fuck the idiots on the left.

We start talking to the old guys, bitching about women and whatnot. One of them starts telling us a story. "Yeah, I was with these two beautiful girls the other night. Wonderful girls. The night was going great until they started using all sorts of horrible four-letter words. Horrible, horrible four letter words, like "can't" . . . "won't" . . . "don't" . . . "stop." Horrible, horrible four letter words." These old guys were cracking us up. Of course, we were quickly approaching Tucker Max Drunk; a dancing Tele-Tubby would probably have had us in tears.

Because I can see the entertainment value from miles away, I start talking to the low-rent metrosexual on my left. I immediately wanted to punch him in the face. He was one of those annoying pseudo-intellectuals; horn-rimmed glasses, drinks Pinot Grigio by the glass at bars, buys poetry books but never reads them, avoids red meat, shops at the Kiehls counter, acts indignantly offended by Howard Stern, likes to drop names like "Foucault" and "Sartre" in normal conversation. We all know one or two. I kept laughing to myself, because he looked exactly like Chachi from *Happy Days*. He thought he was better than me because I was drunk and acting like an idiot, while he was composed and polite. Yeah, I got something for him.

He condescendingly asks me what I do, and I tell him I'm a writer. Then the fun began:

Him "Hmm. I used to be a writer, until I went to law school." A fastball down the middle.
Me "Really? I never would have guessed. Where'd you go to law school?"
Him "The University of Texas."
Me "Well, I guess not everyone can go to a good school. So what did you write?"
Him "Mostly freelance think-pieces for magazines and newspapers."
Me "So you were an out-of-work copy editor?"
Him "Uh . . . no. My last piece was published in the Utne Reader."

IS THIS GUY FUCKING SERIOUS?

Me "I bet you're very proud." I laughed, but he just ignored me. "So what do you do now?"
Him "Uh . . . well, I'm a lawyer. That's why I went to law school."
Me "Suuuper. So, Chachi, where are you from?"
Him "I'm from Texas."
Me "I bet you were real popular there."

He didn't respond. Mark and I order a couple more beers. The game was boring, so I keep fucking with Chachi. His aggravation is growing visibly, but he's the type that signs anti-sweatshop petitions, so I'm not concerned about any forthcoming violence. I continue:

Me "I've been to Texas. I liked it. But I've heard some strange things about the laws there. You're a lawyer: Is it true that you can have open containers in the car, as long there is one less than the number of people in the car?"
Him "Uh . . . I'm not really sure. We didn't really study that in law school."

Me "Did you ever drink?"
Him "Uh . . . yeah."
Me "And you never drove afterwards?"
Him "Uh . . . no."
Me "You don't believe all that Mothers Against Drunk Driving propaganda do you?" He ignored me, so I continued, "Is it true that in Texas you can shoot someone if you find them sleeping with your wife?"
Him "No, that's not true. It's a myth."
Me "I don't know Chachi, I think it's true. What about if you come home, and you find a guy on your porch, nosing around, and your wife is inside, and she's naked. Can you shoot him then?"
Him "No."
Me "What about your wife, can you shoot her?" He didn't answer. "What if there's a guy in your yard, and he's naked, and he's looking at you funny. I bet you can shoot him then."
Him "No, you can't."
Me "What if some guy is on your porch, and he's dancing all funny, like a hippie, and your wife thinks he's attractive? Can you shoot either of them? What is the self-defense standard in Texas—'He needed killin'?'"
Him "What? Are you serious?"
Me "I'm just trying to figure out the law here buddy. You never know when you might have to come out blazing."

He and his friend get up and leave, but he leaves his beer in the cup holder. As soon as he was out of sight, I pour half his beer into mine, finish it off, and head to the bathroom. When I get there, I see Chachi standing at the urinal, so I bust out in song:

"THE STARS AT NIGHT, ARE BIG AND BRIGHT [**CLAP**] [**CLAP**] [**CLAP**] [**CLAP**] DEEP IN THE HEART OF TEXAS!!"

He looks over, not amused. I make a little gun with my thumb and index finger, point it at him, and go "POW!" He is even less amused. Fuck him if he can't take a joke.

The second period comes around, and Chachi doesn't return to his seat, so I finish his beer. He's not going to need it. Mark is busy sucking on the CamelBak, and appears ready to slip into a coma. Then it happens, that defining moment that I wait for every time I go out drinking:

Right before the second intermission, some guy comes up and asks our section if anyone wants to go on the ice and shoot pucks against the mascot,

"OH ME ME ME!! I WANT TO DO IT!! ME ME ME!!"

The guy kinda stares at me hesitantly, but since no one else in the ¼ full section dares get up and challenge my drunken enthusiasm, I become the chosen one. I get down to the staging area behind the penalty box, and the other two participants are a girl who was so skinny she looked like she spent three weeks on the Miami 48-hour Miracle Diet, and a fat guy who uncannily resembled the Comic Book Guy from *The Simpsons*. I asked him if he owns a comic book store, and I guess this is a joke he's heard often, because he got kinda mad at me. Unsure of how to react to his visible anger, I say "Worst. Reaction. Ever." This didn't help.

The waifish usher explains the rules to us: We get a hockey stick and a puck, and are allowed to take one shot against the mascot, this big, furry, dog looking thing. Anyone who scores gets tickets to the next game. I chime in,

Tucker "I don't want to go to the next game. This place sucks."
Usher [stares at me with contempt for a minute] "You can't take your beer on the ice with you."

Once on the ice I flip off the crowd, and start my advance on the mascot. Right before I am about to shoot the puck, genius strikes me.

I hurl my stick at the mascot to confuse him, kick the puck into the goal, tackle the mascot into the net, pull his jersey over his head, and start delivering directed body shots into his ribs.

Raise your hand up if you've ever heard a professional team mascot say "What the fuck are you doing, you asshole?"

I'm not sure if I have ever laughed so hard as when this big fuzzy brown head let loose with a rapid fire barrage of curse words. I am so in tears laughing at him, that I can barely keep up giving him body shots. Of course, my laughter only makes him madder, and I eventually lose the upper hand. He gets me rolled over and ends up on top of me. He is now completely engrossed in the fight, and starts hitting me back, all while I am laughing hysterically.

The crowd went nuts. I mean honestly—picture this scene in your head.

I have no idea who took this pic, it was anonymously sent to me a week or so after the fight. Thanks, I guess.

The entire time, the announcer is standing 10 feet away, completely dumbfounded. He had no idea what to do or say, until the mascot got on top, when he finally comes over and pulls the mascot off of me. It actually took him a few minutes to get the mascot composed. The mascot had completely lost his shit; he wanted to keep fighting me, especially after I got up and threw my hands in the air, receiving boisterous cheers from the crowd.

I was escorted off the ice, to continued cheers, when someone who appeared to be in charge started throwing around a lot of fancy legal words like "assault" and "battery." I paused, staring at him while I composed my thoughts, and said,

Tucker "I'm sorry, but I stand by my decision. I am now a member of the elite club of people that have fought a professional team mascot. You sir, are not in that club."

He stared at me, completely silent, for what seemed like three or four minutes, and then just turned and walked away. I was kicked out of the area, and told not to ever come back.

I had to wait by the car for a good hour and a half until dumbass Mark came stumbling out. When I asked him why he was so late, and didn't leave when I was kicked out, he looked at me strangely and said,

"You got kicked out? What did you do?"

The Absinthe Donuts Story

Occurred—November 2002
Written—November 2002

I used to think that I'd seen everything. I had experienced so many things that I had become jaded with life; nothing affected me anymore. I was world-weary.

That was before I drank absinthe. That devil juice is brewed from the urine of Lucifer. Now I know why Van Gogh cut off his ear and why Toulouse-Lautrec painted funny looking midgets; it wasn't mental illness, it was the goddamn absinthe.

A few weeks ago, one of my old friends, we'll call him "Rich," was in town to visit. This is the story of that night:

6:00pm: Rich shows up at my place. I have not seen Rich in 7 years. He has put on at least 60 pounds of muscle. I am shocked at his size. He is with one of his friends, "Eddie." They are both in an elite special operations unit that is shipping to the middle east in a few weeks. Eddie is Hispanic, tall, angry, and muscular. He looks around my apartment as if deciding what piece of furniture he wants to break first. I consider that perhaps this wasn't a good idea.

6:01: "So Tucker, I hear you finally learned how to drink a little bit?" Rich smiles at me. They have 2 cases of beer with them. I think maybe this is not such a bad idea after all.

7:00: They tell me some of the best stories I have ever heard. Many are tales of clandestine and violent death brought upon unsuspecting international terrorists or stories of sex with third world hookers. I think that this was a good idea.

7:05: We finish our first case.

7:45: I tell them two of my best stories. They are in tears laughing. Eddie tells Rich that he was right, I am the funniest guy he's ever met. I now think that this was a great idea.

8:40: We have finished both cases. I am already 6 beers behind each of them, and feeling the alcohol. They look like they could do an iron man triathlon right now, even after 18 beers. I begin to think that maybe I am not in their league, drinking wise. This worries me. Then I remember that I am Tucker Max. I am no longer worried.

8:45: Eddie thinks my site is the greatest piece of literature in existence. He says that he aspires to be like me. He wants to hear more stories about me ridiculing fat people and hooking up with hot girls. I decide he is one of my best friends.

8:49: We walk to a pasta bar for dinner. The waitress is immediately displeased by our behavior, "We usually don't get people as drunk as you coming in here." I decide her attitude needs an adjustment, "Do you know who these guys are? They routinely risk their lives so you are free to toss your fat ass around Lincoln Park like some haughty tramp, and you question them? Woman, get us some food and liquor, and be quick about it."

8:50: The manager asks us to leave.

8:58: We go to McDonald's. The woman in front of me in line spends more than 5 seconds contemplating her order. This infuriates me, "WHAT ARE YOU LOOKING FOR?? MC-SEABASS?? IT'S THE GODDAMN MCDONALD'S MENU, IT'S BEEN THE SAME FOR TEN YEARS! IT'S ALL MCSHIT! JUST ORDER!"

8:59: She quickly departs the restaurant. One might have described her departure as "fleeing in terror."

9:00: I don't know what I want. I just point at the Dollar Menu and say, "Give me all of that."

9:05: I am displeased with what I get. I try to send back certain items, like the apple pie. The 14 year old Mexican boy working the Friday late shift doesn't understand. I get frustrated and just throw everything I don't like on the floor.

9:07: We decide to play Rich's favorite game: Window Pickle Races.

9:09: We have about 8 pickles on the window, each making ketchup and mustard streaked trips to the bottom. We argue about who owns each pickle. These become intense and profanity laced arguments. Military guys use very creative curse words. I didn't even know I had a "cock-holster" or a "man-pleaser."

9:14: The last people finally flee in terror. The restaurant is empty. We taunt them, and cheer as they leave. They, and their small children, are all cowards.

9:15: The manager comes out and asks us to leave. Eddie is confused, "We can't get kicked out of McDonald's? This is like the DMZ of drunk eating. THIS IS WHY WE CAME HERE!"

9:16: The manager is a frail Mexican woman. She is scared of us. She goes behind the counter, then tells us to leave again. She waves the phone at us, threatening police intervention. We go.

9:45: We arrive at the party. I find the friend who invited me, and introduce my friends.

9:46: We are apparently drunker than I calculated. My friend is appalled, "Dude, man . . . I told you not to show up this drunk." Apparently he is confused. I politely attempt to straighten him out, "Who the fuck are you talking to?" This angers him, "Man—look around. This isn't that type of party."

9:47: I spend a good 45 seconds perusing the scene. It is a large townhome. There is a big bar, with a bartender. There is a table of hors d'oeuvres. I see several button down striped shirts. A few anti-war buttons. A couple guys holding glasses of pinot grigio. I tell my friend, "You sir are incorrect. It most decidedly IS that type of party."

9:48: We walk directly to the bar. I turn to my friends, "Gentlemen—this is going to be a show. You kill terrorists; I destroy poseurs and idiots. Get a drink and watch the artist at work. These people think they're better'n me."

9:48: I order 3 top shelf vodkas. They only have well. This angers me, "WHAT KINDA LOW RENT SHIT IS THIS?" I argue with the bartender. I think he is hiding the good stuff from us. I tell him that my friends kill people for a living, and that unless he produces good vodka, he will become a "target of opportunity."

9:50: An attractive girl comes up and asks what the problem is. I tell her that the rat-fink bartender is trying to make us drink cheap donkey piss. She laughs at this. I shamelessly flirt with her. She flirts back. I tell her that flirting is nice, but it's not getting me drunk. She looks at me seductively, and tells me to follow her upstairs. "Can my friends come?" She smiles, "Of course."

9:51: Eddie whispers in my ear, "Man, I thought your stories were at least a little bullshit, but we haven't even had a drink and we're gonna run train. Rich was right; you are the fucking MAN."

9:52: She takes us to a bedroom. There are a few other people there. They are smoking pot and drinking. There is a solitary bottle on the table with greenish liquid in it. The label has the word "Absinthe" on it. I don't know what absinthe is. Whatever; if it is alcohol, I am not afraid.

9:53: The girl takes three glasses, pours sugar over ice, and then pours the green liquid over the ice. It turns clear. This fascinates us. She hands us the glasses, smiles, and says, "This is better than anything down there."

9:54: I take a sip. Goddamn—my neck muscles flex involuntarily. I can feel my heart start beating irregularly. This shit doesn't fuck around. I drink more.

9:56: The girl starts kissing one of the pot smokers. Eddie whispers to me, "So much for the gangbang." I frown at him, "How long have you known women? Dude—They're all whores. Except our mothers. Just stick to me, I'll find you some pink stink."

9:59: One of the guys tells us about absinthe. He says he brought it back from Europe because it is illegal in the US. Apparently, it is very strong (160 proof) and supposedly has hallucinogenic properties. I tell him he smells like patchouli oil and bong water. Rich and Eddie laugh hysterically. Tucker has an audience.

10:18: Absinthe is the fucking shit. I am on my second glass, and I'm Fucked-in-Half drunk. Rich and Eddie want to see full-on Drunk Insult Tucker. Loaded up with hallucinogenic alcohol, Tucker is happy to oblige.

10:20: We station ourselves in the kitchen. A fat girl walks in. It's game time, "Well, say goodbye to all the leftovers."

10:21: Apparently, this fatty seems to think she can hang. The Iraqi Army made better tactical decisions:

Fatty "What did you say?"
Tucker "Can you not hear me? Are your ears fat too?"
Fatty [Look of astonishment, stares at my friends cracking up] "EX-CUSE ME?"
Tucker "I'm sorry. Really I am. [I open the fridge] Would you like cheesecake or chocolate cake? Probably both, I'm guessing."
Fatty [Turns and leaves in utter astonishment]
Tucker "Hey Sara Lee, I was only kidding! COME BACK HERE—MY FRIEND LIKES TO GO HOGGIN. MORE CUSHION FOR THE PUSHIN! IT'S LIKE RIDING A MOPED!!"

Tucker has arrived.

10:23: Rich knows me from undergrad, and knows how to provoke me, "Come on man, you can do better. There are plenty of people around here to make fun of." Express elevator to hell, going down. I give him my voice recorder and a simple order, "Don't miss anything."

10:26: I see a girl wearing two colored tank tops over each other. This is too easy:

Tucker "Hey 1985 Madonna, are you gonna get the person who did that?"
Girl "Did what?"
Tucker "Spilled 80's all over you."
Girl [Confused look]
Tucker "I know I'd be pissed if I looked like an extra from *Desperately Seeking Susan*."

10:29: Eddie points out a girl wearing the standard anti-globalization outfit. It is topped off with a "No Blood for Oil" button. Rich whispers in my ear, "You gotta get her. Come on man. Do it—for us . . . for your country." Eddie starts humming God Bless America.

10:29: I storm over. Rich says into the voice recorder, "Target acquired . . . we are weapons hot."

10:30: I introduce myself to her as Alger Hiss. She doesn't get the joke. Time to be blunt:

Tucker "Do you hate the World Bank?"
Girl "Uhh, umm, well, I mean, yeah, I feel that . . ."
Tucker "You don't hate the World Bank."
Girl "I don't?"
Tucker "No. You're mad at your father. You just want daddy to hug you more."
Girl "What?"
Tucker "You were a sociology major weren't you?"
Girl "NO!"
Tucker "What was your major then? Cultural Studies?"
Girl [Pauses] "Uhhh, English Literature."
Tucker [Pause—to give her a look of contempt] "Did your parents send you a bill for college? Do those Marxist Literary Critique classes help you at Barnes and Noble?"
Girl "NO—I wor—"
Tucker "Shouldn't you be blocking an intersection right now? How many anti-sweatshop petitions have you signed—EVEN THOUGH YOU HAVE REEBOKS ON. Very-anti globalization to wear those with your animal tested Clinique make-up made in Nepal. Well, at least you're consistent in your shameless hypocrisy."
Girl "What a fascist piece of shi—"
Tucker "Wait—You ever wake up in the middle of the night because a couple of cats are clawing each other to death outside your window? That's what it's like listening to you speak."
Girl [A mishmash of stammered half insults]
Tucker "Seriously—If I stuck my dick in your mouth would that shut you up?"
Girl "Wha . . . YOU ARE SUCH AN ASSHOLE!"
Tucker "HEY—Don't blame me for the wound in your crotch." [As I walk off] "By the way, you owe us a rib."

10:31: I turn to Rich and Eddie: "She'll never recover from that. She'll never be the same. I've completely ruined a human being. Years of expensive therapy and costly drugs can't reverse that kind of damage . . . yeah, I have an upper management role in Hell reserved for me." Rich looks at me and says into the voice recorder, "Damage assessment: Total." I got the joke the next day.

10:32: We spend the next 45 minutes talking to girls. Surprisingly, most do not seem thrilled to talk to us.

11:16: The fat girl from the first kitchen encounter comes over. With reinforcements. Her backup: A small frail dork that looks like he just finished a Magic The Gathering tournament, a heinous Asian girl, and a greasy haired fat doofus in a camouflage vest. I ask you—Am I here right now? Is this my life?

11:17: The girl starts saying something about what a horrible person I am. I stare at her, but I am not listening. I am preparing myself. I am B-Rabbit. This is the final battle rap. I will win the hostile crowd:

[I interrupt the fat girl] "Ward, I think you're being a little hard on the Beaver, [as I point to each in turn] so is Eddie Haskell, Wally, and Mrs. Cleaver."

[To the fat guy with greasy hair in the camo vest] "Look out everyone! It's the Pillsbury Commando! Hey Chunk, when was the last time you washed your hair? Does it give you more hit points to have that grease helmet? I hate to break the news, but +5 defense only counts in Dungeons and Dragons."

[To the ugly Asian girl] "Why you no rike me? You want me frip over? You no piss me off! ME FIND YOU IN POCKING ROT!! YOU NO TAKE MING ARIVE!!"

[To the small frail dork—I notice he has a lazy eye] "Dude—Look at me when I'm talking to you—BOTH EYES AT ONCE. Are you really this ugly or are you just playing? EVERYONE, BE CAREFUL, THIS GUY LURKS UNDER THE STAIRS AND TRIES TO LICK YOUR SHOES WHEN YOU PASS BY!"

[To the original fatty, pause for effect] "Why do you do this to yourself? WHY DO YOU DO THIS TO YOURSELF? Look, I'm gonna give you some advice: Leave the party, take the geek squad with you, go to Denny's, order about 10 Grand Slam Breakfasts, and eat your pain away. Won't be the first time, will it?"

11:19: I am finished. The kitchen is quiet, except for Eddie and Rich laughing. The four freaks are completely speechless. Everyone is staring at me. I blurt out, "WHAT? I'm pretty sure it's what Jesus would've done." Eddie and Rich promptly remove me from the kitchen.

11:42: The absinthe is kicking into third gear. I am feeling euphoric.

Manic even. This is the weirdest drunk I've ever had. I decide it is time to get my little pencil wet.

11:54: I see a hot girl. I walk over and use one of my favorite lines, "Hi. I haven't insulted you yet, have I?" She laughs. I am in.

11:58: I see the large diamond and accompanying gold band on her finger. Hot Girl is Married Girl.

12:06: I talk to Married Girl for a few minutes. I try to think of a good way to broach the marriage subject to find out if she wants to hook up with me. This is difficult, as my mind is a spinning miasma of absinthe.

12:07: I can't think of anything new or good, so I decide to go with my standard married shtick, which has never worked for me, ever, not even once:

Tucker "So you're married?"
Married Girl "Yeah."
Tucker "Is it a good marriage?"

12:08: Married Girl looks at me, looks down, looks back at me, and almost breaks into tears. Married Girl begins pouring her heart out to me. I guess she didn't drink any absinthe. Because she is hot, I decide to be nice to her.

12:23: Married Girl gets to an emotional part and does actually start to cry. I suggest we go into another room so we can "talk in private." Married Girl readily agrees and tells me that I am "so nice."

12:45: Married Girl and I are hooking up. Holy shit this is working! Being nice is great! Who would have ever thought?!?

12:47: Married Girl breaks into tears again. I console her.

12:51: Married Girl and I are hooking up.

12:56: Married Girl breaks into tears. I console her. And undo her bra. With one hand. I got skillz.

12:59: Married Girl and I are hooking up.

1:05: Married Girl breaks into tears. I just stare at her. I suggest to Married Girl that perhaps the best thing to do right now is to go with what feels natural, and not worry about other painful things in her life.

As proof that I am doing this, I tell her that my friends are shipping to Iraq soon, but I'm still at a party hooking up with her. Married Girl agrees with this logic.

1:06: Married Girl and I are hooking up. Clothes come off.

1:12: Married Girl breaks into tears. Again. "I don't know; I . . . I . . . I just can't do this. I'm not like this."

1:13: I get up and return to the party. Tears do not make hooking up fun. Being nice sucks.

1:15: I tell Eddie there is a girl waiting for him in the bedroom next to the guest bathroom. "Really?" I hand him a condom, "Oh yeah dude, she was asking me all about you. She's already got her clothes off and everything. Go to it."

1:16: Rich and I laugh hysterically as Eddie goes into the room. We fully expect Eddie to come out any minute.

1:20: No Eddie.

1:25: No Eddie.

1:30: No Eddie. I want to go in and see what's going on, "Hey—it's my pussy after all. I primed that pump!" Rich convinces me to stay away, "Hey John Maynard Keynes; hold off. This could be the last pussy he's getting for awhile. Military women are ugly."

1:43: The friend who told me about the party has been dispatched to throw me and my friends out, "Dude, everyone here is scared of you. Your friends are huge and you have successfully insulted everyone. That one fucking girl you said owed you a rib or something—dude, she was crying to [the host]. Literally crying. You're like Attila the Hun. You laid waste to this party."

1:46: Rich convinces me that we should just leave Eddie, "Dude, he's an operator. He can find his own way home. The kid made his bones in Bosnia, I think he can find his way around Chicago."

2:04: Rich wants pussy. I take him to a club. I hate clubs.

2:05: We go to a place called Rive Gauche. It should be called Lotsa Douche. Almost as soon as we walk in, some skinny shitbag idiot starts spinning glow sticks right in my face. This enrages me. I shove him down and kick him in the spine.

2:05: Rich bear hugs me and carries me to a VIP booth before anyone figures out what happened.

2:07: I pass out in the booth.

2:30: I wake up to see Rich trying to eat the face of some skank. She looks like something he scraped off his shoe.

2:36: I am not feeling good. Mr. Absinthe is about to send me a bill for his services.

2:44: I make it to the toilet. I can feel the vomit coming.

2:45: My intestines, without subtlety, tell me that I have a higher priority. I nearly pass out on the toilet from my colon's version of Shock and Awe.

2:47: As I am crapping out my internal organs, Mr. Absinthe teams with Ms. Poetic Justice to eject everything in my stomach right out of my face.

2:48: I lean to my left to prevent vomit from getting on my clothes, but my shift moves my ass off the side of the toilet seat and causes me to shit watery diarrhea all over the toilet seat and floor.

2:49: I look over at the shit, catch a whiff of it, and start vomiting again. On top of the shit.

2:53: I stand up, clean myself, and survey the damage. It looks like a tapioca abortion.

2:58: I come out of the bathroom and inform the line that "I am Shiva, Destroyer of Worlds."

3:04: Back at the VIP table. Rich has nearly undressed The Skank and is investigating all of her orifices. His hand will never smell the same.

3:12: The Skank has a friend. She is staggeringly drunk. She makes fun of The Skank and tells me I am hot. Maybe clubs aren't so bad.

3:14: The Friend tells me I am way too sober. I agree. We go shot for shot with vodka.

3:40: After about 3 shots, she tells me, "I think I am getting really drunk. I always do stupid things when I'm drunk." Strike up the band, we have a winner.

3:50: Rich takes The Skank to the bathroom to fuck. The friend says to me, "About time. I'm surprised she didn't just go down on him at the table. That's what she did last weekend."

4:12: The Friend does not mince words, "Let's get out of here. I don't want to fuck in a club bathroom. I have standards . . . well . . . some standards." I can't make this shit up.

4:15: The Friend hands me her keys. I ask her, "You want me to drive your car?" She says, "Well, you're more sober than I am." This statement makes me laugh. I am so drunk I am not sure I could read.

4:40: She lives far away. I don't know where I am.

4:45: We cannot find parking. She has me drop her off at her building and tells me to come up when I find a parking place. I decide that she is a bitch. I think that she will "accidentally" get my dick in her ass when we are fucking doggy style.

4:50: I still cannot find ANYWHERE to park. This is infuriating me.

4:55: I parallel park the car into a space that is too small. I try to force it in. The car gets stuck on the curb. I slam on the gas, the wheels spin until they catch and jump the car onto the sidewalk, crashing it into a storefront.

4:56: I get out of the car. I am INSIDE of a donut shop. With the car. Shattered glass crunches under my feet as I investigate the damage. There are broken and fractured tables scattered all across the store. The car has only a few scratches. I am in shock and completely unsure about what to do. I have never driven a car into a store before.

4:57: Thankfully the donut shop is closed and empty of people. I still don't know what to do. I start laughing to myself. I look behind the counter, but the donuts are all put away.

4:58: I decide that while I find this funny, the car owner, the donut shop owner, and the police would not find it funny. The letters "DUI" leap to mind. The phrase, "destruction of property" also appears. I decide that felony hit and run is not funny anymore.

4:59: I pull the car out of the donut shop, park it in a tow zone, wipe all my fingerprints from the entire car, throw the keys into some bushes, and take off running.

5:01: I get my cell phone and desperately call Rich. I tell his voice mail that under NO CIRCUMSTANCES should he tell The Skank what my name is, who I am, or anything about me. It is Tucker Luck that on the one night when I need to stay anonymous I have someone in special forces to run my operational security.

5:15: I am still running. I lost count of the number of blocks I had traveled somewhere around 30.

5:30: I finally get home. I am completely fucking exhausted and feel like dying. I have probably only run like five or six miles but I know what Pheidippides must have felt like. My feet are bleeding, but I am safe. I pass out.

Epilogue

Rich was smart enough to not only give The Skank a fake name, but a fake phone number. It's standard operating procedure for him anyway. It's been awhile and I haven't seen anything in papers or police reports, so I guess I am OK.

It turned out that Eddie and Married Girl hooked up about 4 times and then they both passed out. The hostess found them the next morning, screamed, both Eddie and Married Girl jumped up, threw on their clothes and tore out of the house. Both were guests of people who were invited, so neither knew anyone who lived in the house.

When asked about how he succeeded with Married Girl where Tucker failed, Eddie simply smiled and said, "That was easy. I walked in and she was already naked. The hardest part was done. After that it was just a little patience and some sweet talking. Come on man; I run black ops for a living—this was cake."

I have no idea what ultimately happened to that girl or her car. Oh well . . . next time she'll stay in the car with the guy until it's parked.

THE MOST DISTURBING CONVERSATION EVER

Occurred—November 2002
Written—December 2002

Part 1: Tucker meets adoring fans, gets cock-blocked

This particular Friday began innocuously enough at The Union, where we drank as much beer as we could pour into our faces, as it was $5 all-you-can-drink from 5-8. The highlight of the early part of the night was when I drunk-dialed one of the MTV producers, Serena [this was about a week before MTV was set to do a documentary about me, which aired in May 2003]. She had made the mistake of giving me her personal cell phone number and telling me to call her "anytime you have any questions or anything." That's like Chamberlain telling Hitler he can have the Sudetenland. You give me an inch, I'm going to take the whole thing.

Tucker "So when you film me, are you going to follow me everywhere?"
Serena "Yeah, that's the plan."
Tucker "Well, what if I hook up and the condom breaks. Are you going to follow me to Walgreen's to get some Ru-486?"
Serena "We'll have to see about that."
Tucker "You have a sexy voice. What are you wearing?"
Serena "A muumuu."
Tucker "What?"
Serena "Tucker, I'm like 250 pounds."
Tucker [Long, drunken pause] "MTV better send a hotter producer."

Thankfully, she is smart and has read enough of my site so she picked up on my drunk sarcasm. And more importantly, she is not even close to 250.

I was drinking at an alarming rate and was well on my way to breaking things and fornicating with hot girls, when some guy came up to me and said, "Aren't you Tucker Max?"

He was a huge fan, and was all excited about meeting the actual Tucker Max in person. I am not a big enough celebrity yet to be used to this, so of course I ignored everything else and basked in the glow of adulation as he introduced me to all his friends. Of course, that adulation might have been from the five tequila shots I had done in the past hour.

I can't remember what he and I talked about, but I'm sure it was about how awesome I am. The funniest part was when he was ready for the next round, asked if I wanted another one, then looked at my unfinished beer, and said, rather condescendingly "Oh. You're not finished." You gotta love it when your own fans are calling you out. I deserved it, and I would expect nothing less. Hey, if I can't take a joke, then fuck me.

As we were talking, this girl came up and basically wrapped herself around me and started almost making out with me. I chatted with her for about 20 minutes, when she said, "Let's go back to your place." A confirming nod later she took my hand and we headed to the door. I like my fans, but I am not passing up pussy for them, even though I am pretty sure that guy said to me as I was leaving, "Tucker, what are you doing? She's a high 2-star at best." I legitimately thought, at the time, that she was a 4-star, and we all know that in these matters, perception truly is reality.

Then came perhaps the greatest cock block I have ever seen. As we were leaving, her friends, seemingly on cue, descended on her from all different directions of the bar. I never even saw them coming. They herded her away from me and into a cab, then piled in after her. The last one turned to me and said, "Sorry, no more room in the cab." The last thing I heard from inside the cab was the girl saying, "But I want to have sex with him . . ."

The bait and no-switch was such a shocking and unexpected turn of events that I stood out there in the cold for awhile, staring at the taxi as it drove off down the street. Eventually I just went back inside and wandered around the bar like a lost vagrant. My mind was having trouble shifting back into "Pursue" mode after being in "Gonna get laid" mode. It was then that my cell phone rang, and part two of the story began . . .

Part 2: Tucker has the most disturbing conversation ever

I answered my phone, still in a daze from having eager vagina snatched away from me. It was my friend Jez.

"Hey what are you doing? Come up and meet us, we're at Felt. It's on Halsted, right north of Belmont." Everyone who lives in Chicago knows what's coming next.

I take a taxi and arrive to find a bar completely packed with dozens of the best-dressed guys I have ever seen, and hardly any girls. Oh, that's fucking great Jez, thanks for bringing me up here, how am I supposed to pick up a girl at this fucking sausage-fest . . . TWO GUYS ARE KISSING IN THE CORNER!!

Jez comes running over and gives me a big hug and a kiss. She is wasted. "Come meet my gay friends. One of them looks just like Christian Slater!"

I am dragged over to the faux Christian Slater and the rest of the gay friends, and introduced "This is my straight friend Tucker. Isn't he so cute!!" They all readily agree, and I desperately feel the need for an alcoholic drink. I tell the bartender to just bring me anything strong. That short-sighted comment is immediately rewarded with a raspberry long island iced tea. I suppress the urge to throw the drink in his face, and then pay him $10 for it. I guess I'm gonna get fucked one way or another tonight.

Having cut my clubbing teeth in South Beach at clubs like Twist and Swirl, I am used to hanging out around gay guys, and thus am completely comfortable around them, but this was a totally different experience. In South Beach, the coolest clubs are the "gay clubs," but it's usually pretty obvious who is gay and who is not. The gay guys are flamboyant and entertaining, real thin, drink bright colored drinks, and wear dazzling, shiny clothes. The straight guys wear tight shirts and hang out in packs, waiting for opportunities to hit on the numerous hot girls that go to those clubs "just to dance."

Not in Chicago. In Chicago, the gay guys look and act just like straight guys, except they accessorize better . . . and, you know . . . fuck other dudes in the ass.

I was at the table with a girl and three guys, each of which looked and acted just like any of my other friends, except they were better dressed. After I got used to it, I was actually thankful to be hanging out with these great looking guys, all of which are gay, because it just means less competition for me. Ask any of the 40 or so straight guys who have attended Vassar over the past decade; having lots of gay guys around means the girls will be desperate. Unfortunately, there were no girls around except for the obligatory fag hags, which did not tickle my loins.

So being bored and Tucker Max, I couldn't resist the temptation to start quizzing these guys. There are just so many questions. I started off by throwing one out to the table:

"Alright guys, seriously, what is it about sucking dick that you like so much?"

They went on to explain that sucking dick is all about imagining it to be your own dick, "You just treat it like a little version of you." They also told me that getting your dick sucked by a guy is much better than by a woman, because, "We know what we want. Women don't have dicks, they don't really know how to deal with them like we do."

It turned out that two of the three guys had been with multiple girls; Christian Slater had been with like 10 or so, and Adam had been with about 8, so they had a reasonable basis for comparison. I guess I'm just going to have to take their word for it.

We leave Felt and decide to go to Manhole. Just by the name, you should be able to discern some things about Manhole. But let me be clear for the stupid readers, like my cousin: Manhole is a famous gay club, and it is famous for a reason, namely, lots of gay "things" go on there.

On the way there, Adam expresses concern for me, "Tucker are you sure you want to go here? This place is very . . . free."

Bitch, please. I'm not about to avoid such great story potential just because of some swinging dicks, "Dude, I grew up in South Beach. I've been to Thailand. There is nothing in there that could shock or disturb me." Truthfully, I've never actually been to Thailand, but I wasn't going to miss out on this.

The club opened into a huge room, and ended in a tunnel that led to another huge back room. The front room had a large, star-shaped bar in the center of it. The ceiling was ringed with dozens of TV's, much like your average sports bar. Unlike your average sports bar however, the TV's were not featuring athletic competition. That is unless you consider vigorous and explicit gay sex between men hung like Tijuana mules to be a sport. The walls were a dark, dingy brown. I stayed at least two feet from them at all times. And my favorite part: Every guy had his shirt off. Except me. And it was going to stay that way.

Jez and I get in line for the bathroom, and every guy in line immediately pushes her to the front. She asks why, and they say, "Because you actually have to go." The door opens and three guys come out of the one-toilet bathroom together. The last one stops, says, "Oh wait, I have to pee," and heads back into the bathroom.

Jez and I decide to go in the bathroom together. We walk in, and I make her close the door, because I don't want to touch it. The walls, which were originally some shade of orange, were now an oily brown, having been re-painted with splooge. Some of the stains were like 10 feet high on the wall. Who was fucking in here, Peter North? I pee in the sink and quickly exit, not touching any surface.

Some random events over the next few minutes: One guy asked me if I liked football, and he said his favorite teams were the Packers and the Titans, though he liked them better as the Oilers.

I asked the only girl in the place other than Jez if I could feel her tits. She said sure, and I gave them a good slapping. It was awesome. She loved it because she thought I was gay and thus safe, and I loved it because I am straight and she had great tits. Everybody wins!

Jez and I took a spot next to the front bar, and her gay friends immediately surrounded us. Jez was mostly talking to Adam and Christian Slater, while the other guys, Lloyd, Dave and Mike talked to me.

The three of them were right up on me, each with their shirts off. They began asking me about the gay porn showing in the TV screens, and whether that offended me or made me uncomfortable.

"No, not really. Porn is porn; I've seen so much in my life I've become inured to it. Most of the shots are up close, too. You can't even tell if it's a male ass or a female ass getting fucked until they pan out."

After they realized I was not averse to discussing gay topics and was relatively comfortable in a gay environment, the fucking floodgates opened.

The first subject was something I knew nothing about, and was actually kind of interested in, in a sort of clinical, sociological kind of way: How do gay guys decide who fucks who? I mean, when two guys go home, do they flip a coin? Play rock, paper, scissors? How does that work?

They explained that there are two types of gay guys: Tops and Bottoms. Tops are the ones that like to do the fucking, the pitchers, if you will, and the bottoms are the ones that like to get fucked, the catchers. Most gay guys have a preference, but can go either way, though there are a certain percentage that are only one way or the other. So if two Strict Bottoms go home together, then no one gets fucked, though there is still the oral sex option. This really was remarkable info to me. I just assumed that when you went home with a guy, you fucked him and then he fucked you, but that is rarely, if ever, the case.

One of the TV screens was showcasing a gay guy tossing another guy's salad, and we began discussing the finer aspects of such activity.

I admitted that I had never eaten out a girl's ass, but that I had had girls do it to me, and that yes, I liked it, especially when the girl jacked me off as she was doing it. They started telling me all these trade secrets about tossing salad and the various ways that one could improve it. They even asked me whether I washed my ass before I had my girlfriend go down there. I told them that I was courteous and did indeed clean myself beforehand. Dave told me I was "well trained," because there is nothing worse than going down there and finding it "all grainy."

Then it got a little weird. Dave started testing my limits. It is apparently a big thing for a gay guy to fuck a straight guy, and he really wanted to break me in:

Dave "So, would you ever let a guy eat out your ass."
Tucker "No, I'm not gay. And that would be weird."
Dave "Right, but if you aren't looking you'd never know if it's a girl or guy."
Tucker "I don't know about you, but I usually look at the people who put their tongue in my ass."
Dave "What if your girlfriend started it out, but then a guy moved in and finished. You would never know."
Tucker "I mean, I don't know, I guess . . . but . . . what kind of girl would . . . look, I'm not gay."
Dave "You know, gay guys give the best head. We teach female porn stars how to do it."
Tucker "I don't doubt that, but it doesn't change the fact that I'm not gay. I don't like dick. Except for mine, of course."
Dave "I like yours too."
Tucker "That's pleasant."

From that point on, it became a game of advance and retreat with these guys. They would test my sexuality with questions like that, and I would have fun talking to them about it, but would always draw the line before they suggested we head into the bathroom. The weird thing was, because I was straight, I had probably three of the hottest guys in there hitting on me, especially Dave. That guy could get so much pussy if he was straight.

It was a very unique feeling, to be so actively and aggressively pursued by guys. Now I know what hot girls feel like, being hounded by multiple guys at once. On one hand, it is a flattering feeling because of the attention and the obvious desire for you, but it kind of leaves a mildly annoying and hollow tang, because you know that all the guys really want to do is fuck, and they only care about you because of what you represent to them, not who you are as a person.

OH JESUS—DID I JUST WRITE THAT?

At one point during a lull in the conversation, a random gay guy got involved in our conversation, and figured out that I was straight and they were trying to get me to have a homosexual experience. He dropped possibly the biggest, most disturbing conversation bomb EVER DROPPED ON ANYONE EVER:

[**WARNING TO ALL GUYS**: You want to stop reading here. The conversation I am about to recount prevented me from sleeping for a full two days, and has permanently and irreversibly scarred me. Save your psyche while you still can. Women have nothing to fear.]

Him "I bet you've already slept with a man."
Tucker "Alright, come on man—I invented Tucker Max Drunk, but not even Tucker Max Drunk makes you switch teams."
Him "How many women have you been with?"
Tucker "I don't know, somewhere in low three digits."
Him "Oh yeah, I bet you've fucked a man."
Tucker [Getting obviously frustrated] "How??"
Him "I have three words for you: Post Op Transsexual."

It took a few seconds for the full meaning and significance of that statement to filter through my drunken brain.

Tucker "What? Get the fuck out of here. I've never fucked one of those."
Him "You wouldn't know."
Tucker "Man, give me some credit."
Him "Have you ever slept with a woman who told you she couldn't naturally lubricate, that she had to use KY?"

Oh no.

Tucker "Well . . . yeah . . . two, actually."
Him "Uh-huh."
Tucker "No. No way. Stacey was one, I went to college with her, she was definitely a woman. Everything about her was woman. And she was like 17 when we fucked. You can't be post-op that young."
Him "Probably not. What about the other one?"

Please no . . .

Tucker "Uhhh, I met her in Miami . . ."
Him "What did she do?"
Tucker "She was a stripper."

Him "Did she have fake tits?"
Tucker "Yes."

This isn't happening. He is fucking with me.

Tucker "No, man, she was not a fucking man. She didn't have an Adams apple."
Him "That is a two hour outpatient surgery. Easily done. Cheap too."
Tucker "But it was . . . she had a pussy. IT FELT LIKE A PUSSY."
Him "Surgery is amazing these days. She probably even had a clit."

WHAT THE FUCK??

Tucker "But she was soft. Her skin I mean. She felt like a girl."
Him "You're smart. You know what large amounts of estrogen do to the male body, don't you?"
Tucker "But what about her voice? She didn't sound like those absurd trannies on Springer."
Him "Again, estrogen. And maybe even vocal chord surgery. It would make sense if she has a lucrative stripping or escorting gig to protect."

I just stood there, too shocked to move, trying to recall every detail about her to refute his argument.

Tucker "Wait, wait, wait . . ."
Him "She gave great head, didn't she?"
Tucker "She was a stripper! They give head for a living!"

THIS CANNOT BE HAPPENING.

Him "Was she tall? Taller than you?"
Tucker "Yeah, but I've dated lots of girls who were taller than me."
Him "But I bet none of them had hands as big as hers."
I AM GOING TO VOMIT.

Him "Did you have anal sex with her?"
Tucker "Yeah."
Him "You ever had anal sex with other girls?"
Tucker "Yeah."
Him "Felt a little different with her, didn't it?"

Oh dear merciful Jesus. He was right. I *distinctly* remember that.

Tucker "FUCK THIS!! NO FUCKING WAY THAT I FUCKED A MAN!!"
Him "I think you did."
Tucker "SHUT UP SHUT UP—I CAN'T BE HEARING THIS!!!"
Him "Don't feel bad, this happens to lots of guys. You'd be shocked."
Tucker "OH MOTHERFUCK!! NO WAY. THIS IS NOT HAPPENING I AM NOT HAVING THIS CONVERSATION!! WHAT IN DEAR GOD IS HAPPENING??? I DID NOT FUCK A FAKE WOMAN!"

I was in SHOCK. I could not sleep or function for the next two days, as I went over every detail I could remember about this "girl." I am still undecided about her. Yes, he made good points, but everything about her I recall as being feminine. The way she smelled, her touch, her appearance, everything. And it was a nice strip club where I met her, Rachel's in West Palm Beach. Don't they check for these things?

He went on to explain that some post-op transsexuals will go to the bathroom before sex, and put the KY in without even telling the guy. Others don't even have fake breasts, because the elevated estrogen levels can give them B cups. He said she might not have been the only one. My brain was completely fried after that conversation. I still don't know what to think.

Gentlemen, all I can say is don't spend too much time cataloging your ex-hook-ups because it will drive you nuts. Just pretend you never read this and move on. You wish you had heeded that warning now, don't you?

SHE WON'T TAKE NO FOR AN ANSWER

Occurred—December 2002
Written—March 2005

This always happens to me, and it pisses me off.

If I dawdle and wait too long to approach a group of girls, invariably the ugliest one "calls" me in the group. I have no idea why. One girl I know told me it was because I am attractive but not great looking, so ugly girls think they have a chance with me. And she added that to people I don't know, I have an approachable air about me. What sweet irony.

One night my friends and I were out drinking, and we were sitting next to a table of girls. One was pretty hot, one was fuckable, and the other was awful. She was a fetal alcohol case, no question. Sunken nasal bridge, thin upper lip, a short upturned nose and smooth skin between the nose and upper lip—all the telltale signs. She looked sorta like she'd been hit in the face with a frying pan.

Before we make our move, one of the girls comes over to talk to me. Do you want to guess which one? Well, it wouldn't be a story unless it was the bag of smashed assholes, now would it?

As my friends talked to the fuckable ones, I tried to make it clear to PanFace that I was not into her. I told her the most absurd shit, things that I was sure would offend her so badly she wouldn't want to even look at me much less fuck me:

- "I will never date you. I won't call you. I probably won't even talk to you afterwards, unless it's to tell you to get out."
- "I am going to cum in your hair. Do you know how hard it is to get cum out of hair?"

- "For real, if I come home with you, you have to eat out my ass. And I haven't showered in three days."
- "I will only want to fuck you from behind. And you can't look at me when I'm fucking you either—I might lose my hard-on."
- "I want you to wear a paper bag on your head, cut a hole for your mouth, and give me head with it on."
- "No seriously, I will probably just cum on your back, then get dressed and leave. And I'll probably break some trinket of yours on my way out, just to show my disdain for you."

COME ON—even a washed up stripper shilling for quarter tips at a topless truck stop would have told me to fuck off. Whether she thought I was joking or not—and I was kinda—some of that shit is just over the line. What girl would keep talking to a guy that said those things? I mean honestly—I told the girl that I would only fuck her from behind because if she looked at me I would lose my hard-on. The girl had to have stopped at some point, right?

Nope. She got all googly-eyed and smitten and told me I was the funniest guy she'd ever met. Doesn't it always happen this way? I would have just ended it for real, but before I could, she discovered my weakness: An open tab.

I couldn't finish my drink before she'd have two more in front of me. Of course, this feedback loop led to disaster:

The constant stream of Red Bull and Goose made me more animated and sarcastic . . .
Which made her more into me . . .
Which allowed me to tolerate her more . . .
Which inspired her to lean into me and expose her cleavage . . .
Which caused me to comment on her nice breasts . . .
Which led to her massaging my crotch . . .
Which made me consider what she would be like in bed . . .
To continue with this line of thought I had to switch to doubles . . .
Yeah, I fucked her.

Oh, but it gets better.

The next morning I wake up in a strange bed with pink silk sheets. For about a minute I seriously wasn't sure who I had gone home with, because there was no girl in the bed. Then Pan-Face came bounding in the room. All the awful memories came rushing back in my head:

Girl "What's wrong? You look upset."
Tucker "Oh Christ . . . I can't believe myself . . ."

Then the rest came back to me—last night this girl had basically promised me the world; breakfast, laundry, fellatio-on-command, everything. Well, I fucked her, I'll be damned if I don't get my side of the bargain.

Tucker "I thought I told you I wanted breakfast in the morning."
Girl "OK! What do you want? I have eggs and bacon and pancakes . . ."
Tucker "All of it. And you also promised to fellate me on command. I want that as my appetizer."

Oh man. Here I go again. I always do this.

Whenever I hook up with some marginally attractive girl I get pissed at myself, for obvious reasons. Then, almost as punishment, I make myself sort of keep seeing/fucking her. Not because I am trying to pretend that I want a relationship—I'm honest with the girl—but because I feel like if I get my money's worth in other areas, then it was worth it to lose a little bit of my soul by fucking some girl I shouldn't even be seen in public with.

After she went down on me [she was really good], I watched *American Chopper* re-runs while she cooked me an awesome breakfast: an andouille sausage omelet with cheese, sautéed garlic and grilled onions, soggy bacon just like I like it, an English muffin buttered just right, skim milk with ice just like I like it, and a cappuccino (she had a machine) with just the right amount of froth-to-coffee ratio. I almost applauded her when I was done—but instead I had her go down on me again.

Over the next few weeks, it got bad. I would go over to her condo at like 2am without calling, drunk out of my mind, fuck her like she owed me money, sleep all day in her bed while she was at work, and then have her make me dinner when she got home. We'd go out and she'd buy me drinks, and then I'd make her leave before my friends or other girls would come out to meet me. When she came over to my place, she would bring Carson's ribs or Harold's chicken or some other delicacy, do my laundry, fuck/suck at command, and then leave without even spending the night. After awhile, even I began to feel bad. Sort of.

Ladies, let me give you some advice. You can throw all your stupid fucking chick-lit, self-help, why-doesn't-he-love-me books out, because this is all you need to know: Men will treat you the way you let them. There is no such thing as "deserving" respect; you get what you demand from people. Let a guy fuck you in the ass, cum on your back, drink all your beer and then leave, and he'll do it. But if you demand respect, he will either respect you or he won't associate with you. It really is that simple.

Or you can just act like Pan-Face, and turn out the same way:

The turning point for me, the exact moment I knew I had to cut the charade off and move on, was the day she showed up at my place in a trench coat. I was in my standard position: sitting on the couch, watching Jerry Springer in gym clothes, with my hand down my pants. She kinda stood there smiling at me, until I looked up:

Tucker "What are you doing? It's 75 degrees outside."

At that, she dropped her trench coat to reveal a tight white t-shirt and panties. Printed on them were these words (she had the shirts made specially at some store):

Shirt "Tucker Max's tits"
Panties "Tucker Max's pussy"

Had I been 17, I would have thought that was the coolest thing I'd ever seen. At 27, I could only see the imminent and now unavoidable disaster that was going to result from this girl falling in love with me.

Of course, I still slept with her that night.

But after that I stopped calling her, and I am pretty sure that as a result, she went bat shit crazy and moved back to wherever she was from. I'm not really sure; I would routinely find 50 missed calls on my cell phone from her and 30 emails in my inbox, so I blocked her email address and changed my phone number. I'll leave that mess for the beta males to deal with.

Tucker Ruptures His Appendix

Occurred—January 2003
Written—March 2003

On the Friday morning that MTV was in Chicago filming me, around 4am, my appendix ruptured. The pain was so intense, it woke me from my sleep. It felt like my lower right abdomen had been stabbed with a rusty serrated kitchen knife and twisted around in my gut.

I'm not sure how many Motrin I took, but it was well above the recommended dosage. If by "well above," I mean "half the bottle." For the rest of the time MTV filmed me, about 2 more days, I was in such incredible pain I nearly finished a bottle of Motrin. There are 100 to a bottle—kids, don't try this at home.

At the behest of my friends, many of them doctors, I decided to go to the ER. This decision was sealed by my conversation with Andrew, a surgery resident, "Dude, you could be in real trouble. You shouldn't play around with internal injuries. You need to go to the hospital. Like drop what you're doing and go immediately." That was at 11pm on Sunday night, and I went to ER right away.

I arrived at Cook County Hospital, parked my car and got in line to register at the desk. Right before the triage nurse got to me, an ambulance pulled up and unloaded a bleeding gunshot victim. I am not sure how many times he was shot, but I saw at least three holes. They even had to call a janitor to come wash blood off the floor.

At this scene, the triage nurse didn't even look up, and handed me my number. It is—I swear to god—187. I looked at my number, watched the paramedic disappear down the hallway with the low-rent Tupac, and walked right out the door. No fucking way. I don't believe in the supernatural and I'm not even the least bit superstitious, but some signs should not be ignored.

I was in agony all day the next day. I was on my sofa at around 10pm when a tsunami of agony crashed over me. Nothing I've ever experienced prepared me for this pain. I have broken an arm, some ribs and a hand, torn a rotator cuff, hyper-extended both knees, severely sprained both ankles, popped an eardrum, torn off fingernails, stepped on carpenter nails, had a plantar wart, etc, etc, so I thought I had experienced a wide and representative spectrum of pain. I was wrong.

It was so crippling, it took every bit of courage I had to reach from the sofa to the table, pick up my phone, and call TheRoommate. He was in his bedroom.

Roommate "Tucker, why are you calling me from the living room?"
Tucker [barely audible whisper] ". . . hospital . . ."
Roommate "Oh shit! OK, OK, hold on!"

By the time we got to Cook County, I was almost in shock the pain was so bad. A nurse rolled a wheelchair out to the car, brought me straight into the triage room and was about to take me back to the ER, when another nurse told her to instead take me to the nurses' station to take my blood pressure and temperature.

On the way there she bumped me into every single chair, wall and obstacle along the way. I groaned in pain at every nudge, each rattling my appendix at what felt like an 8 on the Richter scale. We got to the nurses' station where the nurse, who was Asian and spoke a sort of broken ghetto English, put me in line behind six people.

I gaze at these people, and none seem to have critical, life-threatening internal injuries. This infuriated me. A rush of adrenaline enabled me to muster a voice loud enough to completely silence the entire front of the Cook County Emergency Room:

Tucker "WHAT THE FUCK ARE YOU DOING? WHY AM I HERE? MY FUCKING APPENDIX EXPLODED AND YOU WANT ME TO WAIT BEHIND SLAPPY AND HIS IN-GROWN TOENAIL?"

Nurse "Are you in pain?"
Tucker [This question inspires such utter disbelief I can only resort to my basest reaction] "ARE YOU FUCKING STUPID?"

Nurse [Remember, this is in broken ghetto Asian] "HEY—You don got to be rude. I'n just try-ing to hep you. You don got to disrespect. How much it hurt?"
Tucker "MY APPENDIX EXPLODED—MY FUCKING STOMACH FEELS LIKE SOMEONE FUCKING STABBED ME. HOW WOULD YOU LIKE IT IF SOMEONE STUCK A KNIFE IN YOUR STOMACH? YOU WOULDN'T BE IN A GOOD MOOD EITHER, MAMA-SAN."
Nurse "YOU GONNA STAB ME? [Turns to other nurses] "HEY SHANDA, HE TELL ME HE GONNA STAB ME!"
Nurse2 [Comes over to investigate] "You say you gonna stab her?"
Tucker [I try to be calm about this] "I didn't say I was going to stab her I was describing what my pain was like."
Nurse "HE SAY HE GONNA STAB ME. HE SAY HE GONNA STICK KNIFE IN MY STOMACH."
Tucker [And there goes my patience] "I DIDN'T FUCKING SAY I WAS GONNA STAB YOU. LEARN TO SPEAK ENGLISH GODDAMIT! I WAS DESCRIBING MY PAIN YOU IDIOT!"
Nurse "HE CALL ME IDIOT TOO!"
Nurse2 "Sir, you need to be respectful or we are going to call the police, and you—"

This was my breaking point. I just turned and started rolling my wheel chair towards the ER. The pain was still intense, but my adrenaline was so high I was able to manage it. I guess the nurses decided to go along because the ghetto Asian started pushing me towards the ER. She lectured me the whole way to the ER about respect, telling everyone she saw how I threatened to stab her.

We got to the actual ER area and she rolled me into one of the triage rooms and handed me off to an ER nurse.

ER Nurse "So what's his problem?"
Nurse "He call me idiot and say he gonna stab me."
ER Nurse [Turns to me] "Did you threaten to stab her?"
Tucker "What? My fucking appendix ruptured."
Nurse "He say he gonna stick a knife in my stomach."
ER Nurse [Still looking at me] "Did you say you were going to stick a knife in her stomach?"
Tucker [I am wincing in pain through this whole thing] "What? What is

this? NO! She asked me what my pain felt like and I said it felt like I got stabbed. I'M THE ONE IN PAIN!"

They laid me on a gurney and instead of attending to me and my pain, continued discussing my abusive and threatening behavior. Honestly, does anything ever go normally for me?

Two doctors arrived almost immediately, a male attending and a female resident. They questioned me, poked my abdomen, etc, when the male doctor asked me to roll onto my side:

Tucker "Roll on my side? What for?"
Doctor "I need to check your prostate."
Tucker "WHAT?????? WITH YOUR HAND??"
Doctor "Yes."
Tucker "IN MY BUTT??"
Doctor "I have to, you may have serious colon or prostate problems, and the only way to check those is by hand."
Tucker "Well this is just FUCKING GREAT."

As he put on a rubber glove, the female resident was snickering at my comments, even though I was not finding them very funny at the moment. He turned to her and pointed for her to go on the outside of the curtain. I interrupt:

Tucker "Actually, doctor, can she do it? If I'm going to have fingers up my ass, I'd rather have them be female. You know—they're smaller, more petite . . . you know . . . less gay."

He was completely taken aback at this request. The shock was evident on his face, and for a second I even thought he would agree to it.

Doctor "No. Sorry."
Tucker "Well, she can stay anyway. Fuck it. Might as well invite everyone to my party."

I didn't need this. I really didn't fucking need this. I couldn't stop thinking, especially as he wiggled two fingers into my anal cavity and pressed them against my prostate, about how I'll have to change the part in The Most Disturbing Conversation Ever story about my anal virginity.

The ER doctors eventually decided that I had a ruptured appendix and needed to get prepped for surgery. Never could I have imagined that the words, "prep him for surgery" would have such horrific consequences.

A male Hispanic nurse began prepping me. He took off my clothes, put me in a hospital gown, took various measurements like blood pressure and what not, hooked me up to an IV needle that was only slightly smaller in diameter than PVC pipe, and refused to give me any painkillers, because he said that they might affect the anesthesia.

At this point, I thought it couldn't get any worse. My appendix was absolutely killing me, I had no painkillers, there were numerous needles stuck in me, my ass was still greasy from some guy putting his KY covered fingers in my rectum, some other guy was undressing me—really—what the fuck else could go wrong?

Well, at least one more thing: The nurse told me to pull my gown off my crotch and took out a long tube. It is called a Foley Catheter, and it is used to drain your bladder when it is not under your control, either because you are unconscious (for surgery) or cannot control it yourself (paralyzation). It is exactly 16 inches long.

I took one look at that garden hose he was holding and my heart stopped. I'd rather have a herd of rhinos rape my asshole than take that thing up my urethra. I have heard absolute horror tales about what that thing feels like going up your dick.

Tucker "No, no, no—You aren't putting that thing in my dick are you? Please god in heaven tell me no."
Nurse "Yeah, man. Got to—It's how you piss when you're in surgery."

I didn't even have it in me to put up a fight. I was too scared. I just grabbed the side rails of the gurney and held the fuck on. This is an approximation of my reaction when he started inserting the catheter into my penis:

"AAAAAAAAAAAHHHHHHHHHHHHHHHHHHHHHRRRRRRRRRAAAAAAAAAAAAAHHHHHHH"

It went on like that for a few seconds. When the blazing anguish stopped, I wiped the tears forming in my eyes and looked down, expecting to see a yellow tube sticking out from my penis.

Tucker "What the fuck? Hey man—where is it?"

Nurse "That one was too big, I'm gonna have to go with a 16 gauge instead of a 14."

This did not please me, and I expressed my feelings with a string of furious profanity that would make a longshoreman proud. He eventually got the second one into my urethra, and I wasn't thinking about my abdominal pain anymore. I never really understood the phrase "pissing out razor blades" until this experience. The act of inserting that firehose into my penis was so horribly painful, it made me forget what was, to that point, the worst pain of my life. Even writing this is making my dick hurt. Or maybe that's the herpes. Who knows?

I lay there for another few hours, without painkillers, waiting to get a CAT scan. Every time I moved, the catheter shifted (it was taped to my leg) resulting in a whole new wave of pain and misery. The strangest thing about the catheter was that the collection bag was laying right there on the bed next to me. I watched it fill up with dark yellow urine, yet couldn't control or feel the flow. It was weird. But it felt warm against my leg, which was nice.

Right before the CAT scan, one of the nurses handed me a huge tube of liquid and told me to drink it. I had no idea what it was, but the label didn't sound appetizing:

Tucker "Barium Sulfate?"
Nurse "It's an imaging agent. It's so the CAT scan can get a map of your intestines."

They might was well call it Cum in a Bottle. It was white, cloudy and viscous, with a disturbing salty taste. You know what it tasted like? You know when a girl goes down on you and swallows, and then comes up and wants to kiss you? You try to avoid the kiss, but she is persistent and there is nothing you can do, so you give her a little peck. You know that taste on your lips right after? Hello Barium Sulfate.

This was very nearly my breaking point, "This tastes like semen. Haven't you people humiliated me enough? Should I just dump this on my face so you can get some Bukkake shots for the Cook County website? Would that make you happy?"

I eventually got the CAT scan and waited another hour or so for the consultation with the surgeon. She looked at the pictures and decided they weren't going to operate on me, because my appendix had not burst but rather had ruptured, and a leaking abscess had formed on it. This meant that there was a huge pocket of puss around that section of my colon, and they couldn't operate without having to do an entire colonectomy. The ensuing conversation was alarming, even to me:

Doctor "When did the pain start?"
Tucker "About a week ago."
Doctor "A week! Why did you wait so long to come in?"
Tucker "I don't know . . . MTV was filming me."
Doctor "MTV was filming you?"
Tucker "It would take too long to explain."
Doctor "So you just endured the pain?"
Tucker "Yeah, pretty much. Motrin helped. And lots of alcohol."
Doctor "Hmph. Well, just so you know, you could very easily have died. As it stands, you are going to be fine, but you were about 2 days away from sepsis setting in and killing you. That was stupid of you to wait this long."
Tucker "Yeah, I'm not very smart."

The same male Hispanic nurse came in to de-prep me and get me ready for transport to my room. One of the de-prepping activities was too take out the catheter. The removal hurt, but nothing like the entry. After he pulled it out, this nasty thick yellow discharge followed it out.

Tucker "WHAT THE FUCK IS THAT? DID YOU GIVE ME THE CLAP?"
Nurse "Yeah, you got the clap from a sterile catheter. It's just dehydrated urine. You're fine."
Tucker "Whatever. Dick. You ever have one of those in you?"
Nurse "No. But I'll tell you what—I've inserted hundreds of those and I've never seen anyone scream like more of a bitch than you."
Tucker "So now you're the fucking comedian? Hey Paul Rodriguez—I swear to god, you better not be around when they discharge me. I'll find you, and broke appendix or not, I'll kick your fucking ass."
Nurse "Whatever. You'll just scream like a bitch."

Had I been able to stand, I think he and I would have fought.

Right after this little spat, another nurse came in and shot like 15cc's of morphine into my IV. WOW—I can see why that shit is addictive. I could literally feel the drug course through my veins and almost instantaneously a flowery opiate-induced calm came over me. I went from angry pain to ethereal joy in about two minutes. I even apologized to the Hispanic nurse the next time I saw him.

[Side note about morphine: Everyone who called me or saw me over the next two days when I was in the hospital can attest to the fact that I was the nicest they have ever seen me. If I could find a drug that gave me that feeling on a regular basis, I would be an addict, and happy about it. I now know what it means when heroin users talk about "chasing the dragon." In only a day the normal dosage of that stuff was not enough. I was asking for more and more, pushing that call button like it brought me a fat-titted hooker carrying a plate of juicy pork ribs, screaming at the nurses if they didn't get it to me fast enough. They had to switch me to codeine, which is apparently easier to stop taking. I have what's called an "addictive personality."]

Once I was fully de-prepped, they wheeled me up to my room. I was put in a room with another person, but it was dark when I got there, and I was so flush with morphine that I ignored my roommate and went to sleep.

I woke up to quite the scene. And smell. There were two large black nurses holding my roommate up while they cleaned shit out from under him and changed his sheets. They were not happy:

Nurse1 "Why you keep shitting like this?"
Nurse2 "It's something he ate. What you eat?"
The guy pointed to some Fritos laying on the table.
Nurse2 "No, it ain't no Fritos."
He pointed to a Pepsi.
Nurse2 "No, it ain't no goddamn Pepsi neither. It must be them damn carrots, because you straight up lettin' out vegetation."

They eventually got him cleaned up and left. I looked him over, and the sight was not pretty. He was black, anywhere from 40 to 50 years of age, Tracey Gold skinny, and had half of his head shaved. He didn't seem to be able to use his right side, and did everything with his left hand. He saw me looking at him and nodded his head at me in a "what up" manner. I responded, and said, "What's up man? Having a tough day?"

He opened and closed his mouth repeatedly, each time letting out little grunts. Eventually, with much effort, he got a slurred, "Yeah" out. Shaved head, can't talk, can only move his left side—he either had a stroke or a brain tumor.

He and I talked for awhile, and I eventually learned how to interpret at least some of his affected stroke speech. We were talking about something when a girl I know called my room. I told her where I was and she said she was coming over. My roommate was listening to the conversation and waved at me to get my attention, then pulled his sheet up over his crotch, tenting it, and clearly said, "Me . . . too." I laughed and told her to bring a friend for my crippled roommate.

Later that day his speech therapist came in, and she was pretty hot. She said, "Hello Randolph, how are you today?"

This cracked me up, "Your name is Randolph? RANDOPLH! Your nickname is Ray-Ray, isn't it!?!" Ray-Ray started laughing along with me, and this thoroughly confused the speech therapist.

By this time, I was fairly proficient in interpreting Ray-Ray's stroke grunts, and I spent the half hour telling her what he was saying, hitting on her and making fun of her.

Tucker "You're a speech therapist and you can't understand your own patient? Did you get your degree in the mail? Is there a picture of Betty Struthers on your diploma?"

As she leaves, we have this exchange:

Tucker "So, you're pretty hot, can I get your number?"
Therapist "Sorry, no—I wouldn't give you my zip code."
Tucker "Nice one. That's cool, because I'd rather be deaf than listen to you for another second."

Ray-Ray was nearly in tears laughing at this scene. He eventually got this out, "We . . . we . . . we . . . make . . . a good team."

Watching him eat his lunch really made me empathize with the poor guy. Every time he tried to eat, he would put the food in the left side of his mouth, and then half of it would spill out the right side. He had no feeling on that side of his face, or his entire right side, so he really had no idea what was happening.

On one level it was funny, because there was this guy dumping half his food out of his mouth without knowing it, but on another level it was very depressing, as he seemed like a really good guy that was suffering through a horrible fate.

He was so skinny, presumably from months of inactivity and confinement to his bed, that over the next few days I gave him all of my hospital meals. Granted, it was empathetic on some level, but believe me, it was no fucking loss for me. Every stereotype you've ever heard about hospital food is true. I would have rather eaten medical waste than the shit they served us, though Ray-Ray loved it. I guess brain injuries make you hungry.

Later that night, Stydie and Laura stopped by with, of all things, Harold's Chicken. I don't think I have ever been so fucking happy to see Stydie, as Harold's is nearly my favorite food on earth. That shit stunk up my entire wing of the hospital, but I devoured it without compunction.

After Stydie and Laura left, another girl came to visit me. She brought me a Playboy, and I gave that to Ray-Ray to look at while she and I did things I wasn't supposed to be doing. I believe the term "medicinal head" should be added to the medical lexicon, because I know I felt better.

I heard Ray-Ray hit his nurse call button, and then a very familiar smell permeated the room. Though my curtain was pulled, I heard them clearly:

Nurse "Oh look—you done shit yourself again."
Ray-Ray "I . . . I . . ."
Nurse "You eating Fritos in bed again? Why you eaten Fritos in da bed? Can't you get none in your mouff?"
[The girl and I were laughing at this exchange, and we could hear her moving Ray-Ray to another gurney]
Nurse "Goddammit. I told you to stop eating that damn candy. Look at this bed."
Ray-Ray "I . . . I . . . I want . . ."
Nurse "Shut up!"

The girl who came to see me left halfway through this because we were done, she had to get home to her boyfriend, and the smell was oppressive. After she left and the nurse got everything back to normal, Ray-Ray looked over at me and said:

Ray-Ray "I . . . I . . . I . . . ruined . . . your date."
Tucker "No man, it's cool, she was done anyway."
Ray-Ray [He laughed for awhile before he got this out] "You . . . you . . . alright . . . man."

The Playboy was a pretty good one (the one with the Latin TV stars), and I enjoyed it for our remaining day and a half together. When I was leaving I asked Ray-Ray if he wanted to keep the Playboy. He shook his head yes, and said,

"I . . . I . . . I gonna need it."

THE SEX STORIES

Occurred—various, 2000–2005
Written—May 2005

The pen may be mightier than the sword, but I have found that the vagina is stronger than both. No matter what happens to me, no matter how many girls vomit on me or shit on me or screw me over, I keep hooking up with all kinds of women, seemingly without regard for the repercussions. These are some of my shorter vignettes involving sex that don't fit into any larger stories:

Do you want fries with that?

While I lived in San Francisco I met a girl out at some dot com party. She was cute, the lights were low, the liquor was free, I was horny—always a happy confluence of circumstances.

We ended up back at her place in the South Market district of San Francisco (I lived in Mountain View, which is about 40 minutes south by car, so this was convenient). We start kissing, fumbling with buttons and hooks and straps, things start coming off, when she suddenly pulls back and stops me:

Girl "Before we go any further, I have to tell you something."
Tucker "Umm, OK."
Girl "I just got over genital warts."
Tucker [A blank, unregistering stare]
Girl "This always happens."
Tucker "I'm sorry, I didn't hear you, what did you just say?"
Girl "This always happens...I used to have genital warts, but they're gone now. HPV is usually not transmittable if there isn't a breakout and you use a condom. You don't . . . really have to worry about anything, but I thought . . . that I should probably tell you."

Tucker [Another prolonged, blank, unregistering stare.]
Girl "You were going to use a condom anyway. You won't get them. It's OK."
Tucker [putting my clothes back on] "What's the best way to get back to the interstate from here?"

In retrospect, I kinda feel bad. I probably have every STD known to man, yet this poor girl was honest with me and I totally dissed her. She courageously exposed part of her soul to me, and I callously stomped it. Oh well . . . that's what she gets for wanting to fuck Tucker Max.

Bro's before ho's

When I was in NYC to finalize the deal for this book, I met some friends out for drinks and invited a few girls along that had emailed me asking to hang out. One girl in particular, "Ho," took a liking to my friend Credit, and flirted with him all night. This girl was obviously playing the "girlfriend" game and looking at Credit as boyfriend material: she was nice, a bit coy, not overly aggressive, laughed at all his jokes, and instead of hooking up with him she only gave him her number.

Credit left early because he had to get up for work the next morning, but this girl wanted to go out drinking more, so she took me and my friend Junior with her. Not even two drinks into the next bar, she is all over me: hands on my crotch, seductive looks, the entire slut repertoire. I ignore her, instead paying attention to my vodka clubs, but this only makes her more into me.

Junior lives in Connecticut and we accidentally missed the last train out of the city, so Ho politely invited us to stay at her place. When we got there, she gave Junior the couch and told me I could sleep on the floor in her room.

Riiiiight. Not even two minutes after she turned out the lights I was in her bed and we were tearing the clothes off each other. We both get naked and I slide it in. Things are going great, when she stops and gets all serious:

Ho "Wait, I don't know if we should do this."
Tucker "Why?"
Ho "Well, I don't want to ruin things with your friend Credit."
Tucker "HAHHAHAAHAH . . . I think it's a bit late for that."

Ho "NO! You have to promise not to say anything to him! PROMISE!"

After being a lying asshole during my younger years and realizing how awful it is, it is now a rock-solid policy of mine to never ever lie to a girl . . . but sometimes immediate biological urges force me into situations where I am forced to break this rule.

Tucker "OK . . . fine. Let's keep going, I'm not finished yet."

Of course I ended up telling Credit. I mean—come on. When I am mid-coitus, a girl could extract a promise from me to trade my first-born for a Twix bar. Plus, I had to tell him. God forbid if he dated this girl, fell in love and got married to her. What a shitty wedding that would have been.

Tucker goes a little booty call crazy

I have been saying for years that phone companies should invent a phone with a breathalyzer attached. I cannot tell you how many times I have made awful, terrible drunk dials and not even remembered it the next day. But one time stands out from the rest.

I was solidly Tucker Max Drunk after a long Friday night bar-hopping, and came home alone at around 2am. I hadn't fucked for like four days—a serious dry spell for me—so I started scrolling through my phone, calling every female name I come across:

Tucker "Janet, come over, I'm horny."
Janet "Tucker, I live in Washington DC."
Tucker "So?"
Janet "You are in Chicago."
Tucker "Oh. Do you know any girls in Chicago who want to come over?"

Tucker "Krista, come over."
Krista "Tucker, it's late."
Tucker "My horniness is not relegated to business hours."
Krista "I don't know."
Tucker "I SAID DO IT!"
Krista "Well, maybe."

I don't really recall the amount of time I spent on the phone or even how many girls I called, but I do remember having the distinct impression that I was shit out of luck. I relegated myself to the couch to pass out while watching re-runs of *The Shield*, when all of the sudden there was a knock on the door. It was an irregular fuck buddy of mine, Sandra. Sweet!

She comes in and she wants a beer, so I tell her where the fridge is. We kinda start making out on the sofa a little, and then there is another knock on the door. Who the fuck is at my door at 3am?

Uh oh. It's another booty call, Liz.

Tucker "Well . . . do you want a beer?"

Both of the girls just kinda stood there, alternately staring at each other and at me. There is a way to turn this situation from disaster to triumph, and even though it's a long shot, the only way that you can ever win at the table is to throw the dice:

Tucker "So . . . Liz, uh Sandra is kinda into girls, and I know you've always wanted to experiment. What do you say?"

You know that noise girls make when they are so pissed that they can't even form words? It's a sort of cross between "uh" and a reptilian hiss? Yeah, she made that noise, turned on her heels, and stormed out.

Oh well, at least Sandra was still there, right? I turned to her, and she was setting her beer down and reaching for her purse. Time to act quick:

Tucker "No wait, honey, you don't have to go. I didn't even invite her over, she is a psycho who—"

I was interrupted by some unidentified noise at the bottom of my stairs. It sounded like two girls talking to each other, followed by footsteps, and capped off with the appearance of Krista at my still open door.

Tucker "Oh boy."

I wish I could tell some story about how I turned this into some amazing foursome, but since I have a policy to tell only true stories, I can't. Let's just say that it did not end well. Things were thrown, curses hurled, none of the three ever came over again, and I had to recruit a whole new stable of booty calls. Maybe a better man than me could have turned that night into something out of *Penthouse Letters,* but all I did was end up with my dick in my hand and a mess in my apartment.

Toxic shock

While in law school I dated a girl named "Vicki." A total blonde southern girl; really hot, really sweet, and really stupid. When we'd hang out with my law school friends she'd be very quiet, and whisper things to me like, "I am afraid to talk to GoldenBoy. He uses such big words."

She used Depo-Provera as her birth control, and though it was effective at keeping her from polluting the world with little Tuckers, it caused her to spot occasionally, and she told me this and it usually wasn't a problem. [for the ignorant males, "spotting" is when a girl bleeds when not on her period]

One night we came home drunk and proceeded to fuck the shit out of each other. Sex with Vicki was awesome because she was one of those girls who can cum with virtually no effort through regular sex. Every minute or two she would have an orgasm. I loved this not because she got off so much, but because I could be ruthlessly selfish in bed and it didn't matter. As long as I lasted more than a minute, everything took care of itself.

This bout of drunk sex started off the same as the others; I humped and pumped and she screamed and came . . . but after a short time, my dick started to hurt. I kept pumping away, she kept coming, and the pain kept getting worse and worse. It was a weird moment: Think about what goes through your mind when you are fucking . . . now mix those thoughts with flashes of intense, grinding pain . . . on your PENIS. This greatly confused my drunk brain, but I still plowed on, determined to not let anything—not even obvious and searing pain—prevent me from reaching the ultimate goal of virtually everything I do in life: personal satisfaction.

I concentrated and was able to pinpoint the actual location of the pain: It felt like the head of my penis was scraping up against something hard and abrasive. I was drunk, so my first thought was that my dick was so big it was hitting her cervix and scraping up against that. As if her cervix was made of sandpaper or something. Yes, I can be that stupid when drunk and fucking.

I tried to fuck through the pain. I really tried to convince myself that everything was OK, but when my eyes started tearing up from the agony, I had to stop.

Tucker "Baby—something is wrong with your vagina."
She looked confused, and then kinda hurt, "What do you mean?"
My penis was still penetrating her, so I tried to be diplomatic in my explanation, "Bitch, my fucking dick HURTS. Something is fucked up with your fucking pussy."

She gets up and goes into the bathroom, and I examine my penis. There is a bright red circular area to the right of my urethra (pee hole). Almost all the skin on the right side of the head of my penis has been stripped off. I delicately touch the red throbbing sore, and it burns. I have played many football games on Astroturf, and I recognize exactly what this is: Turf burn.

I have fucking turf burn on my dick? What the fuck? I am confused and pissed off. I mean, how the fuck can I have goddamn turf burn on my dick?

I hear the bathroom door open and I stand up and prepare to yell at Vicki . . . and then I see her. She is crying hysterically, tears streaming down her face, holding something in her hand. Her eyes meet mine, she busts out in an even louder wail, and I look into her hand. I don't really recognize what it is until she says,

"I'm so sorry. I totally forgot I had it in . . ."

In her hand was a reddish-brown, smashed up Tampax.

Vicki had put one in before we went out drinking, and got so drunk she forgot to take it out before we had sex. This was what my dick head was rubbing up against for that 15 minutes of agony . . . a FUCKING TAMPON.

As big of an asshole as I am, I'm still a sucker for a hot crying girl, so I gave Vicki a hug and told her everything was OK. Then she stopped crying and I cut her throat. I'm just kidding. But, true to form for turf burns, I did wake up the next morning with a yellowish brown scab on the head of my penis. Which developed into a small scar that you can still see to this day . . . if you are a hot girl.

What's grosser than gross?

This girl I was kinda seeing worked in a financial services office. On Fridays she had the office all to herself, and once I went in to see her. I tried to get her to fuck me on her boss's desk, that was a no go. On the conference table, no go. In the kitchenette, still a no go.

I can't figure out what her problem is (we'd had plenty of sex before), so I try being nice and start making out. I put my hands down her pants and massage her clit, and she likes it at first but then squirms away, "No, not now."

Getting frustrated, I take my finger which I can feel is covered with her juice, and rub it across her lips, just intending to tease her . . . OH SHIT!

Right across her lips and teeth is a huge red stain! Now it makes sense.

Tucker "Are you on the rag? Is that why you won't hook up?"
Girl "Yeah. I hate to say it, it's embarrassing. How'd you know?"

I just kinda raised my eyebrows . . . and she licked her lips . . . and I wished I had a camera to record the look of shock and embarrassment as she tasted the blood on her tongue. She immediately ran off to the bathroom. I was washing my hands in the kitchenette when she rushed back in:

"You aren't going to write about this are you?"

Fucked up pillow talk

These are some funny quotes or bits of dialogue that are sexually related or happened while in bed, but that didn't occur in the middle of a larger story.

- This happened with a girl I had been seeing for like two weeks:

  Girl "Do you love me?"
  Tucker "I don't understand the question."

- From a girl who had obvious issues with sex:

  Girl "OK, I want you to take your wee-wee and put it on my dirty spot."
  Tucker "What did you just say?"
  Girl "Take your wee-wee and put it into my dirty spot."
  Tucker "What is this, *Sesame Street* foreplay?"

- This from a girl who, for some reason, thought we were exclusive. She didn't get that idea from me:

  Girl "Why didn't you shave. You know I hate stubble."
  Tucker "Oh sorry, I forgot that you were the one who liked me to be shaven."
  Girl "I'M THE ONE WHO LIKES YOU TO BE SHAVEN!!! HOW MANY GIRLS ARE YOU FUCKING??"
  Tucker "Maybe we haven't met: Hi, my name is Tucker Max. You've seen my website. In fact, that's how we met."

- A similar exchange, with a different girl, that nearly ended the fuck-buddy relationship:

  Tucker "Do you like girls?"
  Girl "You ask me that every time I see you."
  Tucker "I forget who answers yes and who answers no."
  Girl "I don't know why I keep fucking you."
  Tucker "Because I am awesome and you can't help yourself."
  Girl "You know, I used to have self-esteem before I met you."
  Tucker "That's what they all say."

- Five minutes later with the same girl:

  Girl "What is your favorite sexual technique?"
  Tucker "Well, I'm not sure. Probably where I pretend like she isn't there, get off as fast as possible, and then she does my laundry, cleans, and then leaves immediately afterwards."

- This was with a total random I picked up at the grocery store. We went home and, with her groceries still in the car, start hooking up. Before we begin sex, she let this out:

  "Don't worry about putting a condom on. I'm already pregnant."

- This one was really depressing. I wish she had told me beforehand:

"You are the first guy I've slept with since I was raped. Thanks for being gentle."

- I was fucking this one girl with music on. I hadn't put anything on intentionally, it was just some mix CD I happened to have in. We are mid-coitus, and a Ludacris song comes on:

  Girl "Can you please change the song?"
  Tucker "Why?"
  Girl "Well . . . I fucked one of Luda's roadies to get back stage, but I never even got to meet him. I am kinda bitter."

- With a girl whose friend I had fucked:

  Girl "You aren't anywhere near as good as [her friend] said you were."
  Tucker "Well with her I actually tried. I liked her."

Miss Deaf Australia

The University of Chicago requires that students take a year of a foreign language in order to graduate, so I took American Sign Language. Our teacher got to like our class, so she invited us to some deaf events in Chicago.

The first one we went to was a dance at a bar that some deaf organization had rented out. We get there a little late and when we walked in the foyer even though I could hear the music I couldn't hear any voices so I thought it'd be empty, but instead the place was filled with like 100 deaf people. I heard nothing except the clink of glasses and some random grunting—everyone was furiously signing to each other. It was kinda spooky.

I was introduced to a girl who had just won the Miss Deaf Australia pageant. She was really pretty and thought that my retarded 4th grade sign language ability was cute. After about twenty minutes of trying to sign and getting frustrated, I asked her to dance, figuring I had to be better at that than her; after all, she can't even hear the music. That was another mistake. She was an awesome dancer. The deaf people picked this club because it had a great sound system, and they dance by feeling the music. Most of them are really good, way better than me. Well, so much for that.

She ended up liking me anyway, despite the fact that I couldn't sign or dance, and we went on a few dates, and ended up having sex on the third date.

I start kinda slow with her, but I can tell almost immediately that she is freaky, so I get freaky with her. She is kinda grunting a little, but nothing all that unusual, until she starts to come.

"AAARRRRRRRRRRRHRHHHHHHHHHAAAAAAAAAAR-RRRRRGGGGGGHHHHHH"

I got so scared I almost went limp. You have not heard a girl scream during sex until you've heard a deaf girl come. It was literally like a cross between a retard scream and the noise a horse makes when it's being slaughtered. I have never heard a more guttural expression of climax in my life.

Sex with her was great, but the rest of the relationship kinda sucked. Not being able to communicate is cute at first, but gets real annoying when you just want to stay in and watch *The Sopranos* but your TV doesn't have subtitles and the deaf girl gets bored.

One instance made it clear we had to break up. We were in my apartment having sex, and it was a particularly intense session, when all of the sudden there was a loud knock on the door. I got dressed and opened the door to find a cop standing there:

Cop "Sir please step back, we could hear the screaming and have reason to believe there is criminal activity going on here."

The naked deaf girl in my bedroom was all it took to send the cops out of my apartment in tears from laughing so hard.

The Chili Pepper Hook-up Incident

Where and how I met this girl is not important. Why I hooked up with her, and what happened the next morning is not even worthy of a story. What she looks like is immaterial (if you care, she looks a lot like the red-head daughter in *Six Feet Under*). All you need to know for this story are three things:

1. I was at a house party in Chicago that was catered by a Mexican restaurant.
2. I was very, very drunk at this party, and at one point, I ate several

of these super-hot jalapeño peppers that Mexican restaurants like to serve, the kind that aren't cut up and pickled.

3. It was at this party that I met the girl who eventually came back to my place with me.

Once at my place, we eventually got down to business. I started playing with her vagina, fingering her and what not when all of the sudden she abruptly stopped me, pulled my hand away from her crotch, and asked:

Girl "Did you eat any of those hot peppers tonight?"
Tucker "Yeah, I had a few."
Girl "Oh no . . . oh no, Oh my GOD! Holy shit, holy shit—IT'S BURNING!!"

She jumped out of my bed, ran into my bathroom and immediately got into the shower.

I was still very drunk, so this confused me. I walked to the door and yelled through it,

"Are you okay? What's wrong?"

She yelled back over the din of the water, "Did you wash your hands after you ate those peppers?"

At this I figured out what the problem was, and immediately erupted into hysterical laughter. I was laughing so hard I could hardly breathe. Then I remember what it was like to have my crotch on fire from capsaicin (remember the Foxfield story?), and calmed down a bit, though I was still laughing.

She yelled through the door, "Shut up! This isn't funny, you jerk! This better not show up in a book!"

Friendly Fire

Karma being the bitch that she is, my activities always eventually catch up to me. The summer before I started law school, I was seeing a girl in Miami named "Courtney." She was incredibly hot—one of those girls you have a physical reaction to as soon as you see her.

One time we were fucking doggy style, incredible sex, and right as I was about to cum I pulled back too far and my dick came out. I didn't realize it, and as I thrust forward again, instead of going back into her vagina my dick stuck in her ass crack (NOT into her asshole, but her crack, between her butt cheeks, like a hot dog in a bun . . . sort of).

I was leaning over her, my face directly above the back of her head, and I looked down at my dick right as I hit climax . . . and shot nut INTO MY OWN EYE.

A direct hit, right into my wide-open eye. I didn't even see it coming . . . literally.

Almost immediately, I developed a personal appreciation for how much cum stings. That shit BURNED. It took me a minute to wash it out, but the sting, and the redness, stayed for a good 4 or 5 hours.

Fuck you, karma.

TUCKER HAS A MOMENT OF REFLECTION; ENDS POORLY

Occurred—April 2003
Written—July 2004

One random Friday I was sitting in my Chicago apartment drinking a beer and watching TV. Around 7, my phone rang. It was "Karen," one of my booty calls at the time. It was early so I was kinda confused; we normally never called each other until at least midnight, even on weekdays:

Tucker "You drunk already?"
Karen "Hehe. No baby. What are you up to right now?"
Tucker "Nothing. Watching Morimoto make some crazy mushroom crème brulee. Battle Porcini on *Iron Chef.*"
Karen "Uhhh, OK. Well . . . I am going on some silly blind date tonight that my friend set me up on . . . but I was wondering if I could swing by your place and get a protein shake first."

Very nice. Karen is obviously making an attempt to move up from Irregular Booty Call to Head Dick Sucker.

Tucker "Yeah, sure. Just come on by. I'll be here."
Karen "Cool. I'll see you soon."
Tucker "Hey baby—bring some beer."

Not even ten minutes later, she rolled into my place . . . with a 12 pack of Miller Light. Karen's going to have to learn the difference between good beer and watered down horse piss if she wants to move up in my Ho Hierarchy.

She got right down to business because her date started in less than 30 minutes. I kept watching the *Iron Chef*, because come on, Morimoto is a genius. Plus, I've already seen the show Karen was putting on. It's really good, but it's been in syndication for months; you don't really need to pay attention until the ending.

I wasn't supposed to meet my friends until 10, so when she left around 8 I just kept drinking at my place. I started thinking about how fucking cool it was that I had a girl coming over to my place to suck me off before she went out on a date. I may not be Hugh Heffner, but I doubt many guys pull something like that off on a regular basis.

Then I started feeling bad for her date. This poor schmuck had no idea that the girl whose chair he was pulling out and buying dinner for and being nice to had her lips wrapped around my cock not even an hour earlier. God forbid if this poor dude kisses her goodnight. I wonder if it'll cross his mind that even with beer breath, her mouth shouldn't taste that salty.

But in a way, I didn't feel that bad for him. You can't make a ho into a housewife, and when you take one out on a date, you aren't helping your chances. I guess some guys never learn.

Of course, he had no idea what she was like; after all, that was the whole point of the date. I guess it just goes to show, you never really can tell . . . **OH SHIT!!**

HOW MANY GIRLS HAVE DONE THIS TO ME??

I shot up from the couch in shock, spilling beer all over myself.

Has this ever happened to me? Have I ever been the sucker that took a girl out after she bought beer for another guy and then blew him?

Oh.My.God—it has to have happened to me. HAS TO. I've been out with so many women, there is just about no way that this hasn't happened to me. And considering the moral turpitude of many of the girls I've hooked up with—suspect at best, wretched prostitute at worst—it is damn near certain that I've been That Guy at least once.

I mean, if Karen does this for me, why not for other guys too? I am pretty fucking cool, but there are other cool guys in the world besides me (or so my friends tell me). Plus, it's not like I've always known what I now know about women. I could have easily been the sucker many times in the past.

And why stop at dick sucking? How many girls have I slept with that were with other guys the same day as me? Or went from another guy right to me? Without even cleaning up? I wouldn't even know, would I? HOW? HOW THE FUCK WOULD I KNOW? There is no way I could tell, short of smelling the semen on her breath. Would I even smell it? Smell it—WHAT ABOUT TASTE IT?

Oh dear merciful God . . . please tell me that I haven't tasted it. I need to go vomit.

My entire worldview was immediately and permanently altered. It was like the first time you turn on a black light in a hotel room and see cum stains covering every surface: For better or worse, your world is never the same.

I stomped around my apartment for two hours until I met my friends out. I explained the whole situation to them and they laughed, made fun of me, and told me to get over it. I wasn't having it:

Tucker "How can you be so cavalier about this? I can't be hooking up with seconds THE SAME DAY. That's for losers and douche bags, NOT Tucker Max!"
Friend "Apparently not, Sloppy Joe."
Tucker "Aren't you the comedian."
Friend "Tucker, haven't you done this to girls before? You know, fucked one in the morning, then gone out and picked up another and fucked her?"
Tucker "SO WHAT? IT'S DIFFERENT!"
Friend "How?"
Tucker "BECAUSE IT'S ME!"
Friend "Wait—didn't you just get YOUR dick sucked tonight? And now you're out trying to get laid?"
Tucker "FUCK YOU!!"
Friend "Dude, it's happened to all of us, and we've all done it to others. Women are women, men are men. This happens to everyone."
Tucker "FUCK THAT. I AM TUCKER MAX. I AM BETTER THAN ALL OF YOU. THIS SHIT DOES NOT HAPPEN TO ME!"
Friend "Oh man; is it going to be one of those nights?"

I drank, and drank, and drank, yet I was still unable to drown the thought that I'd been totally played by multiple women, and I didn't even know which ones had done it to me.

That might have been the worst part—not knowing. Well, that and the prospect that I have at some point kissed a girl who still had semen caked to her teeth from 45 minutes ago. I know of at least one ex-girlfriend that cheated on me, but we were long distance and I fucked more than Caligula when I was dating her, so I wasn't pissed about that. But what about all those girls I thought were all wrapped up in me? How many of them fucked other people behind my back?

What also fucked me up was that women were doing the same thing to me that I was doing to them, except I didn't even know they were doing it. For the entirety of my life up to that point I thought I had the upper hand, that I was the player and not the playee when in fact, I was possibly just another chump. The illusion of control was shattered. Needless to say, this little revelation colored my perspective for the rest of the night. If by "colored my perspective," I mean "totally and irreversibly fucked me up beyond all repair."

Sometimes, too much to drink is still not enough. I needed therapy to bury my anxiety, and alcohol was going to be my counselor. Yes friends, this was going to be one of "those" nights.

At the first bar, I went around quizzing girls about how often this sort of thing happens:

Tucker "Let me ask you a question: Have you ever sucked off one guy, then went on a date with another guy right after? Like that same night? Or fucked another guy right after you blew a different guy, but without telling the second one?"
Girl "EXCUSE ME?"
Tucker "Don't play coy with me."

As you can imagine, this made me very popular with the ladies.

At bar two, I ordered at least three rounds of shots in the first ten minutes. I kept making toasts like this one:

"Roses are red,
Violets are blue,
The bitch gave me head,
And some other guy too."

My toasts to cuckoldry got the attention of a group of girls, and they came over to talk to us. My friends, who had not yet consigned all the women of earth to a fiery death and eternal damnation, made up a story about me to explain my behavior. They told the girls that I had just broken up with my girlfriend who I was in love with and to not pay attention to anything I said. It was my first night out and I was bitter and mean. I helped enforce this lie with the toast I gave to the next round of shots:

> "This shot feels so good, this shot feels so right,
> I can't believe she blew me and another guy tonight.
> To drown my pain, I bought this drink at the store,
> Because let's face it: All women are whores."

Greased by the bullshit story that I had been dumped, the girls actually thought that I was funny. One of them tried to console me by switching the subject to music. I told her I was a country music fan, which is not even remotely true.

Girl "Really! I like to make up my own lyrics to country music songs. Like, you know that one song, 'Let's Get Drunk and Screw?' I like to pretend the lyrics are 'Let's Wait in Line for Shoes.'"
Tucker [I stare blankly at her for a good ten seconds]
Girl [Still trying to be cheery] "Isn't that funny?"
Tucker "You are making me stupider."
Girl "What!?!?"
Tucker [Wait for it . . . wait for it . . .] "I bet you've sucked miles of dick."
She immediately turned away and as she walked off stuttered, "You're, you're . . . a JERK!"
Tucker "Have another shot? DON'T MIND IF I DO!"

That pretty much sealed our fate at bar two. Bar three presented some ample targets, but I was still too head-fucked to do anything, so my friends planted me at a table and went looking for girls on their own.

After about three seconds, I got bored and started wandering around. I snatched some pink drink off the bar as the girl who owned it looked the other way, took a sip, and immediately spit it out. A girl on the other side of me used this to initiate conversation:

Girl "Gross?"
Tucker "Yeah, it tastes like ass."
Girl "I like ass."
Tucker "What's your name?"

Had it been any other night, I would have turned this little gem into a 'tongue up my ass' crack. Not tonight. Tonight, it was only a matter of time before I fucked it up.

Tucker "But be honest—would you ever eat out one guy's ass and then kiss another guy the same day?"

And I'm spent.

My friends were doing well with this one group of girls and looked to be on the way to hook-up victory...until I decided that I wanted to hear the sound of breaking glass, and we all got kicked out.

We ended up going to a late night club. When we got there, I was so drunk the bouncer almost didn't let me in. My last clear memory is my friend grabbing me at the bar after I ordered a double something, and trying to calm me down:

Friend "Dude, you've had too much. This is bordering on dangerous."
Tucker "The only dangerous amount is none!"
Friend "How many drinks did you have at the last place?"
Tucker "You're counting MY drinks? If you want to act like my liver accountant then you can pay the fucking bill too!"
Friend "I PAY YOUR BAR TABS ANYWAY!"
Tucker "I'M FAMOUS—WOMEN CAN'T DO THIS TO ME!"

They sat me in a corner and went back out on the prowl. One or two more drinks later, I decided that I was going to dance. Completely immersed in my indignant self-pity on the dance floor, I found my savior.

In the corner of the club, dancing alone, I found the person that I could trust. I found my one. My soul mate. The person who would never betray me and who would love me forever and never fuck anyone else behind my back without telling me.

This was the most gorgeous person I had ever seen. Piercing blue eyes and sandy blond hair. Great body. A deep, penetrating stare that revealed a wisdom and understanding beyond the average person. Great charisma. Someone who would hold me. And we had immediate chemistry.

We danced for an hour, exchanging seductive looks, coyly flirting, seductively whispering sweet nothings at each other. Every smile was met with a smile, every caress with an equal response.

I finally found someone to fall in love with.

I was too drunk to realize this at the time, but my friends were watching me the whole time . . . and all they saw was me dancing in front of a huge mirror.

By myself.

No one else within ten feet of me.

Let me emphasize: I was so drunk, I was dancing WITH MYSELF in the mirror. For AN HOUR. NO ONE was near me.

Not only did I never once realize it, the only thing I remembered the next morning from that club was thinking that I'd fallen in love. For real, it took several of them to convince me that I was dancing alone, and not with the most amazing girl I'd ever met.

My friends also told me that later when the lights came on indicating closing time, I staggered out of the club onto the street, ran away from them, and their last sight was me careening down the street, bouncing off store fronts and parked cars, yelling:

"IF YOU WANT TO GO OUT ON A DATE WITH ME, YOU CANNOT FELLATE ANYONE ELSE FOR AT LEAST TWENTY-FOUR HOURS BEFOREHAND! DO YOU HEAR ME?? AND I WANT YOU TO SHOWER TOO! I HAVE STANDARDS!! YOU HAVE TO DOUCHE!! IF THE GLOVE FITS, THE GIRL IS A WHORE!!!"

Now THAT is Tucker Max Drunk.

But unfortunately, Tucker Max Drunk is not free. At some point the bill comes due. How expensive is it? Let's tally the total:

You know it's been a hard night when you wake up dehydrated and still dizzy.

You know it's been a really hard night when you wake up dehydrated and dizzy and don't know where you are and have no memory of how you got there.

But it is only when waking from a truly Tucker Max Drunk night that you are completely dehydrated, too dizzy to stand, and though you don't know your exact location or how you got there, you do realize that you have just woken up OUTSIDE, in a PUBLIC PARK, with a stray dog LICKING YOUR FACE.

Raise your hand if you've ever had that happen to you.

I clawed my way to a park bench, pulled myself up onto it, and saw a huge Tin Man statue. For a split second, I honestly thought I'd died and gone to hell, and it was sponsored by Warner Brothers. That was a bit of a shock, because I'd always thought Disney would rule hell. Then I remembered: I lived right by a park called Oz Park, though until this moment, it had not occurred to me where it got its name.

Encouraged by the fact that I was close to my apartment, I started walking. After falling a few times and finally getting that damn dog to stop following me, I found Halstead and followed it back to my apartment.

I was so concerned with keeping my balance and navigating correctly, I didn't really notice till I got home that my face and scalp were itching something terrible. I was reaching up to discover the source of this itch as I stumbled in my door. My roommate took one look at me, audibly gasped and got that "Oh my god" face I've seen so many times. He usually lets out a laugh when he sees the aftereffects of one of my binges, but this time he was so shocked he could only cover his mouth and utter "Go look in the mirror."

I felt my face, and there was definitely something sticky and hard crusted onto it. Thinking that it was possibly blood and I had sustained a head injury, I rushed to the bathroom, and there in the mirror was rock bottom:

The "love of my life" stared back at me with a face covered in hardened, crusted vomit. Yellow and brown bile matted my hair, chunks were in my eyebrows and ears, my cheek and neck had pieces of grass stuck in the vomit crust. I looked like some sort of botched special effect. So much for being too good for whores' sloppy seconds.

But the pièce de resistance lay on the top of my head, at the edge of the crusted vomit, precariously stuck to the vomit in my hair:

A small, dry dog turd.

Postscript

The repercussions of that night did not end there. First off, my (now ex-) roommate will call me shit-head for the rest of my life, and I deserve it.

Second, I will never look at women the same way. Ever. This event, combined with a story my friend told me right after that about his ex-girlfriend letting herself get gang-banged by Mexicans in front of him to get even for him cheating on her totally ruined me. Now, every time I look at or talk to a woman, I can't help but think to myself, "Has she already sucked a dick today? How recent was her last migrant worker gang-bang?"

Granted, I've done horrible stuff also, but anyone in the world can read this book and know what I've done. It's the not knowing that really messes with me. What fucks me up is to think that girls I'm casually dating are fucking around on me, and not even just on other days, but right before they see me. I don't really go on dates anymore since I learned that you don't need to spend money to get pussy, but when I did, I wonder how many girls came out with sperm breath? And how many of those did I kiss? And even now I wonder how many women have I met out at a bar who fucked a guy before going out, and then went home with me?

I talked to all my female friends about this, and the response was varied.

- The dumb ones were like, "Ohhhh—can I come over and suck you off too?" Yes you may. And bring beer.
- The naïve ones were like, "A girl came over and sucked your dick before a date?? No girl does that!!" Riiiiight . . . and you've never had a boyfriend cheat on you. Go back to reading books you buy at the grocery store and leave reality to the rest of us.
- I finally got some usable feedback from my smart female friends. Most of them were like, "This is news to you? That there are women who do what you do? Tucker, I thought you were smarter than this." Thanks for making me feel better.

One friend in particular summed it up: "At least you had this realization. Most guys go through life being blissfully ignorant. My girlfriends who juggle a lot of guys are the ones who don't give off any slutty vibe . . . which is how they totally get away with it. Every guy they are with thinks they've got the perfect situation—a sweet girl who comes over at midnight once or twice a week because that's all she wants. They don't understand that she's got the same perfect arrangement with four other guys."

I tried to explain that giving me head was so good that women actually wanted to do it and didn't care about getting anything back, but she just laughed.

Not that sucking my dick is some chore, but the idea that any guy is so much better than other guys that he is above cuckoldry is ridiculous. Believe me, guys: No matter how good you are, some girl has played you . . . and you probably didn't even realize it.

Don't think about this for too long fellas, or it will drive you nuts. I fixated on it for a whole night and ended up dancing with myself in a mirror for an hour and then woke up in a public park with vomit crusted to my face and dog shit stuck to my head—you can trust me on this. Just move on.

The Dog Vomit Story

Occurred—April 2005
Written—April 2005

As I write this I am sitting in my cousin Josh's apartment in Dallas, Texas. I am fighting a hangover and an intense desire to vomit myself to sleep so that I can get this down now, when it is fresh, because even though it's not the most absurd thing I've ever done, it is up there.

Last night we go to a place called The Corner to meet a group of girls who had been emailing me. This is Josh's first experience dealing with my website groupies, and even though he understands what I do in the abstract, he can't fathom that I get laid this way.

Josh "So let me get this straight: Girls email you, then meet you out, and have sex with you?"
Tucker "Yeah. Lots of them."
Josh "Why?"
Tucker "I don't know. I am awesome. Some women are sluts. Who knows?"
Josh "All the women in Dallas are sluts."
Tucker "God bless them, every one."

The girl who emailed me, Lindsay, shows up. She is even better looking than her pics; blonde shoulder length hair, cute button nose, that sexy Texas twang, light eyes—a total Southern hottie. Her four other friends ranged from "really cute" to "what happened to her face," so predictably, I focus all my attention on Lindsay. Tucker Luck being what it is, my cousin not only has a girlfriend but is also a great wingman, so he was happy to handle the group, leaving my flank protected and me free to talk to the hot girl. About five minutes into the conversation, she drops this:

Lindsay "Can we just be friends?"
Tucker "What do you mean?"
Lindsay "Well, I just don't want you to think that I'm here to have sex with you."
Tucker "When did I bring up the subject of sex?"
Lindsay "Well, you didn't, but . . . well . . . you know . . ."
Tucker "Don't sweat things like that. Let's just hang out and have fun and everything will work itself out."

Let me translate that conversation from GameSpeak to common English:

Lindsay "I want to fuck you, but I don't want to feel like a slut when I do it."
Tucker "I won't make you feel like a slut, even if you act like one."
Lindsay "Good, because even though I think I want to fuck you, I want you to run good game on me first. You have to earn it."
Tucker "Relax, I have everything under control."

Now, even though the odds were good that Lindsay was going to fuck me, I still had to play my cards right. I do know women as a group very well, but I don't ever claim to completely know any one individual woman. As soon as you think you have a woman totally figured out, that's when you walk in on her being triple teamed by the yard workers.

Lindsay did some of my work for me by getting really drunk. I was drinking Goose and Red Bull doubles, and she was lapping me. Then out of nowhere, she brought up my number of sexual partners.

Lindsay "How many girls have you been with?"
Tucker "I never answer that question. That answer never leads to anything good."
Lindsay "I've only been with two people."

I openly laughed in her face. [note: She is 24]

Lindsay "IT'S TRUE!"
Tucker "OK, whatever."
Lindsay "IT IS TRUE!"
Tucker "I don't really care, but let me tell you something I have learned about women: They lie. A lot. Especially about that."

Lindsay "I'm not lying."
Tucker "OK, I believe you. It doesn't really matter either way. We're just friends."
Linsay "Oh stop it."

Again, from GameSpeak to English:

Lindsay "Ask me if I'm a slut."
Tucker "No."
Lindsay "I was testing you to see if you'll treat me like a slut for fucking you the first night we meet."
Tucker "I know. Now I will show you how edgy I am."
Lindsay "You passed the test. And I like your edginess."

As the night went on, she got hammered. Housed to the point where she was stumbling into people at the bar and speaking in tongues on her cell phone. Her friends were telling me that it was the drunkest they'd ever seen her. Not to be outdone by a small girl, I did shots with half the bar until I was as drunk as, well, Tucker Max.

But just being drunk and foolish wasn't enough for Lindsay and me, so we started making out. Yeah, we were that drunk couple that everyone hates, the ones eating each other's faces at the bar. She kinda stops and pulls me aside:

Lindsay "I never do this. I cannot believe I got this drunk."
Tucker "You ready to go home?"
Lindsay "That's a good idea."
Tucker "You obviously can't drive. Do you want me to call you a taxi or get your friends?"
Lindsay "No. Are you sober? You can drive me home. I live just like a mile away."

Translation:

Lindsay "I want to fuck you, but I need to get drunk as an excuse, so I can explain this away when I sober up."
Tucker "Do you want to back out now? We don't have to do this."
Lindsay "I know, but I want to fuck you. Let's go."

I drove her home and was immediately met at the door by her ankle-biting yippy dog. I normally love dogs, with the notable exceptions being those brain dead little rat dogs that are fashionable with the I-wanna-be-Paris-Hilton crowd, and this was one of those.

Lindsay "Hey Tucker! How are you?"
Tucker "His name is Tucker?"
Lindsay "I've had him for a year, way before I saw your site."

We eventually get down to business and start fucking. I am not even inside her for a minute when she stops me. OK, no big deal, sometimes girls just need time or whatever. We start fucking again . . . and she stops me again.

Tucker "Are you OK? Is everything alright?"
Lindsay "Yeah, it's fine."

So I start fucking her again . . . and she stops me AGAIN.

Tucker "OK look honey, either shit or get off the pot. If you don't want to do this, that is totally fine and I have no problem respecting that decision, I'll even leave if you want. But you need to decide one way or the other, so I know what to do, because this game has to end. I only start and stop when I'm in traffic."

She decides that she does in fact want to have sex, so we start fucking, and to her credit she was really good in bed and managed me well. Without direction I am selfish and dominant, but she knew what she was doing and was able to mesh her desires with my style. We finish, and I turn to her:

Tucker "So how many people have you slept with?"
Lindsay "Two."
Tucker "Yeah, you don't lie about that."
Lindsay "NO! I meant three. I wasn't counting you!"
Tucker "AHAHHAHAHHAHA! What are you, an Enron accountant?"
Lindsay "JERK!"

She goes into the bathroom to do whatever it is that women do after sex. I had been feeling queasy during sex but had managed to force it down until I came, but I couldn't hold it any longer. I had to vomit. And this wasn't going to be normal vomit; this was make-your-eyes-water, burn-your-sinuses, I-want-to-die vomit. Thank you tequila shots.

Then I panicked: where was I going to vomit? She was in the bathroom. There was no porch. I tried to open the window but there was a screen on it. That's a no-go; I've tried vomiting through screens before. It doesn't work.

Suddenly, I had an epiphany: still laying on her bed I pushed it away from the wall, hung my head between the wall and mattress, and blew all over the place. I couldn't have thrown a bucket of vomit on her floor any harder. Thankfully her room is carpeted, so there was no splashing and minimal running, it all just kinda streaked down the wall and piled up under her bed.

By the time she came out of the bathroom I had moved the bed back and recovered, so we fucked again. Thankfully she was drunk and didn't notice my rancid vomit breath. Or maybe she did and just didn't mention it.

The sex the second time was even better. But then in the middle of us fucking, I hear this weird slurping noise. At first I think maybe something is wrong with her pussy, so I stop for a second, but the noise keeps going. Then I hear a jingle associated with it . . . it sounds like when my dog it wants to go out—I think her dog is under the bed eating something . . .

HOLY SHIT—THE DOG IS EATING MY PUKE!

What the fuck do I do now? I can't get up and stop the dog, because then I'd have to admit that I threw up all over her floor and didn't clean it up or tell her. The only solution I can arrive at is to kinda push myself up and down on the bed, thinking that maybe he'll get the picture. The slurping stops and the jingling increases.

Lindsay "Tucker, what are you doing under there? I think he is licking himself. That dog is crazy."

The dog takes maybe a three second break and I hear the slurping again. This is great. Now I am simultaneously trying to:

1. Suppress my laughter,
2. Push the thought of the dog eating vomit out of my mind so I can avoid getting sick on top of her, and
3. Maintain my erection and keep fucking her.

Seriously, picture this scene in your mind's eye: I am mid-coitus, drunk out of my mind, vomit on my breath, on top of a girl I just met six hours ago, her dog under the bed loudly feasting on my barf. What the fuck? What would you do? What could I have done? When in doubt, just fuck harder. It's what I did.

But it got better. I did manage to finish and we both fall asleep. Sometime in the middle of the night, I woke up to piss and as I step off the bed, my foot lands directly in something musky.

Oh man . . . there is only one thing that feels like that as it squishes through your toes.

The lights were out but there was enough glow from a street lamp coming through the window for me to clearly see doggy diarrhea all over the floor. I used the floor to wipe the shit off my foot which left a huge brown streak on the egg-shell white carpet. After playing hop scotch to get to and from the bathroom, I just went to sleep and pretended nothing was wrong. It's not my dog, plus she'll see the poop in the morning.

She got up an hour later maybe, and stepped in the same shit I did.

Lindsay "OH TUCKER! You shit on the floor! Why did you do this?"
Tucker "He's probably jealous that he doesn't get to sleep in your bed tonight."
Lindsay "You never poop in the house! What happened?"
[she turned the lights on]
Tucker "How did he leave that huge shit streak on the floor? That is like two feet long."
Lindsay "OH MY GOD—how did you do that? LOOK AT THE FLOOR! BAD DOG! BAD!"

Tucker crawled up to her, and gave her a few vomit-flavored licks in the face.

Lindsay "OK, I forgive you. But you are still a bad bad dog."

Postscript

The next day I got this email from her:

"I was being a good hostess because you're from out of town—but that is the drunkest I've ever been in my life so I'm not counting anything that happened last night."

Do I even need to translate that from GameSpeak to English?

She didn't find the vomit, and of course I didn't tell her about it, so we ended up going out the next night.

Tucker "So, was it fun cleaning up all that crap?"
Lindsay "UH! What a mess. I had to buy all these cleaning supplies at Walgreens and I scrubbed and disinfected and cleaned for two hours, and it STILL stinks in there."
Tucker "Maybe he ate something. You should check the rest of the room; he might have crapped or vomited somewhere you didn't find. Dogs are weird like that."

THE MIDLAND, TEXAS STORY

Occurred—April 2005
Written—April 2005

Midland, Texas is awesome. Not because it is fun or peaceful or has lots of hot girls. Midland is awesome because it is incredibly and irreversibly fucked up. Remember the scene in *Midnight in the Garden of Good and Evil* where John Cusack calls his editor and says, "This place is like *Gone with the Wind* on mescaline. Everyone is heavily armed and drunk. New York is boring." Welcome to Midland, Texas.

I went to Midland to visit my friend Doug. I had met Doug at a party in Austin. He came up to me, huge dip in his lip, oil-stained jeans tucked into his dirty cowboy boots, wide grin on his face and said, "HAY! Yur Tucker Max!" and handed me his business card. It said:

[his full name]
Oil Wells Dug

Also: Revolutions started, Orgies Organized, Uprisings quelled,
Tigers Tamed, Assassinations plotted, Virgins Converted.
Also preach and lead singing for revival meetings.

I know, my first thought was the same as yours: This kid is a fucking tool. But in spite of the absurd business card, I ended up hanging out with him several times, and he turned out to be a pretty cool guy. When he invited me to hang out with him for a week and work with him in the West Texas oil fields that his family owned, I took the opportunity.

I landed at Midland airport and walked out of baggage claim to see Doug sitting in his massive truck, its engine making that obnoxious KNOCK KNOCK KNOCK KNOCK diesel engine idling sound. I have to reach up for the door handle because the truck has huge 45 inch tires as well as lifted suspension, putting the baseplate at like four feet. I open the door to find the seat at eye level for me. He hands me a beer before I can even pull myself up into the truck.

"WOOOOOOOOOOOOO!! WELCOME TO MIDLAND MOTHER-FUCKER!!"

It is 3pm on Sunday and he is at least six beers ahead of me. Scattered all over the floor are empty tins of Copenhagen, crushed up cans of Keystone Light, Chilean surplus 7.62 rounds and .45 magazines loaded with Mag-Safe hollow point rounds. On his gun rack—yes, his truck had a gun rack—is an M-14 assault rifle and between the console is a holstered H&K USP pistol. If you don't know guns, let me explain it this way: With just the arsenal in his truck, Doug could go round for round with just about any cop in the country, SWAT included, and probably outgun many of them.

It's a 20 minute drive to his place, and there is nothing resembling civilization on the road there. Every direction is flat, arid brush land scattered with mesquite "trees" (they look like bushes but Doug insisted that they are trees) and the occasional tumbleweed blowing across the road. The only exception to this wasteland is the huge sign that reads:

"Welcome to Midland: Home of George and Laura Bush."

Not even 20 minutes on the ground, and I begin to understand what General Sheridan meant when he said, "If I owned Hell and Texas, I'd rent out Texas and live in Hell."

We get to Doug's place and the first thing I see is a Colt .45 sitting on his kitchen counter, pointing right at me. I notice that the hammer is back, and upon closer inspection I realize that the pistol is FULLY LOADED WITH A ROUND CHAMBERED. I grew up around firearms and know how to use them, so I instinctually pick up the gun and make sure the safety is on—which much to my relief it is—then immediately clear the weapon.

Tucker "DUDE—why was there a round in the chamber with the hammer cocked?!?"
Doug "The safety works better that way."
Tucker "Better than if there were NO BULLETS IN IT?"

Upstairs in my room, there is an HK 91 assault rifle just laying out, also locked and loaded. There was enough ammunition scattered throughout the apartment to re-enact the Son Tay raid.

Tucker "Dude, why do you have so many guns?"
Doug "Well, just in case, you never know. Plus, we got some rowdy Mexican neighbors."
Tucker "WHAT? Who do you live next to, Pancho Villa?"

He hands me a beer:

Doug "Start drinking motherfucker, there are some bitches coming over."
Tucker "Do you think maybe we should unchamber the rounds from the rest of these firearms and safely store them before we get rip-roaring drunk with girls around?"
Doug "What for? The safeties are on all of them."
Tucker "Are you kidding?"
Doug "What if we want to go shootin' tonight?"
Tucker "Oh.My.God."

I immediately called my friend PWJ and told him to tell everyone that I love them, because I wasn't coming home alive. But I didn't get to where I am by fretting about these things, so I just said "fuck it," slammed a few beers and relaxed. After all, alcohol always makes everything better.

[SIDE NOTE: I came to learn during my visit that everyone in Midland is armed, and that they have a very different notion of gun safety than the rest of the world. Basically, if the gun is not going off at that exact moment, then it is safe. Even the women ride around with loaded firearms in their cars. I consider myself a minor gun enthusiast, but Midland is ridiculous.]

The girls arrive and I can immediately tell that they are all teenagers. How do I know this without asking? Well, the game of quarters they started playing was the first indication. The conversation about the newest Lizzie Maguire movie was probably the second. And this conversation sealed it for me:

Tucker "What are you drinking?"
Jenny "Chilled wine."

Tucker "You have ice cubes in it? No way. You're kidding right?"
Jenny "I like it that way. It's how we serve it."
Tucker [jokingly] "What are you, a stripper?"
Jenny "No, I only work in a strip club. I don't strip."
Tucker "AHHAHHAHHAAH—YOU ACTUALLY DO WORK IN A STRIP CLUB!! Yeah, there is a bright line distinction between the strippers and the waitresses."
Jenny "IT IS DIFFERENT!"
Tucker "Let me guess—that is white zin. And you are probably mad because Doug doesn't have any straws."
Jenny "Excuse me jerk; it is CHABLIS." [to her credit, she pronounced it correctly]
Tucker "My mistake. I apologize, you are obviously very cultured. You only partake of the finest of the boxed wines."
Jenny "It didn't come in a box! It came in a jug!"
Tucker "Oh right . . . make sure to say hi to Carlo Rossi for me next time you refill."

Doug comes out of the bathroom and joins the conversation.

Tucker "Dude—who is this girl?" [pointing to Jenny] "Don't you know me well enough yet not to bring girls like this around?"
Doug "What? She is hot."
Tucker "Yes, she is hot. But she is painfully dumb and desperately needs braces."
Jenny "Excuse me, I've had braces."
Tucker "Then why do your teeth look like you've been chewing on rocks?"
Jenny "Because I lost my retainer."
Tucker "Left it on the dashboard of a truck, right? Don't you hate it when that happens?"

I almost felt bad after this exchange. Fucking with 18 year old girls is like kicking cripples; it's just too easy. Of course, the other two girls with her thought this was the funniest thing they'd ever heard. One is cute and skinny with no tits, and one is cute and kinda fat with huge tits. You want to guess which one threw herself at me? Whatever; just give me another beer. I've fucked worse.

As the night moves on, I continue to abuse the dumb one for the entertainment of everyone else. If that girl didn't hate herself before that night, she did after it. The two girls that thought I was funny invited me to go drinking with them at some friend's house. Jenny—the dumb, hot, crooked toothed stripper—doesn't want to hang out with me, and asks Doug to take her to a bar. He kinda looks at me surprised for a second, and then realizes the lesson I just taught him: there is more than one way to be a good wingman. You're welcome Doug.

Now, I assumed that when they said "a friend's house" these two girls knew where the house was. And what happens when you rely on the cognitive skills of 18 year old females? You get lost. After two hours of riding around back country roads, we come to the sign:

"Pavement Ends"

Skinny Girl "Emma, do you know where we are?"
Emma "No."
Skinny Girl "Tucker, do you know where we are?"
Tucker "Is this a fucking joke? I LIVE IN CHICAGO!"

We eventually find our way to someone's house who has beer. It rained the night before, and I am drunk and bored, so I throw Emma into this huge mud puddle. She doesn't take that shit, and flings a handful of mud at me. We wrestle and before I know it we are both covered in West Texas filth.

Still dirty, we drive back to Doug's place and get in the shower to wash it off . . . and then we start hooking up in the shower . . . and it moves to the bed . . . I put my hand down her panties, and feel something gritty. I pull up and find a handful of mud. We get back in the shower, this time with all our clothes off . . . and we start hooking up again . . . and move to the bed again . . . and I start to fuck her . . . grit again. In her pussy. No matter how much we tried to clean it off, it just would not all come out.

I might as well have been fucking a dirt pile. Welcome to sex in Texas.

Doug woke me up early the next morning, because I was going to go work with him in the oil fields. He knocks on my door, opens it and sees Emma in my bed.

Doug "Shit. Get that land beast out of my house."
Tucker "I hope you have an elephant gun ready. You'll only get one, maybe two shots before she tramples us."

Aside from the random hookups with little girls, the really funny thing about Texas are the people you meet. These are not normal people. I can't call them redneck, because that word implies a sub-standard level of intelligence and sophistication, and that isn't really fair to these people, some of whom are very smart. I grew up in a pretty rural part of Kentucky, and those people are rednecks, but the Texans I met weren't like that. Perhaps I should just refer to them as "country." If you ever grew up or spent time in a southern state, you know the difference between country and redneck. These are some of the people I met in Midland:

- The Sheriff of Midland lives in Doug's apartment complex. When he gets drunk, which is pretty much every day, he sits in his car and tries to pull people over for DUI. In the parking lot of the same complex he lives in. He doesn't even bother going out into actual streets.
- When they are bored, Emma's friends will do what is called "spotlighting." West Texas is basically all brushland that is overrun with jackrabbits, so hunting them is legal year round. To hunt them, you go out at night in the fields with your truck and shine your spotlight around until you catch one. When the light hits them they look right into it and freeze, thus making easy targets.

  But because it is so easy, just shooting them isn't enough for some of these people. One guy told me a story about how he got bored with shooting them with a rifle, so he started using a bow and arrow. That got boring, so he would run them over with his truck. That was simple, so he started getting out of his truck and beating them to death with a tire iron. When that got too easy, he chased them and stomped their heads. When that lost its luster, he threw his tool box at them. Then he took the 50 or so rabbits he'd killed and laid them out in his ex-girlfriend's yard, spelling the word "Ho."
- One of Doug's friends got kicked out of his house at 18 because he was a total fuck-up and his parents couldn't deal with him anymore. This kid is either too poor or too stupid to get a normal apartment, so he instead moved into a storage unit. He sleeps in an empty, gutted Bronco, and uses hundreds of boxes of Keystone Light as insulation. You don't believe me? Look at the picture:

These people are funny, but they've got nothing on Doug's co-worker, Wayne. Wayne works with Doug in the West Texas oil fields, and we spent a few days with him on the rigs. The first time I met Wayne, he drove up in his truck when we were doing something manual:

Wayne "You two look like monkeys fuckin' a football."
Doug "Fuck you redneck."
Wayne "Proud of it, you knob-slobber. Want some beer?"
Doug "Yeah, gimme one."
Tucker "Should we drink when we work?"
Wayne "Sheeet. Son, this tha country, this ain't no got-damn New Yourk City or no fuckin' She-Ka-Go. In the country, it ain't called 'drankin a beer,' it's called 'improvin' yer work.'"
Tucker "Well . . ."
Wayne "Come on. It's rodeo cool."
Tucker "Well, OK, if it's cold I guess . . ."
I take a sip and immediately spit it out.
Tucker "DUDE—THIS BEER IS HOT!"
Wayne "Whudda fuck duhya thank 'rodeo cool' meens?"

Watching Texans work is funny.

We went to lunch with Wayne. He took out his tooth to eat—one single tooth—and regaled us for hours with some of the funniest stories I'd ever heard.

Wayne on occupational hazards: "Yeah, them oil rigs ain't to be trifled wit. One time we was changing the heads on a pump and the fucker blew. Throwed me bouta hundred yards and killed two other guys workin' with me. That was some shit. I had to take a whole week off work."

Wayne on drinking: "I knew I should slow down my drankin when I was going through half a fifth a day, just on the drive home. Now I just drank a few beers on the ride and save the hard stuff for when I git home."

Wayne on West Texas flora: "This one time I got throwed off a Bronc and landed in a mesquite bush. You know them mesquite thorns is long and thin as hell. Well, I stood up and brushed miself off, but I felt blood dripping down ma face. I wiped it off but I couldn't find no cut, then ma son told me it was coming from ma eye, so I reached up and felt a lump under my eyelid. I pulled a three inch thorn out of my face. That fucker had gone in vertically and missed tha eyeball, but had gotten sunk deep behind the eye. I got lucky on that one. You can still see the scar—just look right her. What's wrong wit you boy? Why you squirm'in' like a ki-ote caught inna snare?"

Wayne on whiskey: "I don't drink JD; it gives me gout." [we crack up laughing] "Fuck yall, you'll be old soon."

Wayne on West Texas fauna: "Don't let no one tell you cows ain't mean. Thems some fuckers. Another time I got throwed trying to

Watching Doug work from the cool shade of the truck is even funnier.

break'a horse, and a cow done shit all over my head when I was laying on the ground. I got up and whupped his ass. Punched that fucker right'n his face. He didn't shit on me no more after'at."

Wayne on cunnilingus: "Just because it smells bad don't mean it tastes bad. I ate out all kinds of pussies, and I liked ever one. Cept them Mexican hookers. You don't go down on them, you'll come up seeing stars and have a green tongue and shit. Other'n that though, I'd eat the hymen outta dead donkey. I love it!"

The second day in the fields I had to get suntan lotion, because I wasn't used to spending 10 hours a day in the sun. While we were at the store Wayne called Doug looking for him:

Wayne "Where the hell you faggots at?"
Doug "We had to get Tucker some suntan lotion."
Wayne "SUNTAN LOTION? Well god damn! I been'ta two world's fairs and a goat ropin' contest and I ain't never seen no shit like this."

After that, he called me the "World Champion Goat Roper" all week. I didn't figure out what it meant for a few months. Think about what kind of person spends time holding goats down, and you'll get it.

One night we were out drunk and called Wayne. Doug dialed his number, the phone answered, but it was a good minute before any voice came on. Even though I was standing next to Doug and not on the phone, I could hear the Hank Williams Jr. blaring on the stereo in the background.

Wayne "Whut'dda fuck dyew want?"
Doug "Hey Wayne, you want to come get some beers with us?"
Wayne "Who's dis?"
Doug "It's Doug and Tucker."
Wayne "FUCK NO! I ain't watchin you two faggots suck dick all night. I can turn on the cooking channel and see plenty of homos."

Here I am, in the West Texas Oil fields, on the phone with my agent. Only Tucker Max.

Doug "Come on Wayne, we—"
Wayne [He yells away from the phone to his 12 year old son] "HEY—YOU FUCKING DITCH MONKEY, GET ME ANOTHER BEER 'FORE I HIT'CHA WIT MY BOOT."
Doug "Wayne?"
Wayne "Ain't you got some goats to poke? Ah hell, where is my beer? YOU BETTER HURRY UP YOU LITTLE SHIT OR YOU'LL BE SLEEPIN ON THE PORCH WIT'DA DOGS."

Wayne is awesome, but Doug has other country friends that may be even funnier. Doug is big into off-roading and rock crawling and similar redneck activities involving big tires and loud engines, so one day he took me to hang out with some other off-roading friends of his, Mike and Cliff. He said I would like them because "they call themselves a 'drinking team with an off-roading problem.' "

We met Mike and Cliff at a maintenance shop that one of their friends owned. It looked just like the American Chopper shop, except the place was a mess. I kept expecting Paul Sr. to storm out of the office and start screaming at Paulie and Vinnie about the shop being dirty.

Mike was about 40, had an orange "Daytona Bike Week" hand band, a white goatee and was covered in axle grease or some other dirty mechanical fluid. Cliff was about 35, in a plaid lumberjack jacket, a gold rope chain and I think had at least two dips in, if not more. They both looked like tow truck drivers (and I don't mean that as an insult, it's just the impression they gave off).

At first, we just sat around and drank beer and bullshitted. It took awhile but once they realized that I wasn't some city-boy prima-donna who thought he was better'n them, they warmed up to me.

Tucker "So Mike, on the ride over here Doug said that his truck was a lot better than yours."
Mike "Sheet. His little girl truck couldn't pull a tampon out of a sick whore's pussy."
Tucker "Doug said that your truck is just like bad pussy—it stinks."
Mike "There ain't no such thing as bad pussy."
Tucker "You haven't had enough pussy to say some shit like that."
Mike "Well you must fuck a lot, 'cause you ain't had a long enough dry spell to thank pussy can be bad."

Tucker "Touche."
Mike "Don't use no goddamn French round me, boy."
Tucker "Holla."
Mike "I guess nigger's better'n French."
Tucker "You shouldn't say nigger. If you must, at least say 'urban.' "
Mike "You got too much education, boy."

Doug had something broken on his truck and his buddies helped him work on it for a few hours. I just stood around drinking Keystone Light and watching because I don't know shit about anything mechanical:

Mike "Tucker, hand me that crescent wrench."
Tucker "What is a crescent wrench?"
Mike "Goddamn. You bout as useful as tits on a bull. All that education and you don't know nothin'."
Cliff "He sure know how to drink my beer without paying for it."

But the highlight had to be listening to them talk shit to Doug:

Doug "I only have 40,000 miles on that thing; I don't know how the U-joint broke."
Mike "Right, 'cause having a dumbass driver who's always hopping curbs and smokin' his tires don't got nuttin' to do wit it."
Doug "Fuck you, bitch."
Mike "I hope you brought some tequila Doug. We ain't doin' this for free."
Tucker "All it takes is a bottle of tequila to pay you off? This is some serious mechanical work you are doing."
Mike "Hell no. But tequilas the only thang that's gonna wash the taste of dick outta Doug's mouth."
Cliff "You'd know bout that wouldn't you?"
Mike "Well I was in the fucking Navy, asshole."

After they got Doug's truck fixed, we headed to Cliff's house to drink more beer and blow things up. Cliff's place was hilariously redneck. As we drive up, three dogs that look more like coyotes come running up barking and jumping around. Sitting on a nice two-acre piece of land is a big double-wide trailer, very nice by trailer standards. It is flanked by two huge storage sheds with ATV's, boat hulls, a beer fridge, animal skins mounted on the wall and all order of tools and sheet metal and what not. In the huge back yard is a rock pond that is really nice and well put together, with a working fountain in the middle. Next to the pond is an old three wheeler . . . up on blocks. No, really it was up on concrete blocks. Awesome.

All the way in the back is an animal pen that has donkeys and goats. We go to the pen because Cliff wants to show everyone something behind it.

Mike "Hey Cliff, what the fuck is wrong with that billy?"

The male goat, called a billy goat, had a torn and bleeding ear. We walk into the animal pen, and laying on the ground is a dead goat with half its face missing. Across the pen are two dead baby goats, both dirty and mangled. Everyone just kinda stands there for a second, when one of the dogs—the big male one—sticks its head through the gate, sees Cliff standing there, and takes off running with his tail between his legs. Cliff explodes.

Cliff "CHEVY GET BACK OVER HERE! YOU GODDAMN MOTHERFUCKER GET OVER HERE!"

Cliff stomps across the yard after the dog. He is PISSED.

Mike "Oh shit. Here he goes."
Tucker "Why is he so mad?"
Mike "You see the goats, Helen Keller?"
Tucker "That goat's been dead a long time. It's face is half decomposed."
Mike "No no. That goat was alive this morning."
Tucker "Then how did its face get like that? It's decomposed."
Mike "You dumbass. The dogs ate it."
Tucker "NO WAY! Are those dogs wild?"
Mike "Hell no; they just normal house dogs."
Tucker "Normal dogs wouldn't do that."
Mike "Sheet. You got dogs?"
Tucker "Yeah. I grew up with them and have one now."
Mike "Well, your dogs'd do the same thang. They are all sweet and nice around humans, but you get them in a pack and they go fuckin nuts. Domesticated or not, them's wild animals at heart. Chevy is the ringleader, and he's done this before, that's why Cliff is so pissed. He should know better."

A gunshot rang out, and I kinda jumped. We turned towards the yard, and saw Cliff, red as a beat, screaming and chasing his dog around, a shovel in one hand and a .22 in the other. The dog was scurrying this way and that, dodging gun shots and shovel swings. It looked like a *Hee-Haw* skit:

Cliff "YOU STOO-PID STOO-PID DOG!" [swings the shovel and misses] "WHY THE FUCK DA YEW KEEP DOIN' THAT!" [another gunshot rings out and misses] "GET OVER HERE AND GET'CHER WHOOPIN!" [swings the shovel and misses] "HOW MANY TIMES AM I GONNA HAVE TA BEAT YEW?!?" [another missed gunshot]
Tucker "Is he really shooting at his dog?"
Mike "Oh hell yeah. Cliff is a pretty level guy, but when he gets mad, you better watch out. He'll calm down after he tones the dog for a little while."
Tucker "Tones the dog? What does that mean?"
Mike "Wait'll he catches him, you'll see."

A few seconds later I see Cliff swing his shovel and hear the distinctive "TONG" of metal against skull as he clocks the dog flush in the head. Much to my surprise, the dog took the hit and ran off with no noticeable damage. I didn't know whether to laugh because of the absurd comedy inherent in watching a fuming redneck chase his dog around his yard with a shovel and a gun, or be sad because some guy just hit a dog in the head with a shovel.

Mike "You hear that sound the shovel made on his skull? That's why we call it 'toning'."
Tucker "Wow. I mean . . . I've never seen anyone work a dog over like that. I've never even seen anyone work over a person like that. Pimps don't even beat hookers like that."
Mike "Chevy'll be fine. He's tough, but he's obstinate. Dogs is like women; sometimes talkin' don't work."

After Cliff was too exhausted to chase the dog any longer, he stormed back to the animal pen, shovel in hand but no rifle, sweat pouring off his brow, still muttering to himself.

Tucker "Why is he so mad? It's just a goat. He can buy another one."
Mike "Well, he ain't got much money, and them goats is worth bout $150."

Mike goes behind the animal pen to what can only be described as a small pet cemetery. There is a pine cross up with a goat's name, and rocks over the grave. Cliff starts digging a new grave next to the old one. The digging eventually calms Cliff down and all of us start trading drinking stories. I tell them a few of my classics and they laugh.

Doug "Cliff, tell Tucker some of your stories."
Cliff "Well, there was that weekend I tore my intestine from beer. I went into the doctor and he asked me how many beers I drank. I said I had about an average Saturday, bout 50. A pretty hairy Sunday, had bout 70. They called in two more doctors and a whole mess'a nurses. Them fuckers didn't believe me. I asked'em: How the hell else am I gonna tear my intestine from beer unless I drank me a shit load of it?"
Tucker "You drank 120 beers in two days? No fucking way."
Cliff "You sound like the fucking doctors."
Tucker "That is over 1400 ounces of beer! That's like . . . 10 or 11 GALLONS! IN TWO DAYS!?!?"
Mike "Well thank you Mr. Wizard, we know how much fucking beer it is."
Tucker "I am in awe of that."
Cliff "Shit. That ain't nothing. Around here, 120 beers is what we call 'tha weekend.'"

After awhile Chevy came over and sort of crawled near us but stayed out of reach, obviously not wanting to get another whipping. He laid about 10 yards away, licking his crotch.

Tucker "I wish I could do that."
Mike "I don't think he'd let'cha."

Doug and Cliff digging a hole for the dead goats. Notice that Doug is "supervising." He's such a lazy shit.

Cliff finished digging and paused to stare at the dead goat for a minute.

Cliff "I kinda want to keep that goat head and mount it above my fireplace . . . but I cain't."
Doug "Why not?"
Cliff "Cause evertime I look at it I'd hit my dog."

We threw the goats into the grave, and Mike jokingly took a full Keystone Light and threw it in the grave before he filled it in.

Mike "That's for the trip, you stupid goats."
Cliff "The sad part is, when I'm broke jones'in for a beer, I'm gonna dig that motherfucker up and drank it."
Mike "Boy, that'd really git your goat."
Cliff "Fuck yew."
Mike "Cliff, you feelin alright? You look like you just buried a goat."
Cliff "Im'ma tone you in a minute if you don't shut da fuck up."

THE WORST TUCKER STORY EVER

Occurred—April 2005
Written—April 2005

[WARNING: If you enjoy carefree, guiltless sex with multiple partners and want to continue having lots of it, stop reading right now. Don't say I didn't warn you.]

I know I say things like, "Is this my life?" all the time, but honest to fucking god, every time I think my life is as weird and perverse and fucked up as it can possibly get, I trump myself. It never fails. This just happened on April 3rd, 2005 as I was finishing up the material for this book:

"Sarah," one of my regular fuck buddies, calls me and asks if she can come over and spend the night. It was a Sunday and I was going to stay in to do some work anyway, plus she is real cool and laid back and doesn't require any attention from me except for sex, so I agree. Sarah said she'd be over around 9pm. Right after I got off the phone with Sarah, I got a call from an irregular booty call of mine, "Mimi." Mimi was very drunk and making all sorts of promises about coming over. She gets hammered and calls me all the time promising to come over and never shows, so not taking her inebriated call seriously, I tell her she can come over.

Sarah gets there and instead of fucking, she wants to talk:

Sarah "Tucker, I went to the hospital yesterday. I'm 5 weeks pregnant" (we had been fucking for at least two months).
Tucker "Aren't you on birth control? You told me we didn't have to use condoms because you were on birth control."
Sarah "I was. I still am, but remember when I got pneumonia from you?

The doctor said that the antibiotics messed with my birth control, and I guess I got knocked up."

We talked about our options for awhile. I am always hesitant to say anything in these situations, for many reasons, but Sarah made it easy on me:

Sarah "Well, no matter what, I have to get an abortion. I don't really have a choice."
Tucker "I mean, OK, but what do you mean you don't have a choice?"
Sarah "Well, I start chemotherapy next month."
Tucker "Chemotherapy?"
Sarah "I wasn't going to tell you this, but . . . well . . . I have ovarian cancer. I found out two weeks ago."
Tucker "Fuck. You are having a great month . . . are you going to live?"
Sarah "Yeah, I should be fine. But I obviously can't be pregnant during cancer treatment."

The great irony in this: The entire reason she found out she had ovarian cancer early enough to treat it was *because* she was fucking me. It is pretty rare to get ovarian cancer that young (she's 20), but it's even rarer to catch it early enough to treat it effectively. We had unprotected sex because she was on birth control, but after considering the fact that she was fucking me without a condom, she kinda freaked out and went to her Ob/Gyn for a complete STD test and pap smear. Turns out she has no STD's, but came up positive for cancerous cells. I guess sometimes fucking me can actually be healthy.

But this wasn't all:

Sarah "You don't know any private abortion clinics do you? I need to go soon."
Tucker "You don't have insurance?"
Sarah "Yeah, but I am on my parents' policy. If I use my insurance, they will find out and flip on me. I'm not sure I even have enough to pay for it."

Before I can even recover from the cluster bombs that Sarah dropped on me, an enfilade is fired at me from my flank: Mimi picks tonight to actually make good on a booty call promise. Oh boy . . . this night just got as awkward as a mule on rollerskates.

Still very drunk, Mimi crashes into my place and falls on the floor. Maxie (my dog) licks her face until she gets up onto the couch, where she proceeds to lay a litany of her own problems on Sarah and I. Well, she doesn't actually tell us per se; she calls some other guy she is fucking and we learn these facts from her loud and drunken conversation with him:

- She was five months pregnant, but just had a miscarriage four days earlier [note: in this, she is telling the truth. We have many friends in common, and I saw her a few weeks before and she was clearly pregnant. Now she clearly wasn't, and our friends had told me about her miscarriage yesterday].
- Her husband blames the miscarriage on her.
- She is pissed at her husband for blaming the miscarriage on her.
- She is very unhappy with almost everything about her three-month old marriage, and thinks she wants a divorce. [Yes, she was already two months pregnant when she married him.]
- She admits that the baby might not even be her husband's.
- She says that the only reason she married her husband was because she was pregnant, not sure who the father was, and he had the most money of anyone she was fucking at the time.
- She is at my place to fuck me mainly because her husband hates me [note: He hates me because I once embarrassed him at a party].

Wow; this night just went from awkward to full-on Tucker Max surreal. There isn't this much concentrated misery in a pediatric burn unit.

But even beyond the wretched circumstances surrounding these girls, I really don't know what to do. Both girls are totally fucked up and both want to fuck me. How do I resolve this situation? I was totally baffled. I don't even know what my options are. Could I just leave? Could I call the cops and pretend one of them hit me, and have her taken away? Could I somehow turn this into a perverted, prego threesome?

Remembering that the only way to defeat an ambush is to charge into it attacking, I decide that fucking at least one of them is the solution. But should I screw the slut who is cheating on her husband and just miscarried a 5-month old fetus, or the one who has cancer and is currently carrying my child? I do a cost-benefit analysis of sex with each:

Mimi Pro

- Mimi is great looking with huge fake tits
- Mimi is good in bed

Mimi Con

- Mimi just had a miscarriage
- Mimi is a revolting slut who should be ground into pig slop

Sarah Pro

- Sarah is very pretty also, but no fake tits
- Not only do I actually like Sarah, she is probably better in bed than Mimi

Sarah Con

- Sarah is pregnant . . . with my child
- Sarah has cancer . . . right in the hole where I put my penis

I cut the Gordian Knot and decide to fuck Mimi. I figure that if I give her a good dicking, she will either leave or fall asleep, and then maybe I can salvage something with Sarah. If I fuck Sarah first, Mimi will get pissed and immediately leave, probably stealing and/or breaking my stuff on the way out.

All of us still sitting in the living room, I grab Mimi and lead her towards my bedroom. I turn to Sarah and say, "Stay here. I just need to fuck her to sleep, then I'll be back up." Sarah is not happy. As in "Hell hath no fury" pissed. Whatever; it's too late to worry about that now. I've committed to the charge, the only thing I can do now is finish hard.

We go downstairs and start fucking. Mimi fucks like a professional, and is on her game tonight (I know what escorts fuck like because I dated several when I lived in Florida). When I am with her I usually get off multiple times, not really because I like her but because I have an almost pathological fake tit fetish.

I shoot my first load pretty quickly; like five minutes. It usually takes me only a few minutes to reload, so I massage her clit and finger her until I am ready to go again. But two minutes pass, and I can't get hard. Four minutes, I am still a wet noodle. After like ten minutes, some jacking off that required a surprising amount of concentration, I am finally half mast, so slide in her and start again.

But it won't start. In fact, it deflates a little. What the fuck is wrong with my dick? The only time it ever does this is when I am truly Tucker Max Drunk or after I've cum like 5-6 times in a night.

Then I realize what is happening. Sometimes when I fuck, especially when I fuck demon sluts like Mimi, my subconscious tries to fuck with me. It has a nasty habit of creeping up on me and attempting to sabotage my journey to orgasm. But my conscious mind, which has the power of my penis behind it, usually busts the subconscious in the mouth and quickly shuts it up.

This time was different. After everything that had happened tonight, my conscious mind was like George Foreman in the fifth round of The Rumble in the Jungle: exhausted, punched out, and stunned by an opponent he underestimated. My subconscious, seeing my conscious mind on the ropes, did exactly what Muhammed Ali did to Foreman: Finished him.

Subconscious "Tucker . . . are you having fun? You like that soft supple flesh on your penis? That pussy you are penetrating . . . it is the same hole that just passed a dead 5-month old fetus. Isn't she supposed to wait at least two weeks after that happens to fuck again?"

As my conscious desperately tries to fend off my subconscious, Mimi is no help. She keeps moaning and screaming. This only makes me more disgusted. My dick is not big enough to make a girl scream "FUCK ME WITH YOUR HUGE COCK" during sex, especially considering that I was barely hard. The only type of woman who would say that is one who is accustomed to propping up the egos of men who pay for sex.

Subconscious "I wonder how much she charges? You could be getting thousands of dollars of value here, all for free. Do you think she fucked anyone before you today? Her pussy does seem a bit slippery, doesn't it? I wonder how much she made. After she passes out, check her purse."

Mimi "OH TUCKER, JUST LIKE THAT! I LOVE YOUR GIANT COCK!"

Subconscious "Tucker, you realize that the only way a girl gets this whorish is because she was raped by her step-dad at age 10. Do you think your dick is bigger than the guy who sexually abused her as a child? I bet it's doesn't feel that way, even if it is."

Mimi "FUCK ME HARDER! OH MY GOD!"

Subconscious "You know, she just miscarried . . . I wonder if there is still any embryonic fluid down there. That's probably why she's so wet. I bet she didn't even miscarry. I bet she got a vacuum and sucked that nearly third trimester baby right out. That's why she feels especially good—a pussy gets tenderized when its stretched for a dead baby head."

Mimi "OH GOD YES! FUCK ME RAW! SHOOT YOUR CUM ALL OVER MY TITS!"

Subconscious "And if it was a partial birth abortion, there is probably still some brain juice coating her pussy. That stuff is REALLY slippery. I bet you can feel it if you concentrate."

There was the knock out punch. No standing eight count, no saved by the bell: My conscious mind was on the canvas looking up at the referee.

My dick went totally limp. Wouldn't respond at all; it was like trying to get a marshmallow into a slot machine. I was done.

Not even pretending to cum, I roll off her and leave the room. I checked on her 10 minutes later, and she was passed out exactly where I left her, naked, laying on her back, her huge fake tits just sitting there on her chest. I momentarily considered waking her up to try again, but the immediate gag reflex that followed that thought stopped me. I don't want any more of my subconscious tonight.

Sarah was indeed pissed, but she stayed around anyway. After the night I'd had, all I wanted was to be alone. I couldn't kick her out, but I just couldn't be cooperative:

Sarah "Did you take a shower after you fucked her?"
Tucker "No."
Sarah "Well, would you take one?"
Tucker "Why?"
Sarah "Cause I want to have sex with you."
Tucker "Do we have to?"

She left after that. But not before she asked me to cut her a check for half the cost of the abortion. As I wrote the $200 check, I momentarily considered asking her if she was sure the kid was mine, but I just couldn't. I was still on the canvas.

After everyone left, I stopped and fully considered what I had just done:

I invited a girl over to have sex . . .
who is pregnant with my child . . .
AND has ovarian cancer.

While she was at my place hanging out with me seeking moral support for her difficult times ahead, I invited another girl over to fuck me . . .
That girl is married . . .
And just had a miscarriage . . .
AND only wants to fuck so she can have something to throw in her husband's face.

Then I fucked her, but had to stop because I couldn't remove the image of dead fetus brains spilling out of her vagina from my mind . . .
Then I refused to fuck the other girl because I was too disgusted with myself to get hard again.

Seriously, think about this scenario for a second, and ask yourself: Is it possible to be a worse person without breaking the law? Forget an upper management role in hell; I think I have the CEO position in my sights.

Well, I just hope that they serve beer in hell. Even if it is rodeo cool.

APPENDIX 1:

THE TUCKER MAX FEMALE RATING SYSTEM

As an alternative to the "how many beers" or the "1 through 10" rating system, my friends and I came up with the following 5-star scale to rank physical appearance only. There are three things that you must remember before using this scale:

1. Though personality is very important in evaluating females, in this scale it can only hurt. Too many men are the type that once they start fucking, they think the girl is cool because she likes having sex with them, and want to raise a woman's rating. This scale is for accuracy of physical appearance only, so keep your feelings for her personality out of this rating. People generally agree more when a woman is a bitch, thus making that more of an objective factor (personality is obviously important in deciding whether or not you want to date the woman, but not in conveying her physical attractiveness on this scale).

2. Bonus stars can only be given under the following circumstances:

- A woman financially supports the man, or at least buys him everything he wants; capped at a half star.
- A woman is into other women, and lets the man participate in some way (including watching); capped at 1-star.
- Sex drive can help, but it can only bring a marginal candidate up a level. For instance, a high 2-star can be elevated to a low 3-star, but an average 2-star CANNOT go to a 3-star, no matter what her sexual habits are.

The scale:

1-star (aka, common-stock pig): No redeeming qualities. This girl is ugly, usually fat, boring and sucks in just about every way possible. If you don't know a common-stock pig when you see one, you are destined to spend the rest of your life with one.

2-star (aka, respectable pig): One redeeming quality, like large breasts, nice ass, cute face, great dick-sucking lips, etc. If you concentrate on that one redeeming physical quality, and you get shit-housed, you're not too upset with yourself waking up next to a respectable pig. Of course, you still make her crawl out the window when she leaves, because you don't want your friends to see her, but at least you don't want to gargle bleach and scrub yourself like a rape victim after she leaves.

3-star (aka decent/attractive/pretty): Acceptable to be seen with in public. She is average when sober, but looks MUCH better after only about three beers. You'll admit to your friends that you're fucking her, but you still make fun of her behind her back, and tell them lies about her sexual prowess and bi-sexual tendencies to justify your dealings with her. She's not bad overall, and will do if nothing better comes along, but could be left in a heartbeat if the opportunity for a hot chick arises. Sadly, most guys end up having to settle for a 3-star, as these are the most prevalent type of women.

4-star (aka girlfriend material): This is the girl that is very attractive, but not super hot. You will be seen with her in public at any point in the day, even before drinking. You think twice before ditching this girl for a hot chick, especially if she has special powers (tongue ring, double jointed, etc.). Ascension to the 4-star level can only be attained through use of a petition. The candidate must secure 75% of the vote from those polled. (NOTE: Bonus points only make a candidate petition eligible. She still must garner 75% of the vote.)

5-star (aka super hottie): This is the hot chick. Hopefully no further explanation is necessary. It's kind of like the Hall of Fame. VERY FEW WOMEN ARE 5-STARS, about 3-5% of the population. A declaration that someone is hot is assumed to be true, but can be rebuked if 25% of those polled vote against her 5-star placement.

Other category: 0-star (aka, Wildebeast): The lowest of the low. A 1-star (common-stock pig) with a terrible personality qualifies as a Wildebeast. They should all be put to sleep. This is that loud, disgusting fat girl in the bar that smokes, orders complicated drinks and then spills them on everyone, and is generally just so annoying that you have to actively restrain yourself from kicking her in the crotch and stomping on her throat until she drowns on her own blood. There is no insult too mean or crude for her, and basic human rights do not apply to her.

APPENDIX 2:

THE TUCKER MAX DRUNK SCALE

When describing how drunk I get, I use my own scale that my friends and I devised:

Buzzed: is after a few beers, when I can feel the alcohol affecting me, but I think I can still drive reasonably well. My brain generally works like normal, though perhaps a little slow.

Inebriated: is when I start feeling good, but I know my ability to drive is impaired, and so I give the keys away. I begin to doubt my ability to make good judgments. I am usually a much nicer person at this stage of drunkenness, though this changes quickly.

Drunk: is when I start feeling overly confident about myself and all of my abilities, I argue about who drives, but eventually give the keys up anyway. Other people begin to seem much funnier and more interesting. This is also when the ability to socialize in an appropriate manner starts breaking down.

Fucked-in-half (aka "**shit-housed**"): is when I believe that my abilities have become nearly superhuman, that I am the best looking man in my geographical area, and that that hunchback girl over by the bar is really hot too. As far as I am concerned, there is no road, policeman, or possibly even army, that can contain me. It is at this point that I cannot differentiate between an appropriate comment and an inappropriate one, so I just say whatever I feel like.

Tucker Max Drunk: is the ultimate drunk stage. Never mind about operating heavy machinery; I have trouble figuring out doorknobs. The only benefit is that I don't have to worry about driving because I can't